Cornell '77

Also by Peter Conners

NONFICTION
*JAMerica: The Oral History of the Jam Band
and Festival Scene*

*White Hand Society: The Psychedelic Partnership of
Timothy Leary and Allen Ginsberg*

*Growing Up Dead: The Hallucinated Confessions
of a Teenage Deadhead*

POETRY
The Crows Were Laughing in their Trees

Of Whiskey and Winter

FICTION
Emily Ate the Wind

EDITOR
PP/FF: An Anthology

Cornell '77

The Music, the Myth, and the Magnificence of the Grateful Dead's Concert at Barton Hall

Peter Conners

Cornell University Press
Ithaca and London

First published 2017 by Cornell University Press
Printed in the United States of America

Design by Scott Levine

Library of Congress Cataloging-in-Publication Data

Names: Conners, Peter H., author.
Title: Cornell '77 : the music, the myth, and the magnificence of the Grateful Dead's concert at Barton Hall / Peter Conners.
Description: Ithaca : Cornell University Press, 2017. | Includes bibliographical references and index.
Identifiers: LCCN 2016052331 (print) | LCCN 2016053083 (ebook) | ISBN 9781501704321 (cloth : alk. paper) | ISBN 9781501708565 (pbk. : alk. paper) | ISBN 9781501712562 (ret) | ISBN 9781501712579 (pdf)
Subjects: LCSH: Grateful Dead (Musical group)—Performances—New York (State)—Ithaca. | Deadheads (Music fans) | Cornell University.
Classification: LCC ML421.G72 C64 2017 (print) | LCC ML421.G72 (ebook) | DDC 782.42166092/2—dc23
LC record available at https://lccn.loc.gov/2016052331

Cornell University Press strives to use environmentally responsible suppliers and materials to the fullest extent possible in the publishing of its books. Such materials include vegetable-based, low-VOC inks and acid-free papers that are recycled, totally chlorine-free, or partly composed of nonwood fibers. For further information, visit our website at www.cornellpress.cornell.edu.

For Aimée

Contents

Prologue: Grown Up Dead   1

The Sex Pistols, Disco, and the Dead   11

Cold Rain and Snow   23

Sonic Experiments   35

Just the Right Night   61

First Set   81

Second Set   105

Betty Boards   129

The Show That Never Happened   147

Epilogue: A Band Out of Time   173

Listening and Reading   181

Acknowledgments   197

Notes   203

Index   215

Grown Up Dead

The bus came by and I got on, that's when it all began.
—Bob Weir, "The Other One"

Following the Grateful Dead as a teenager in the mid-'80s it was easy to feel like I'd already missed too much. Even as the Dead were pumping out stellar shows there was always the sense that "in another time's forgotten space"—as Jerry sings in "Franklin's Tower"—things had been better, looser, freer . . . in '67, in '72, in '77, in '78, . . . in Egypt, at the Fillmore West, at the Matrix in San Francisco, at the Capitol Theatre in Passaic, and at Barton Hall in Ithaca.

Part of that feeling came from listening to bootlegs and hearing how far out on the sonic ledge the Dead had gone over the years. In a twist on Ram Dass's term "spiritual materialism," rather than jonesing for spiritually charged items that bring one closer to the source of one's devotion, it was easy to crave those transcendent musical moments that I'd never gotten to experience, despite the fact that I was experiencing plenty of my own. But another part of that longing came through having older Deadheads tell me that, yes indeed, things used to be better—and I had missed it. Deadheads can be cruel to each other that way.

It was thrilling to join the lineage of a band that had hit so many inimitable musical moments over twenty-five-plus years of playing live. After all, the magic was still regularly happening, and, particularly in the late '80s, the band was reaching a new peak, albeit a more refined one. But it was hard to escape the craving for the new, the desire to be on the ground floor with a band just starting out. Yet the only new music I heard growing up in my cozy, isolated little suburb came from the radio—and to my ears, all of it fell short. There was no danger, no recklessness, no feeling of exploration or even humor. What little I did catch that had some of those qualities—bits of early rap, some punk, a little CBGBs-style New Wave—was ultimately overwhelmed by waves of prepackaged synthetic rock coated in hair spray and served up limp, cold, and bloodless.

The Dead may have been playing long before I hit the planet in 1970, but in the 1980s they were still around, still delivering the most interesting music I had ever heard within a cultural milieu that I found fascinating. To paraphrase a famous Bill Graham band introduction: the Grateful Dead weren't the best at what they did, they were the only ones who did what they did.

But by the time Jerry died, I had gone through and back out the other side of the Dead touring scene. My last show in Buffalo on 6/13/93 left a bad taste in my mouth. The band sounded worn-out, like they were just going through the motions, and the scene was a shell of its former self. There was no camping or vending allowed anymore, and it was hard to spot a decent freak through the crowd of baseball hats and store-bought tie-dyes.

By then—owing to a combination of the slack music, the changes in the surrounding environment, and my own need to move into a new phase that wasn't focused on following the Dead—the whole scene felt like a drag. Or perhaps I was the one who was a drag on the scene. It happens that way sometimes.

When I first discovered the Grateful Dead in the mid-'80s, the entire experience—the music, the culture, the history, the rituals—was a complete revelation. In a very real way, the Grateful Dead became my religion and other fanatics my fellow congregants. Their music opened my ears to the possibilities of artistic expression and the insights into our humanity that can be accessed through improvisation. Nothing had ever opened me up that fast and that widely. Not only did I learn that I was an artist through the Grateful Dead, but I learned how to be one. For a writer who didn't yet know I was allowed to be one, Robert Hunter's lyrics were my gateway to the world of language, and the Dead's music modeled narrative arc better than any English class lesson I'd ever taken. Their music was Freytag's pyramid on acid.

As a fifteen-year-old kid listening to Dead bootlegs and albums over and over on my bedroom tape deck, I was struck dumb. Years later, I would read an interview with poet and publisher Lawrence Ferlinghetti in which he states, "The first thing a poet has to do is to live that type of life which doesn't compromise himself." As I began to live inside the Dead's catalog and world, it became clear to me that following the path being laid out for me—school, religion, career, walking the straight line—would indeed be compromising myself. If I wanted to use words to re-create the world in the hopes of unearthing an utterance that needed to be spoken, I would need to be brave and honest to myself. Even if it meant rejecting much of what I'd been raised to believe. The truth is, those institutions didn't want me any more than I wanted them. I just didn't know where else to go until I found the Grateful Dead.

Although this is a book about a specific show that the Grateful Dead played in 1977, it's also a book about the larger world of the Grateful Dead. Whether fans believe Barton Hall was one of the best Grateful Dead shows ever played, or that it's an overhyped stuffed sausage of a show, the root of those opinions is an unyielding passion for the music of the band. In honoring that passion, I have approached the legacy of Cornell '77 by looking at three main factors that have driven this one show—among more than twenty-three hundred shows—to be the subject of copious amounts of discussion and debate among music fans. First, 1977 was an exceptional year in the career of the band, and the musicians had reached, both personally and professionally, a high mark. Second, there is the matter of how the show in Ithaca was recorded and what that taping meant more generally to the experience of any given show and its subsequent dissemination in the tape-trading community. Third, there is the matter of where Cornell '77 fit in an ambitious spring tour schedule and how the Dead's touring operation functioned at that time. These points will not be addressed in linear order. Rather, the story will be spun out through vignettes, quotes, facts, figures, and opinions that, once combined, create a larger portrait of the majesty, myth, and magnificence of the show often referred to by Deadheads simply as "Cornell '77," "5/8/77," or "Barton Hall."

You will hear from Deadheads who went to the show. You will hear from non-Deadhead Cornell graduates who were responsible for putting on the show in the first place. You will hear from record executives, academics, scholars, Dead family members, tapers, traders, and trolls. You will hear from those who still live the Grateful Dead every day. You will hear from those who would rather keep their Grateful Dead passions private for reasons both personal and professional. You will hear stories about the early days of being a Deadhead and what it was like to attend, and perhaps record, those early shows, including Cornell '77. You will read fresh perspectives selected from the dozens of interviews I conducted while researching this book. You won't hear new information from any band members, however, because, as Bob Weir told me by e-mail, "I'm not sure I'm going to remember the sound check, or even that show. I'll try to find some time at some point soon to listen to it, and see if any memories come back." The memories must not have come back. I never got a direct statement about Cornell from Bob or any other band member, despite multiple approaches from me and from other sources close to them. Hell, even Weir's yoga instructor asked on my behalf.

It's all good, though. Namaste. As Mark Pinkus, president of the Dead's record label, says, "It's not that they don't care, it's just that their priority is always what they're doing next. They've always been a band that looks forward."

Thinking about all of the time that has passed since 1977 and the band's grueling tour schedule that spring, I would be more surprised if Weir or any of the band members actually did remember specific details about Cornell '77. After all, at the time, it was just another gig on the road. Cornell was just another college trying to put on rock 'n' roll shows in a terrible-sounding multipurpose field house that also served as training grounds for their branch of the ROTC. How terrible sounding, you ask? The story goes that in 1980 when the Dead came back to play Barton Hall, an immense field house built in collegiate gothic style around the time of World War I (complete with heavy fieldstone walls, crenellations, and narrow windows reminiscent of a French cathedral), Garcia called the space a "toilet bowl," and Weir changed the chorus of "Playing in the Band" to "playing in the barn." (Even the local reporter from the *Ithaca Journal* would write after the 1977 show that Barton was "never known for its ideal acoustics.") Please don't underestimate the significance of Bob Weir changing key lyrics to comment on the terrible acoustics of a hall. They played a lot of bad-sounding places that he never commented on during a show. Apparently, Barton Hall stands out for both positive and negative reasons.

Despite the silence from the band members on Cornell '77, the common denominator that ties together everyone who appears in this book is the impact of the show played on May 8, 1977. Whether it was hearing a recording of the show for the first time or actually attending it, each person interviewed for this book had his or her first encounter with Cornell '77 long ago. In one way or another, they have all grown up Dead. In many cases, that encounter became the impetus to a musical passion that persists to this day. It's a passion that has caused East Coasters to pack up and move west. It has formed the basis for life-defining relationships. Other relationships it has destroyed. That passion has made good people do bad things and bad people do kind things. The music has been spiritual, recreational, devotional, disappointing, elevating, and, a surprising number of times, revelatory. Whatever it is, it is always inimitable. It is always, singularly, the Grateful Dead. It is a passion I know well.

Yet when an editor and the publisher at Cornell University Press first approached me with the idea to write a book about the fabled Barton Hall show, I was dubious. Cornell '77 was amazing, of course, but an entire book about a single show? Seems a little extreme, no? The other personal hurdle I faced was that, frankly,

I thought the next night's show at Buffalo was better. In my opinion, that "Help > Slip > Frank" opener was one of the most vigorous sprints-out-of-the-gate that the Dead ever played. There was no sense of tentatively dipping their toes into the water. There was no getting acquainted with the venue, encountering the first of the night's equipment bugaboos, or remembering where the F♯m goes. The Dead were so *en fuego* with "Help > Slip > Frank" that it might as well have come during the second set of the previous night. Interestingly, during a phone interview for this book, a similar idea was suggested by someone who has thought a lot about the Grateful Dead. Two people, in fact. Bestselling author and Deadhead Steve Silberman told me that his friend the journalist and Deadhead Sam Gustin believes that Buffalo 5/9/77 is best understood as the third and fourth sets of Cornell 5/8/77. It's all one big show that just happens to occur at two different venues on two different nights. Silberman found this concept compelling. I do too. It's trippy, right?

So it goes with Cornell '77. The legend grows. The debate rages on. Deadheads are never short of opinions, and everyone has one about Cornell. As this book is published, Rhino Records will issue the first official release of Cornell 5/8/77 as a standalone show and also as part of a box set, *May 1977: Get Shown the Light*, that includes New Haven 5/5/77, Boston 5/7/77, and Buffalo 5/9/77. Because those releases weren't available while writing this book, I settled for listening to the show literally hundreds of times online. My personal favorite pre-Rhino version is the matrix recording that combines Steve Maizner's audience recording with Betty Cantor-Jackson's board recording remastered with audience splices by Rob Eaton. It's got all the amazing clarity and instrument delineation of the "Betty Board" recording, but with enough dashes of crowd noise that you feel like you're standing on the rail at Jerry's feet.

However, with Rhino's new release of Cornell '77, the gold standard has been reestablished. Prior to that release, there were seventeen different versions online, and collectively they've been streamed more than 1.8 million times. Compare that to, say, 380,000 streams for the next night's show in Buffalo, or 36,000 for the early show of 2/13/70 at the Fillmore East, and you get a sense of how many ears have sought out this particular gig. It's also been packaged and sold illegally in bootleg versions by shady record labels around the world, such as the widely circulated three-CD set from the shamefully successful British-based Silver Rarities company. Whether you think the show deserves its praise or not, if you add up the new official Rhino release with all those streams and bootleg album sales, plus the unknowable number of physical copies that have been dubbed and shared, it's fair to conclude that Cornell '77 is one of the—if not *the*—most listened to Dead shows of all time. For certain, it's the only one that's been deemed worthy of inclusion in the Library of Congress's National Recording Registry.

With so many years on the road and miles beneath their feet and wheels, the Grateful Dead has origin myths that are oft told and more colorful with each telling. If you're looking for a straight account of the band focused on the key personalities, your best bet is to read *A Long Strange Trip: The Inside History of the Grateful Dead*, by Dennis McNally. Dennis was the band's publicist from 1984 until the end of the Grateful Dead and, more important for these purposes, was also hand-selected by Jerry Garcia to write an official biography of the band. His book is the most detailed, well-researched, and well-written one available. I was fortunate enough to conduct a wide-ranging interview with Dennis for this book. His thoughts about 5/8/77, including what Jerry might make of the reverence for the show, and other Dead-related topics are sprinkled throughout these pages.

The origin myths return again and again. Yet by 1977 there was a frequently aired opinion that the best years of the Dead were behind them. They were older, if not old. They were tired. Their music was not changing the times as New Wave, disco, and punk appeared to be doing. Some said the Dead had devolved to a nostalgia act. A good listen to the shows of 1977 and *Terrapin Station*, released that year, disproves much of that skeptical bluster. But, no doubt, the writing on the Dead is more voluminous and more robust covering the late 1960s and early 1970s eras. There is definitely more space to add to the revival stories of the band's resurgence in the late 1970s.

This book adds to that cause. Yet my assumption when writing this book is that if you're interested in finding out more about one particular show, like Cornell '77, you're most likely already familiar with the Grateful Dead in a wider sense. In some cases, "familiar with the Grateful Dead" may be a massive understatement— once one goes full-blown Deadhead, the buy-in tends to be pretty steep. This is not a detailed history of the Dead in 1977, so for newer fans and seasoned vets alike, if you'd like to know more about the history of the Grateful Dead, I suggest you peek at the "Listening and Reading" section at the back of this book. There you will find a list of publications that I consulted or quoted from while writing *Cornell '77*. Each one has its own merits and offers up new insights into the history and legend of the Grateful Dead; a story that is deep, nuanced, and that—more than two decades after Jerry Garcia died—continues to unfold.

Barton Hall, Cornell University, Ithaca, New York, 5/8/77. Sit back and listen to the crowd mill around the cavernous space of the hall. Daylight fades outside the massive windows as evening falls swiftly over central New York. Blazing house lights illuminate the stage and shine down on the mass of fans already pressed up against the front rail. It's almost show time. The floor of the hall is packed and buzzes with anticipation. The house lights come down as Candace Brightman's light show takes over. Jerry walks on stage; there is no fanfare, just a man in a black t-shirt going to work. Phil drops a few test bombs on his bass. Keith makes a run down the keys. Bob strums three chords and then steps back to adjust his gear. The drummers, Mickey and Billy, are cracking jokes with the crew while Donna paces back and forth at the front of the stage. The air is electric, the Grateful Dead are in town, the show is about to begin. . . .

The Sex Pistols, Disco, and the Dead

I'm not that taken with my own ideas. I don't really have that much to say, and I'm more interested in being involved in something that is larger than me. —Jerry Garcia, 1977

The Grateful Dead had nothing to do with 1977. They were anachronistic, out of step, out of vogue, and, excepting the ether used to cut their cocaine, out of cultural gas. Fortunately, no one who loved them gave a damn. Including the band themselves. In a friendly 1981 interview on Tom Snyder's *The Tomorrow Show*, Snyder asked Bob Weir and Jerry Garcia, "If you could hold your music, as they say, up to the light now after sixteen years, what changes do you see in what you've done over the years and how have you managed to be evolutionary and stay current?"

After a couple seconds of silence and one raised eyebrow from Garcia as he gazed down at Weir's shoe, Weir sounded off: "I don't think we've stayed current. I don't think we ever were current." Garcia perked up, nodding, and furrowing his brow in agreement as only a worldly West Coast beatnik can manage with sympathetic grace, "Yeah, right, that's about closer to the truth, yeah.

We never were current." Weir, encouraged by Garcia's nod—the two very much playing out their interconnected onstage dynamic in front of the TV cameras—continued, "I think we've been sort of singular in our whole endeavor. And probably stay that way. I mean, all we're trying to do is just satisfy our own standards." Then Weir stared straight at Snyder and, with utter and complete sincerity, concluded of the band's standards, "They're pretty steep."

In a twisted funhouse parallel, five years before the Dead were on *The Tomorrow Show*, the Sex Pistols were part of an incendiary television interview on a show called *Today*. The interview destroyed a journalist's career and elevated the Pistols into naughty gods. The host was Bill Grundy, who was, allegedly, drunk, and certainly disdainful of the band. He began the interview by describing the previously reigning bad boys of rock, the Rolling Stones, as "clean by comparison," and setting up the interview environment by saying, "They're a group called the Sex Pistols, and I'm surrounded by all of them." Once he had established his under-siege, "surrounded" mentality, Grundy began to lash out in an attempt to deflate the Pistols' dangerous image. He continued, "I am told that that group have received forty thousand pounds from a record company. Doesn't that seem, er, to be slightly opposed to their antimaterialistic view of life?"

Steve Jones, the band's guitarist, replied, "We fuckin' spent it, ain't we?"

And that was that: with a single "fuckin'," the Sex Pistols had launched their sneering, snot-nosed pose into mainstream Britain's face. Once the cork was out of that bottle, the band and their mates proceeded to smash it across the nose of Grundy and his viewing audience. Bourgeois culture enthusiasts would never be the same.

Grundy landed one weak, parting blow as he signed off from the broadcast. "I'll be seeing you soon. I hope I'm not seeing you [the Sex Pistols] again. From me, though, goodnight." But the damage had been done. Bill Grundy was off the air the following day, and the UK's *Daily Mirror* newspaper ran a headline about the interview titled, "The Filth and the Fury!" The Sex Pistols were legends. The culture wars of the mid-1970s had staked out a new beachhead, which, make no mistake, had the remnants of hippie culture in its bull's-eye every bit as much as straight, mainstream culture.

In many ways, mainstream culture wasn't the antithesis of mid-1970s punk. Subcultural hippies like the Grateful Dead were. In his book *Lipstick Traces: A Secret History of the Twentieth Century*, Greil Marcus writes about attending the Sex Pistol's final concert at the Winterland in San Francisco on January 14, 1978: "That was how I felt when Johnny Rotten sang 'Anarchy in the U.K.,' 'Bodies,' 'No Feelings,' 'No Fun.' When he finished that last number, his last performance as a member of the Sex Pistols, when he threw it all back on the crowd—which was, to him, no more than a representation of a representation, five thousand living symbols of Scott McKenzie's 1967 Love Generation hit, 'San Francisco (Be Sure to Wear Flowers in Your Hair),' symbols of mindlessly benevolent hippies who knew nothing of negation—when he said, leaving stage, gathering up any objects of value, 'Ever get the feeling you've been cheated?,' that was how I felt." Ironically, the Grateful Dead played the last concert ever at Winterland Arena less than one year later on New Year's Eve 1978. Far from being cheated, the crowd that night was treated to a five-hour-long concert, which included the appearance of some very special guests (Dan Aykroyd and Ken Kesey, among others), and which ended only when Bill Graham distributed free breakfast to the entire audience at dawn.

The labels "hippie" and "counterculture" are synonymous because hippies largely operated against—or counter to—mainstream culture. Said another way, many hippies were "against" what mainstream culture represented. While "subculture" and "counterculture" are often also used synonymously, there's an important distinction between groups that operate "counter" to a dominant culture and ones that operate "sub" or below it. Hippies who were against the war, against discrimination, against drug laws, against government laws that impinged upon personal freedoms, and so forth, were operating within a countercultural context. They were using their energies to push back against the values, mores, and laws of their day. Hippies who simply wanted to "drop out" and be left alone by mainstream culture were operating on a subculture value system. They didn't strive to change the world—they just wanted to be ignored enough not to get hassled.

Backed into a corner following a raid on the band's house in San Francisco in 1967 that resulted in several arrests for possession of marijuana, the Grateful Dead held a televised press conference in which their then co-manager, Danny Rifkin, read a statement on behalf of the band. The statement was written by Rifkin's friend Harry Shearer. Although Shearer would go on to become a comedy hero for his character voices in *The Simpsons* and for his role as bass player Derek Smalls in the spoof rockumentary film *This Is Spinal Tap*, the statement was no joke. Shearer's words, and the more spontaneous question-and-answer session that followed, encapsulate both sides of the hippie ethos, using drug laws as the jumping-off point. While the Dead maintained a largely subcultural mentality throughout their career, the marijuana bust forced them into a more defensive, countercultural position. Rifkin began his statement by saying, "The real danger to society, as well as to thousands of individuals, comes from a law that is so seriously out of touch with reality. The law contains an even greater evil. It encourages the most outrageously discriminatory type of law enforcement."

As he stiffly read aloud, it became clear that Rifkin's (and, by extension, the band's) discrimination argument hinged on the belief that if all the "lawyers, doctors, advertising men, teachers, and political office holders" who smoke marijuana were arrested, the laws would change immediately in their favor. But, as it stood, the police were targeting young men and women who fit the hippie profile. Rifkin went on to state that hippies were largely a construct of a media that too easily labeled a group of people who were simply "individuals trying to develop styles of life as free men and women" and that the stereotype resulted in institutional discrimination. Finally, despite Rifkin's statement about this "outrageously discriminatory type of law enforcement," when he was asked whether he would participate in a group who organized to fight against unfair drug laws, Rifkin responded, "I don't participate in movements." Here, in a single press conference, we witness the Grateful Dead at the crossroads of counter- and sub-cultures. They wanted to see the drug laws that resulted in their arrests changed but didn't wish to actively fight against such widespread, institutional discrimination. Instead, they simply wanted the problems—the culture at large—to go away and leave them, as "individuals trying to develop styles of life as free men and women," in peace.

For most of their career, the Grateful Dead staunchly maintained that antipolitical, subcultural stance. While they played the occasional benefit for a good cause, they made it known that they did not view their band as a vehicle for sociopolitical change. Peter Richardson, author of *No Simple Highway: A Cultural History of the Grateful Dead*, asserts, "When it comes to politics, I think they belong in the Buffalo Bill Cody camp. As the first global media superstar, Cody had strong views (about slavery, for example) about politics and society of the late 19th century. But like the Dead, he opted for politically vague symbols after a very divisive Civil War." Garcia summed things up more offhandedly in a 1989 interview in *Rolling Stone*: "For me, the lame part of the Sixties was the political part, the social part. The real part was the spiritual part."

In an open letter / free-verse poem written after he "caught" his friend's funeral, Ken Kesey would praise Garcia for opting out of the politics of the day: "Nobody ever heard you use that microphone as a pulpit. No anti-war rants, no hymns to peace. No odes to the trees and All Things Organic. No ego-deaths or born-againnesses. No devils denounced no gurus glorified. No dogmatic howlings that I ever caught wind of. In fact, your steadfast denial of dogma was as close as you ever came to having a creed." Likewise, on the cusp of Phil Lesh, Mickey Hart, and Bob Weir reuniting for a 2008 concert at the Warfield Theatre in San Francisco in support of young presidential hopeful Barack Obama—a rare political moment for the band members—Weir offered reporters this insight and reminiscence about how John F. Kennedy's assassination may have shaped the band's antipolitical stance: "The last time hope was in the air, it was ended by a bullet." He made clear: "We've been reluctant to do political events all along."

By 1977 the Dead were more than a decade down their subcultural artistic path. In an interview that year, journalist and Grateful

Dead expert David Gans asked Bob Weir what he listened to on his own time. Weir responded, "Elton John listens to everything that comes out, I've been told, and he keeps up on it that way. I like to listen to, like, African music or classical music or jazz or North Indian classical music—anything that I might not normally run into. It just seems like my own little obsession with getting away from where I am now. It seems kind of pointless to listen to nothing but rock 'n roll and then try to come up with an original approach to anything. That's kind of beside the point, because what you really need to get an original approach is that good old-fashioned flash of inspiration, no matter what your sources are. I like to bring other kinds of stuff into what I'm doing." While the answer gives some measure of the band's dissociation from the music of their time, it's also revealing to hear Weir clarify that he seeks out music that he "might not normally run into."

As all can attest to who have ever heard themselves humming the catchy-as-hell earworm hook of a popular song they seemingly can't stand, it is extremely difficult to fully disengage from the music of your time, much less the times themselves. Like it or not, if you are in any way socially engaged in the outside world, hit songs have a way of seeping into your brain. This would have been especially true at a time when radio ruled and things like personal cassette players—much less iPods, iPhones, or i-anything—hadn't yet been invented. Even if it was only during a cab ride from a restaurant to your boyfriend's house, you were bound to hear the latest smash hit. Despite the long-standing cultural impact of punk, we aren't talking about the Sex Pistols either. The Sex Pistols—much like the Dead—didn't earn their following thanks to radio play. The music that ruled the airwaves in 1977 was largely in two genres, what we currently define as "easy listening" and, more culturally significant, "disco."

According to the *Billboard* Year End Charts, the songs dominating the radio in 1977 were

1. Rod Stewart: "Tonight's the Night (Gonna Be Alright)"
2. Andy Gibb: "I Just Want to Be Your Everything"
3. Emotions: "Best of My Love"
4. Barbra Streisand: "Love Theme from *A Star Is Born*"
5. Hot: "Angel in Your Arms"
6. Kenny Nolan: "I Like Dreamin'"
7. Thelma Houston: "Don't Leave Me This Way"
8. Rita Coolidge: "(Your Love Has Lifted Me) Higher and Higher"
9. Alan O'Day: "Undercover Angel"
10. Mary MacGregor: "Torn between Two Lovers"

Falling just below the top 10, at spots 11 and 12, were the disco hits "I'm Your Boogie Man" by K.C. and the Sunshine Band and "Dancing Queen" by ABBA.

If punk was one half of the mid-1970s underground, disco was the other half. The difference was that disco knew how to dress up nice when it needed a seat at the larger table. Or, in this case, a ranking on the *Billboard* charts. But disco didn't start out mainstream. In fact, as with so much American music, it was birthed by the very people most marginalized by those who would one day colonize it completely. In this case, it was homosexuals, African Americans, and Hispanics. As editor and journalist Adam Mattera writes, "John Travolta flares, hen parties off to *Mamma Mia!* and grown men dressing as schoolboys for wacky school disco nights. Now that is not what I call disco." Moving beyond the look and the posing, he observes, "In its proud and glorious mid-70s Manhattan heyday, disco was far more than that. It was a four-on-the-four bassline, euphoric strings, fierce cowbells and a soaring vocal straight out of the church and on to the dancefloor. More importantly it created a place—or rather it soundtracked a space—outside the mainstream. A place where black, Hispanic, gay and any combination thereof could come together and dance, love and just be without fear."

Mattera goes on to outline the crucial validation and safety that the early disco scene provided key members of its community. "Early clubs such as David Mancuso's Loft and Nicky Siano's Gallery, now whispered about in reverential tones by true discophiles, were always so much more than the sum of their parts," he writes by way of showing that the social scenes that became possible after the repeal of the New York bylaw criminalizing two or more men dancing together were as critical to the early gay rights movement as the more overt political events and protests. Musical and culture writer Jesse Jarnow draws an even clearer line between Mancuso's Loft and the psychedelic world of the Grateful Dead: "While the Dead played five blocks to the north at the Fillmore East, a Timothy Leary follower named David Mancuso threw a soiree at his loft, calling the party Love Saves the Day and DJing soul and funk and rock records for his friends. As the name suggested, the punch was well zapped. . . . If one can tentatively trace several major religions to psychedelics, one can confidently do the same with disco and the entire genre of dance music that follows, and pinpoint the explosion to David Mancuso's Loft, which quickly becomes capitalized."

Although it originally referred to speakers who could move back and forth between different languages, the term "code switching" has evolved to mean a communicative style that shifts between different identities based on who the speaker is addressing and the information he or she is trying to convey. Because individuals within disco's groups of origin were often forced to code switch for their very survival—presenting themselves in a manner more in line with the dominant culture's communication style in order to make it easier to earn a living, get an education, avoid an assault, etc.—the music that represented them also adapted the ability to code switch and thus became palatable to a wider audience than its origins would indicate.

In short order, disco *was* mainstream music. It was unavoidable and, depending on whom you were speaking to, even insidious. So insidious, in fact, that with the November 15, 1978, release of the Grateful Dead's tenth studio album, *Shakedown Street*, a derogatory term began being floated around by Deadheads to describe the band's new sound: Disco Dead. The critics were no more enamored of the Dead's crossover sound than were their hard-core fans. Rolling Stone's review of the song "Shakedown Street" on their eponymous album noted, "The disco tinges in the latter merely add to the catastrophe."

However, the Dead weren't disco, they weren't punk, and, as was so often the case, their new album offered barely a glimpse of the true musical depth of the songs. In fact, three tracks on the album, "Shakedown Street," "I Need a Miracle," and "Fire on the Mountain," became staples of the Dead's live shows, and "Fire on the Mountain," in particular, was a vehicle for some of the band's most creative, evocative, harrowing, haunting, and exhilarating musical passages. The song made its live debut at the fabled Winterland Arena, in San Francisco, on March 18, 1977. That night, as happened numerous times in the months and years to come, the band musically linked "Fire on the Mountain" to the song "Scarlet Begonias" and used that powerful combination to end the first set of their three-night run at the arena.

Two months later, the band would continue to employ the same combination (featured so frequently it would often be referred to in Deadhead shorthand simply as "Scar-Fire") on their spring tour of the East Coast, beginning at the Spectrum, in Philadelphia, on March 22, and through and beyond the May 8 show in Ithaca.

Cold Rain and Snow

I remember it being one of these great hippie social experiments
like . . . when in the absence of actual authority people just get
together and do the right thing and it all just comes together.
—JoAnne Narad, 2015

Snow hadn't factored into Robert Wagner's plans at all. It was
a little cold, sure, but after all it was upstate New York, where
spring can be nothing more than a lovely, fleeting moment between
winter and summer. But even for upstate New York, snow in May
was rare. Besides, going to college in North Carolina had allowed
him to weed out most of the winter wardrobe he'd relied upon while
growing up in Long Island. But now he was back in New York and
using his time between college graduation and the start of medical
school to do what he loved best—go to Grateful Dead concerts.

The spring 1977 tour fell at a reasonably good time for Wagner's schedule. He had shot back east to catch a couple of shows at
the Capitol Theatre in Passaic, New Jersey, in April, and then he
had a little free time between the end of classes and the start of
his summer job when he could do a mini-tour in early May. His
plan was to see the Dead in New Haven, Ithaca, and Buffalo. But,

as with the April shows, he'd have to move fast to make it back to North Carolina in time to meet his commitments. He would have preferred to stay on tour with the Dead, but his parents were coming from Long Island for his graduation ceremony, and he couldn't blow them off. College graduation is a big deal for parents. Even bigger than catching an epic version of the Dead's new masterpiece, "Terrapin Station."

Wagner's first shows were at the Academy of Music in 1972. The Dead were about to embark on their legendary first tour of Europe, but before leaving they were playing seven consecutive shows for their fiercely devoted New York City fans. In Long Island in the early 1970s the Grateful Dead were omnipresent in Wagner's high school rock 'n' roll circles. Wagner had heard the band's name and caught flashes of the music buzzing among his buddies, but after sitting in the cafeteria and hearing his classmates rave about the shows they'd seen at the Academy the previous night, he was more determined than ever to see this band for himself. Needless to say, by the time the Grateful Dead pulled out of New York City, they had yet another fan for life.

After the Academy shows in 1972, Wagner saw the Grateful Dead whenever he could. He saw them in 1973 at the Springfield Civic Center in Massachusetts. That same year he saw them at Dillon Stadium in Hartford, Connecticut, and in 1974 he caught them at Roosevelt Stadium in Jersey City, New Jersey. He also saw them at Duke University in 1976. To fill in the gaps between concerts—including the painful two-year drought between Roosevelt Stadium and Duke—he began tracking down bootleg recordings of the band. It wasn't easy; the bootleg taping community was still very small at that point, and North Carolina wasn't nearly the Grateful Dead hotbed that Long Island was. But Wagner had a subscription to a new magazine called *Dead Relix* that contained a classifieds section for people looking to trade tapes, and he slowly began making connections and building his own small library of choice recordings. He hadn't started recording his own tapes yet—that wouldn't happen until 1978—but show by show, tape by tape, Wagner was joining a close-knit community of similarly die-hard fans.

The difference between the shows that Wagner was seeing in May 1977 and the ones he had seen in the past was that he wasn't returning to his usual life in between them. He was staying on the road with the Grateful Dead. He and his road partner were camping along the way, and, being poor college students, they were committed to keeping expenses as low as possible. Since they weren't going to the May 7 show at the Boston Garden, they had a couple of days to drive from the show in New Haven on May 5 to the scenic campus of Cornell University in time to see the band on Mother's Day.

As they drove across central New York and neared Ithaca, it got colder at night. Uncomfortably cold—down into the low forties. But those wide differences in daytime and nighttime temperatures were typical of the region in that season. While planning the trip it had never occurred to Wagner that snow was even a possibility. If they had had a weather report out of Ithaca, they would have learned that on Saturday, May 7, skies were clear and temperatures had reached 77. But on Sunday it got no warmer than 54 and low clouds rolled in over Cayuga Lake. By the time Wagner and thousands of other Deadheads exited Barton Hall after the show, flurries were in the air. It was unseasonable, yet kind of beautiful. Peaceful even. It was all just a part of the trip.

What Wagner hadn't factored into his plans was that meteorological aftershocks were looming from a brutal winter in central and western New York. Winter 1977 had seen a record-setting blizzard hit the region. The storm had claimed twenty-three lives across the state, with most being recorded in western New York close to Lake Erie. Between January 28 and February 1, daily wind gusts reached from forty-six to close to seventy miles per hour, and an accumulation of more than a hundred inches of snowfall created drifts as high as forty feet. Even the weather-toughened residents of western New York, and particularly the city of Buffalo and Erie County, were staggered by the ferocity of the season. Ithacans had not endured the snowfall that Buffalo residents had that late January weekend, but temperatures were in the single digits for them. It was another tough weekend in an already grueling winter.

By May, people in places ranging from Ithaca to Buffalo were ready to get outdoors and celebrate spring, Mother's Day, and the end of the semester. At Cornell on Ithaca's East Hill, Mother's Day weekend was traditionally an activity-filled one. The wide expanses of lawn stretching between the architecturally eclectic clusters of buildings were filled with students celebrating the home stretch of another semester. In addition to the Dead, Dr. John played a concert on campus that weekend, and there was even a showing of a then-rare 3-D movie. If the weather took a turn before the concert, Cornell students and Ithaca townies (unlike Wagner, who was coming to town strictly as a fan) had the option of retreating to their dorm rooms and homes for shelter. JoAnne Narad, a Cornell student who took advantage of that option, fully embraced the wide range of activities the weekend had to offer: "My experience started at midnight the night before. The show was on a Sunday, and on Saturday night, at the hall kitty-corner to Barton Hall, they were having a midnight showing of *Creature from the Black Lagoon* in 3-D. In those days, 3-D was very trippy. We figured the thing to do was to get ourselves properly prepared and go see this movie in the middle of the night and then just walk over to Barton Hall and spend the night hanging out with the tour rats who would surely be gathering by then."

The weather had cooperated just fine for the early part of Narad's plan. But by the morning of the Dead show, the sky was beginning to turn gray, and it was clear that the weather was changing. What had seemed like a great idea—hanging outdoors with all her fellow Grateful Dead fans and "tour rats" who were following the band—no longer seemed as appealing as heading back to her dorm for a few hours of sleep. When she returned to Barton in the afternoon, the weather had already turned rainy and cold. Yet instead of cursing the dreary weather, Narad and her fellow fans came together to make the best of it.

"By the time we came back that afternoon it was getting nasty. By the time the doors opened, it was raining and it was cold. I remember it being one of these great hippie social experiments," Narad remembers. "All the people who were there in front who had been hanging all night had blankets and sleeping bags and tarps and stuff, and when it started to rain everybody lifted them up over their heads and we made like a patchwork of blankets and tarps over everybody's heads. But the thing was, you couldn't hold your arms up for that long. They'd fall asleep and get tired. So at any given time there had to be a certain percentage of people with their arms up and a certain percentage of people with their arms resting. But at any given time if there were too many people letting go, the thing collapses and we all get soaked. So we had this system going of taking turns and letting people rest and other people stepping up and holding up the tarp." For Deadheads and college students gathering at Barton Hall, even a reprise of winter couldn't sour the fact that the Grateful Dead were in town and springtime had finally arrived.

That ebullient mood would carry into the hall. One of the unique aspects of a Dead show, no matter the venue, was the high degree of interplay of energy between the band and the crowd. Because each show, each set list, each performance of any given song was unique to the night it was performed, it is not a reach to think that the performances themselves might reflect the ambience of the venue and the mood of the crowd. The Cornell students, Ithaca townies, and itinerant Deadheads were ready to supply as much positive energy as was needed.

As a group, the Grateful Dead first explored the invisible but still somehow material connections between themselves and the audience during their performances at the so-called Acid Tests in the mid-1960s. The Acid Tests were a California phenomenon initiated by Ken Kesey as a way to explore the creative and social potential of LSD. The Grateful Dead were the "house band" for the tests. The experiences that they had playing under the influence of LSD found its literary representation in a popular science fiction novel published in 1953. As Phil Lesh describes, "The word 'blesh' is used in Theodore Sturgeon's novel *More Than Human*, which is essentially the story of how certain human beings communicate with each other telepathically and form a greater organism." The concept had its experiential equivalent at those early Dead shows, Lesh remembers. "And when we first started playing together at the Acid Tests and in the bars it slowly became apparent that that's what was happening to us on the musical level in the sense that we were manifesting this togetherness or this unity or this single organism and it just grew and grew in that direction."

Bill Kreutzmann expanded the concept of the "blesh" experience to include the audience and even some divinity: "That's why I started playing music. To make people feel good, because it made me feel good too. That's what the Grateful Dead's all about—communication between the band and the audience. They're really the seventh band member. There is some great power, be it God or whatever, that enters the Grateful Dead on certain nights, and it has to do with us being open and getting together with the audience. If we can do that, then it comes . . . and spreads everywhere."

If Lesh, Kreutzmann, and legions of Dead fans are correct, it follows that performing shows in central and western New York on the heels of one of the region's most intense winters in history would undoubtedly flavor the music being played. Locales that experience hard winters are often gripped by what is commonly referred to as "spring fever," as the promise of warm weather hangs just out of reach while yet more snow falls into March . . . April . . . even May. The Dead's May 1977 tour schedule brought the band into the heart of one of the most snow-punished areas in the United States. In retrospect, one can imagine a buzz of "spring fever" in the air, particularly among college students. Thankfully, as Narad's story and that of many others who attended the show attest, not even a final flurry of winter activity could diminish that rejuvenating spirit.

What Wagner, Narad, or any of the other attendees of the concert most likely never realized is that without the inspired, diligent work of the students on the Cornell Concert Commission, the show never would have happened at all. The impediment was not the weather but an unfortunate situation at a Deep Purple concert four years previous that had soured the Cornell administration on hosting rock concerts on campus.

Once upon a time, outdoor concerts were planned as regular events at Cornell's Schoellkopf Field, a large outdoor stadium where football and lacrosse games are played. Built in 1912 and

1913, the crescent-shaped bleachers on the east side of the field can accommodate more than twenty-five thousand people—the size of the crowds when Big Red football was routinely winning national championships in the early part of the twentieth century. In the early 1970s those glory days were long past, but the new "poly-turf" field surface was perfect for outdoor concerts. Thousands of stamping feet would barely bend a blade of synthetic grass. So audiences could fill the field and swell up into the stands, and that is just what Cornell students and administrators planned in 1973 when they inaugurated the Cornell Open Air Concert Series. It was a grand vision for outdoor fun during the central New York summer.

In June 1973, Deep Purple had been scheduled to play the first concert of the summer series cosponsored by the Cornell Concert Commission and two outside promoters, Concerts East and Festival East. The show had been postponed earlier in the month due to inclement weather. Unfortunately, it was raining again on Tuesday, June 12, when Deep Purple arrived in Ithaca, and there were reports of nearby lightning strikes. Because the temporary stage that had been erected was made of metal, the band members were concerned about getting electrocuted. Their opening act, a promising young band named ZZ Top, braved the storm and performed their set, but Deep Purple refused to play. The crowd got restless as time passed and Deep Purple failed to take the stage. To make matters worse, power to the PA system had been cut following the band's refusal to play, thus making it impossible for the concert's organizers to adequately communicate the situation to the increasingly agitated, and inebriated, audience. When it finally became clear that the concert was not going to happen, the crowd of more than twelve thousand erupted in violence.

Turf was torn apart. A beautiful Steinway piano worth more than $10,000 was destroyed. The police and anyone even remotely associated with the production were pelted with rocks and bottles. In perhaps the strangest twist of all, because the tentlike structure around the stage couldn't be staked to the artificial turf, two architecture students had used thirty waterbeds as ballast for it. When the riot started, all thirty waterbeds were slashed open, unleashing massive pressurized waterspouts onto the field and the crowd. As one of those students, Nicholas Goldsmith, recounted, "We thought it was going to be a Woodstock, but it turned out to be more of an Altamont." The brutal 1969 stabbing death of Meredith Hunter at a Rolling Stones concert in Altamont, California, had set up a polarity between Woodstock (mystical, magical) and Altamont (tragic) that haunted the conscience of the baby boom generation. For Goldsmith, the riot at the Deep Purple concert at Cornell brought those associations of violence and mayhem rushing back.

The Deep Purple riot lasted two hours and resulted in an estimated $75,000 in damages. Those expenses were covered by the co-promoters' insurance companies, ostensibly shielding the Cornell Concert Commission from any losses, but for reasons ranging from public safety to finances, the university administration soured on rock 'n' roll concerts. They were adamant (and remain so to this day) that no more concerts would be held outdoors at Schoellkopf Field. The Open Air Concert Series had only that one show before it was declared defunct. Rock shows continued at indoor campus venues like Bailey Hall and Barton Hall, but administrators were worried about another incident, and the CCC was on a short leash, its autonomy in question and its finances subject to scrutiny.

By 1975 the Cornell administration was wading warily back into the murky backwaters of rock 'n' roll. The college hosted sporadic rock concerts, including 1974 shows by Yes and Jefferson Starship, both at Barton Hall. What the administration was looking for, though, was an established concert promoter to bolster the efforts of the Cornell Concert Commission. The CCC had sustained significant financial losses on other concerts, in addition to the riot, and the administration didn't want to continue throwing good money after bad. At the urging of Mike McEvoy, the CCC's Selection Committee chairman, the college allowed a concert to be held at the two-thousand-seat Bailey Hall on October 27, 1975, with the participation of East Coast concert promoter John Scher. The concert was performed by the Jerry Garcia Band.

Much like the members of the Cornell Concert Commission he worked with to bring the Dead and other bands to campus, John Scher began promoting concerts while still a college student. During his time at Long Island University, Scher began working with a company called Monarch Entertainment Bureau, which was owned by a man named Otto Steinberg. (Scher would eventually take over Steinberg's company.) By his junior year of college, Scher was so successful as a concert promoter that he decided to drop out of school and pursue promoting full-time. When Bill Graham, in 1971, closed the Fillmore East—a venue that had all but locked-down the market for rock concerts in New York City—Scher moved quickly to step into the void Graham had left behind.

Roughly six months after Graham closed the Fillmore East, Scher opened up the Capitol Theatre in Passaic, New Jersey. The thirty-two-hundred-capacity theater—a former vaudeville house—became a must stop for touring rock bands coming through the New York City area. Although by the time the Capitol closed in 1989 it had lost some of its luster, throughout the 1970s touring bands from Chuck Berry to Alice Cooper to the Allman

Brothers to the Kinks all made stops there. One band that Scher took a particular role in helping book, promote, and launch into public consciousness early in his career was Jersey's own Bruce Springsteen and the E Street Band. In fact, Scher and the Cornell Concert Commission leveraged the success of the Dead's 1977 show to put on a Springsteen show at Barton Hall on November 7, 1978. Both shows were, at the time, rare sellouts for the Cornell Concert Commission. Along with Springsteen, the Grateful Dead were also closely aligned with both the Capitol Theatre and John Scher. As much as Bill Graham was the Dead's man on the West Coast, John Scher was their man in the East. With new ties to Scher, then, the CCC had access to some of the best national rock acts and a partnership with a promoter with acumen and skill. That professionalism surely allayed fears among Cornell administrators.

When Jerry Garcia played Cornell in 1975, the Grateful Dead were on a touring hiatus. But as soon as the Dead hit the road again, McEvoy and the CCC set their sights on bringing the band to campus. "In working with John, it was something we as the Concert Commission were very interested in doing—a Dead show at Cornell. Prior to the May '77 show we had done the Garcia Band at Bailey Hall in October of '75. That's a two-thousand-seat hall. So we were kind of working in the direction, greasing the skids if you will, to try to get the Dead into Ithaca at some point," McEvoy recalls. "After a lot of cajoling and arm twisting and trying to get all the pieces in place we were finally able to make it all happen."

An article in the *Cornell Daily Sun* titled "Dead Sell-Out Helps Commission Pay Debt" further illuminates the connection between Scher and the CCC. It appears that without Scher's intervention there may have been no future concerts at Barton Hall at all. "A portion of an anticipated $5,000 profit from the May performance by the rock band The Grateful Dead will partially offset the $94,700 owed to University Unions by the Commission as of last June. . . . Until fall 1975, the Commission was part of the University Unions. At that time, it was almost $99,000 in debt to the unions, which refused to continue sponsoring it. . . . Under its present contract with promoter John Scher, only Scher incurs losses from unsuccessful concerts. However, the commission must still pay for its operating expenses." The Dead show of May 1977, with budgeted costs of just $11,245, was then a triumph for McEvoy and the CCC. A show of this stature, and with a large anticipated crowd, would show that rock was alive and well on the Cornell campus. And the expected profits would help put the CCC back in good financial stead.

Sonic Experiments

At one of the Acid Tests—I don't know which one it was, it might have been Watts—it was a very strange experience where all of a sudden I was *looking* at sound coming out of the speakers. —Bear, 1991

After Jerry Garcia's funeral, Ken Kesey wrote a poetic note to his old friend titled "Message to Garcia." In it, he recalls hanging out with Garcia, Phil Lesh, and Ken "Intrepid Traveler" Babbs after the Muir Beach Acid Test. Kesey wrote:

I remember standing out in the pearly early dawn after the Muir Beach Acid Test, leaning on the top rail of a driftwood fence with you and Lesh and Babbs, watching the world light up, talking about our glorious futures. The gig had been semi-successful, and the air was full of exulted fantasies. Babbs whacks Phil on the back.

"Just like the big time, huh, Phil."

"It is! It is the big time! Why, we could cut a chart-busting record tomorrow!"

I was even more optimistic. "Hey, we taped tonight's show. We could release a record tomorrow."

"Yeah, right"—holding up that digitally challenged hand the way you did when you wanted to call attention to the truth or the lack thereof—"and a year from tomorrow be recording a 'Things Go Better With Coke' commercial."

The day Kesey was recalling was December 11, 1965. Kesey and his band of Merry Pranksters were experimenting heavily with audio and video recordings as a way to both chronicle and enhance their psychedelic adventures. Given his vocation and activities at that time, it is wise to interpret Kesey's admonition, "Get them into your movie before they get you into theirs," both metaphorically and practically; a man of both vision and action, he operated on both those levels simultaneously.

With regard to Grateful Dead recordings, his action ("we taped tonight's show") was certainly one of preternatural vision ("we could release a record tomorrow"). It was much more than an "exalted fantasy," though. In fact, fifty years later, it is not uncommon for fans—particularly those in the "jam band" musical community that was spawned by the Grateful Dead's improvisational live performances and touring model—to leave a concert having purchased a jump drive or URL password that will allow them to listen to a pristine, sound-board recording of the night's concert. For that matter, fans who were unable to attend the concert can buy a recording of the show, too. Chicago-based band Umphrey's McGee has pioneered such stage-to-ears purchasing, experimenting with different methods over the years. Their current sales model revolves around the website UMLive.org, which they call "The Definitive Live Home of Umphrey's McGee" and which boasts well over one thousand shows available for purchase for either a monthly or yearly fee. At the band's website you can create listening queues, playlists, download single songs or entire shows, and search for such minutiae as which song was played where, when, how often, and perhaps even extrapolate from those details where a song will be played next. It's the sort of obsessiveness that only true fanatics—Deadheads, for example—can appreciate. In short, Kesey's acid-fantasy of a live show being converted into a record release the following day was nearly spot-on regarding what people wanted and what technology would soon be able to offer.

At the time the Grateful Dead were touring, though, they did not yet have the ability to immediately release live concerts for sale. They recorded most shows directly off their sound board, but those recordings were kept largely within the band's inner circle. Instead, their fans assumed the role of making live recordings on their own equipment and circulating the tapes among themselves. Those recordings were traded among fans at no charge to each other, but with strict terms of protocol. That "bootleg" trading process would almost inadvertently build the Grateful Dead's fan base in ways the music industry proper had never anticipated. Although it took the band years to officially sanction the practice, by eventually ceding potential record sales in favor of allowing audience members to record their shows, the Dead broadened their audience base and also freed up fan dollars to be spent on merchandise and ticket sales. In so doing, they became one of the most profitable bands of all time.

But while the Dead's business strategies are interesting to examine, it would be pure rock 'n' roll blasphemy to reduce the "bootleg" legacy around their music to such crude parameters. Deadheads know the truth: bootleg recordings spread the gospel of the Grateful Dead. They were the cornerstone of the Deadhead community. Grateful Dead lyricist John Perry Barlow made clear that taping was "one of the most enlightened, practical, smart things that anybody ever did. I think it is probably the single most important reason that we have the popularity that we have. . . . [Tapes are the] article of currency for this economy, our psychic economy to say the least. . . . And by the proliferation of tapes, that formed the basis of a culture and something weirdly like a religion." Dennis McNally, the Grateful Dead's former publicist and official band historian, concurs: "The whole decision to allow taping—although it wasn't formalized until after Cornell—had all these unintended consequences. One of which was that it indicated a lot of trust with the audience. The assumption was that it wouldn't be used for commercial purposes. These tapes became, in anthropological terms, talismans. They were fragments, they were reliquaries, they had religious connotations, or tribal connotations." Indeed, the way that Deadheads traded and revered bootlegs was ritualized to the point of religiosity. A high-quality, first-generation sound board was close to a holy relic.

Within the Deadhead community, bootleg recordings were traded, debated, celebrated, and, in the case of the Grateful Dead's show at Cornell University on May 8, 1977, consecrated. If it wasn't for tapers and tape trading networks, it is unlikely that that particular concert would have risen to the top of the twenty-three-hundred-plus shows the Grateful Dead performed, to be inducted, thirty-six years later, into the Library of Congress National Recording Registry. The registry was created to preserve recordings that "are culturally, historically, or aesthetically important, and/or inform or reflect life in the United States." As far as Cornell '77 goes, Deadheads have long recognized its importance as a recorded artifact. As far as they are concerned, the Library of Congress is coming late to the party.

The status of the Barton Hall show owes a lot—some would say everything—to the quality of the recording. During the spring

1977 East Coast run, Betty Cantor-Jackson was working with the sound board, making a master recording of each show, "mixing the soundboard feed directly onto a two-track tape as the music was being performed." The recordings, which include the famed run of shows at Boston on May 7 and Buffalo on May 9—have an integrity and clarity that most audience bootlegs lack. They also convey a certain acoustic personality. "I can always tell when a recording is mine," Cantor-Jackson told Nick Paumgarten in 2012. "It has my tonalities. My sound is beefy. My recordings are very stereo, very open, with a lot of air in them. You feel like you're standing in the middle of the music. My feeling is everyone wants to play in the band." Somehow or other, whether it is the fidelity of the recording or the personality of the sound engineer who did the mix, there is something special about those tapes.

Longtime Deadhead Howard F. Weiner wrote about the powerful, and controversial, legacy of Cornell '77 in his book *Grateful Dead 1977: The Rise of Terrapin Nation*: "In a poll of Deadheads, 5–8–77 Cornell was ranked the greatest show ever. However, this by itself did not outrage academics and fanatics. *Deadbase* also made the mistake of polling these crispy critters on what their favorite versions of various songs were. Few were surprised that the 'Morning Dew' and 'Scarlet' > 'Fire' from 5–8–77 were top ranked." Then he digs into the controversy regarding opinion about Cornell '77 by noting that "what did incense the intelligence of knowledgeable fans was that the Cornell renditions of 'Jack Straw,' 'Estimated Prophet,' 'New Minglewood Blues,' and 'Lazy Lightning' > 'Supplication' finished in the number one spot as well. These rankings are a farce that can be chalked up to the fact that Cornell was the most popular and circulated tape of its time—the common denominator factor. Almost everybody voting in the *Deadbase* poll had a phenomenal copy of 5–8–77. Few other tapes had the circulation and sex appeal of Cornell." The legacy of Cornell '77, Weiner contends, has almost as much to do with the recording of the show as it does with the show itself. The experience of the sound, the capturing of the sound, and the sharing of the sound are equal parts of what turns a Dead show into a legend long after the band's gear is packed and the bus is gone.

The Grateful Dead's decision to allow recording at their concerts was a concession to the dogged persistence of Deadheads. The fans simply wore the band down. The reality was that some Deadheads were going to tape the shows whether the band wanted them to or not, so it made more sense to give them a section of their own, keep them out of the way, and let straightforward concertgoers enjoy the show without worrying about screwing up some obsessive taper's microphone setup. As Jeff Mattson, longtime Deadhead and guitarist for the Grateful Dead–inspired band Dark Star Orchestra, describes it, "The thing from a non-taper's point of view was you didn't want to be sitting next to a taper 'cause they were really anal. You couldn't make any noise. At least if you're in a taper section, you know what to expect. But if he is sitting next to you in a regular section, you can't make noise or walk in front of him. It can be a real drag." Divisions between regular concertgoers and tapers—who were, essentially, "working"—was stark and could be charged with animosity. It was certainly not the environment the Dead were looking to create with their music.

Despite the fact that recordings of the Grateful Dead go back to the band's origins, the band itself did not officially sanction taping until 1984. For example, on the band's contract rider for the Cornell 1977 show, page 4, clause 17, states: "Employer shall not permit any form of recording, filming or taping of the performance(s) of [sic] the taking of any photographs without the

Artist's prior written consent and shall take reasonable measures to insure such prohibitions. No filming or video or audio taping shall be permitted during or after or before performance, and no visitors with cameras shall be permitted in the Artist's dressing rooms or backstage without the Artist's explicit approval." The beginning of that clause also references page 3, clause 14, which, in pure-blooded legalize, stipulates: "Artist shall have the sole and exclusive right to film, record, tape, or otherwise reproduce, embody or transmit any and all performances by Artist, including without limitation audio tape, visual tape, and any other audio-visual process or solely audio or solely video process, and the performances embodied thereon shall be entirely and exclusively owned by Artist, together with all rights to manufacture, produce, sell, transfer, lease and otherwise exploit and deal in the same by any means, methods, in any media, and by any devices whatever now or hereafter known throughout the world, free from any claims whatever by Employer or any person deriving any rights or interests from Employer." Despite the labyrinthine language, the message is direct: The music is ours.

The Dead were wisely protecting themselves from predatory employers who might think that hiring the band to play a gig gives them some claim to recording and profiting on sales of the music being played there, ad infinitum. It is also clear that the onus was on the venues to keep fans from openly taping shows. The venues succeeded to a greater or lesser degree based on their staffing and familiarity with the band. Despite the band's best efforts though, Deadheads were simply too persistent to dissuade. So while the legal language was strong, the practical effect was uncertain and even weak. Could college students working for the Cornell Concert Commission readily identify and then challenge a hardcore taper in Barton Hall? And did the band really want to crack down on its fans, the people who flocked to their shows and kept them going night after night on the road?

Band publicist McNally remembers the situation well. "The real reason, and I witnessed this a number of times, that they made that decision to finally formalize it and create a taping zone was . . . because they were lousy cops, and to ban taping would have meant destroying the ambience of the show. But the other [reason] was that, literally, [soundman Dan] Healey couldn't see the stage anymore. There were so many mike stands in front of him that he literally couldn't see the stage. And large portions of the audience couldn't see the stage! At which point it was time to segregate, which worked well. It made everybody happy. The tapers didn't need to see the show. They were looking at dials!" Control was, in the end, practically impossible.

Given the band's Bay Area community origins, it is appropriate that the first show where taping was officially sanctioned was at the Berkeley Community Theatre on October 27, 1984. Grateful Dead staff member Steve Marcus was part of the decision about where to place the taper section. "I said, 'Why don't we put them behind the soundboard?' We never sold the seats behind the sound board anyway. Then they discussed charging $5 more for taper's tickets, but I said no. So we did an experiment. And it was a hit." Tapers had come out of hiding and now had dedicated places to set up their gear on the floor.

Previous to the band's sanction, tapers had to be ingenious when it came to getting the best possible recordings. Rob Eaton— sound engineer, seasoned Grateful Dead taper, and founding member of Dark Star Orchestra—tells of the early taping efforts. "I taped my first show with a rigged-up tape deck I borrowed from my high school. I rewired it so I could put a real microphone on it. Of course it didn't work out too well, but I kept working on it and evolving with it, and by '77 I made some good tapes, and by '78, '79 they were pretty good!" As Eaton describes, many Deadheads were inventive to the point of ruthlessness when it came to getting their recordings made. "We had a lot of creative ways to get in. We had girls with harnesses between their legs. The best, most creative but not too politically correct, was the wheelchair, where you would have a guy in the chair with a blanket over his lap and hide the tape deck and mike stand in pieces to fit on the side. We would go early and through the handicap area, and the guy in the wheelchair wouldn't get patted down! Barry Glassberg was a genius. He would come in a three-piece suit and a briefcase with a tape deck, stand, and mic inside the briefcase. You had to be creative." But the band was more or less passive about the tapers and let the show's promoters call the shots. Eaton remembers how "at Dartmouth College, no matter how hard I tried, I couldn't get in. Back then it was the venue. The band didn't care, but they didn't go to the venue and say, 'Let the tapers in.' They would be saying, 'No audio. No video.'" When the message was mixed, people had to be creative—and they were.

As an early taper, Eaton served as a witness to the birth of taping culture: "There weren't many of us back then, maybe four to six people with a mic, at most. It was hard to get in, too. You had to smuggle them in. There was Barry Glassberg, Jerry Moore—he was one of the first tapers and the founder of *Relix*. It was a very small community. We all knew each other, and we traded with each other. It exploded in probably the early eighties when people started buying tape decks." Then, by the early 1980s, he continues, "there were tons of tapers, and they would be up front, and they would have their mic stand, and that started to piss Healey off 'cause he was looking at the stage in a sea of microphone stands. I think it was the fall of '84 when they had their first taper section to try to alleviate that, and they said if you're up front, we will throw you out. That's when people used to get binaural heads with the mic built in. They put a bandanna on it and put it up on a stand, so it just looked like a six [foot]-three guy in the tenth row." The creativity of the tapers pushed limits and tested people's tolerance.

"There were some really aggressive tapers that were really mean, and that gave all tapers a bad name," Eaton says, underscoring the sometimes contentious relationship between listeners and dancers and the tapers. "That's kind of what put us off the scene. They would go and find the perfect spot on the floor, even if it wasn't their seat, and when people came they wouldn't give up the seat. They would say, 'Here, take these tickets and go sit somewhere else.' They would do some very passive aggressive things to get that spot, and it put a sour taste in my mouth."

But, as Eaton concludes, the fruits were worth the labor. "It's improvisational music, which is what the whole jam scene is based on—the jazz concept, which is no show or song is played the same, and there is no right or wrong way of doing it," he says, making a crucial point about why the Dead's live performances were more revered than their studio releases. "So you can collect all those tapes, and they are all valid to their own degree. Their own personality. So that's why you taped, because you didn't want to miss the 'good one.' That's why you taped a lot of them, although the tape never did it justice."

Eaton's early compatriot, Jerry Moore—one of the original tapers, and a cofounder of *Relix* magazine—tells his own story of becoming a taper: "I'm a native New Yorker, almost, I was actually born in Ireland, but I've been in New York most of my life. I got into the taping world ass-backwards, because there was no taping world at that time. I was in high school, this was long-about 1971, and one of my friends brought in a Grateful Dead bootleg album.

I had never seen such a thing before. So I said: This is interesting, where did you get this artifact?" With that question began a long, obsessive career of taping. Moore recounts that his friend said he got the bootleg in the Village around Sheridan Square where some guy had an armload of these things and was selling them. "So I said, Cool," he continues, "I'm gonna go get me one of those things. Except I couldn't. I never saw that guy. Believe me, I haunted that neighborhood too, looking for him! I could not find him. I've never been good at dealing with frustration, so, somehow or other, this eventually led to me making my own, because the stuff just wasn't there. What there was of it wasn't very good quality. So one thing led to another. If you want it done right, you do it yourself."

Moore's first taping efforts didn't turn out too well. In 1971 and 1972 there were a lot of poor tapes, and the quality was so bad that he didn't keep them for himself, let alone trade them with other tapers and collectors. "By the time I got into the middle of 1973, they were doing okay," Moore says. "The first ones I made that turned out okay were made with a Sony 110 mono portable cassette machine and an AKGD 1000E. For a while there I started carrying around an Atlas mic stand. Not one of your latter day mic stands, but the old cast iron solid steel ones. I'd hold that up at chest level with a boom for hours. It worked!" He remembers that, loaded down with equipment, "you had to keep an eye out for everybody. Even the environment itself was unpredictable. Random audience members could do some really erratic things even without active opposition." A false step or collision with a dancer could ruin a recording and bring both the taper and his equipment crashing to the floor.

Moore also offers some firsthand information on the early relationship between the band and the tapers. "There's this myth that the Grateful Dead encouraged taping. It's a crock of hooey," he says. "They totally didn't encourage taping. At least they didn't in the early days. They tried their best to stop it. They couldn't stop it. Basically they lost the war, then struck a compromise deal somewhere down the line." Like others, Moore sees the Dead as having been worn down by the tapers. And, like others, he sees this moment of concession to that taping community as a turning point for the band's larger reputation. "So the party line changed over the years to, 'Yeah, we encouraged it! Yeah, yeah, we're all for it!' It was a great deal for them. They should've been all for it earlier, because it's probably what made them what they were. I mean, definitely the music made them what they were. But what blew the whole scene into mammoth proportions was all the tapers!"

Grateful Dead expert David Gans concurs on the fan-making power of bootleg recordings: "When I was a young Deadhead in the early '70s, I went and saw the Dead at the Cow Palace in March of 1974, and a week later my buddy Feldstein had a reel of that show. There was this moment in 'China Cat Sunflower' when they get to the bridge, that E chord in the bridge, and Phil hit this note that rattled the whole building. And when we listened to it on the tape it distorted the tape too! It was like, 'Oh my god, that's so cool!' And then later that summer, a friend of mine had moved to New Orleans, and he met up with all these Deadheads at Tulane, and through them I started meeting all these guys. Those guys would send reels out, so I was hearing stuff from the summer '74 tour before the tour was over. It really was a great way of deepening this relationship with the music—and turning new people on to it." Person by person, ear by ear, Dead bootlegs made converts across the country. In addition to spreading amazing music for free, tapes were an exceptional advance promotion tool for the next time the band came through town.

Well before the band gave its OK to tapers and set space aside for them on the concert hall floor, random tapers cohered into a loose community of passionate traders and fans. They formed a network, small at the beginning, no more than a half dozen or so people, including one of the first tapers, Marty Weinberg. Along with Weinberg, Moore was among that network of early tapers that formed small "tape clubs" within their social circles of fellow fanatics. The next phase began when members of these tape clubs began exchanging business cards with each other to widen their networks. Once those networks began to expand, Moore, Les Kippel, Arty Carlyle, and some others within their network of early Deadheads formed the Free Underground Grateful Dead Tape Exchange to help tapers find each other. At that point, most within the network—the founders included—had no more than a few dozen hours of recorded live Dead shows—a number that, a few short years later, would barely constitute a tape collection at all. The taping, trading, and collecting grew almost exponentially; if you were a serious collector your collection was in the hundreds, and you were always on the lookout for that rare, excellent-sounding recording few others had.

Kippel recalls, "It was very important for us that we use the word 'free.' We did not want to buy and sell music—it was bad karma to do so, it wasn't our music. We wanted everything to be based on the concept of 'free.'" And this nonmonetary system of exchange attracted attention. "After we formed the Grateful Dead Tape Exchange, Charlie Rosen wrote an article about me in *Rolling Stone* where he called me 'Mister Tapes, king of the Grateful Dead Tape Exchange,'" Kippel continues. "I got about seventy-five letters from people all over the country who wanted to get involved in collecting tapes. All these people felt the same thing: that the Grateful Dead records that were out at the time did not give a true representation of what the Dead sounded like in concert."

In 1974, Moore and Kippel took their collaboration further and formed *Dead Relix*, primarily as a one-stop, handmade newsletter publication for tape collectors, to help them meet each other, learn more about taping, and to chronicle the Grateful Dead and its surrounding culture. Eventually, the "Dead" part of *Dead Relix* was dropped, and the publication morphed into a more professionally produced and written magazine. The magazine expanded and contracted its scope over the years to include musicians as far afield from the Grateful Dead as Ozzy Osbourne, but today it holds its focus on the "jam band" heirs of the Grateful Dead scene such as Phish, Widespread Panic, moe., the Disco Biscuits, and so forth. *Relix* is now recognized as the second-longest continuously published music magazine in the country, behind only the Dead tapers' early friend, *Rolling Stone*.

While tapes would become a currency of cool within Grateful Dead culture, tape trading itself was as obsessively geeky as any small, exacting subculture. Steve Silberman, longtime Deadhead and author of *Neurotribes: The Legacy of Autism and the Future of Neurodiversity*, notes that for some tapers, obsessive collecting and trivia compiling may have had as much to do with being on the autistic spectrum as it did with the Dead's music: "Several of the really senior tapers whom I met over the years, now that I know what autistic people look like and sound like and seem like, I look back and I think, 'Well that guy certainly had Asperger's syndrome.' It was quite striking. Deadheads would say, 'Oh he's a taper geek,' or something." But now we have new concepts for that behavior, and it seems likely that some of these guys might have had a page in the *DSM-5*. The perception of obsessiveness and geekiness, Silberman states, was "the appearance of someone on the spectrum before there was a spectrum. Because the spectrum didn't come into effect in the world of psychiatry until, really, the early '90s. All these people were out there in the wild who were on the spectrum, but they weren't yet recognized by medical science."

For most all who participated, on the spectrum or not, tape trading was an important way for Deadheads to form alliances that stretched from coast to coast. Dennis McNally recalls, "The community of meeting people periodically at shows, being in a relationship with them, and then exchanging lists, and doing that very slow, real-time, tedious copying of shows, generated a relationship that is profoundly different from being able to simply get a tetrabyte hard drive and download all the shows. That is not community." As with the rest of the music world, things were different in Deadheadland before the Internet and digital downloads. The materiality of the tapes mattered. As McNally says, the sense of community "was facilitated by the exchange of ritual objects, which was the tapes, and [having] a legend to be able to attach to the tape."

Thinking about that community, McNally raises the subject of his first meeting with Dick Latvala, legendary archivist of the Dead's tapes. They met about a week after what is known as the "Bobby Sands Show" at the Nassau Coliseum, in Uniondale, New York, on May 6, 1981. Sands was a British member of Parliament and a member of the Provisional Irish Republican Army who had been arrested by the Royal Ulster Constabulary after a bombing run in Belfast. He died in Maze Prison in 1981 while on a hunger strike. Bob Weir dedicated "He's Gone" to Sands—an uncharacteristic foray into revolutionary politics—and then, after "He's

Gone," McNally remembers, the band "went into this ten-minute blur of a jam that was just brilliant. Really one of the best things they'd played in years. This ten-minute fragment of music was just phenomenal. I'd already heard about it from people—no computers, no Internet—I'd heard about it from people on the East Coast. Dick had heard about it." But to get a copy of the show, you had to be connected. You could not just go and download it. Dick had those connections, and "he'd already gotten a tape of course, because he was Dick. When I met him, he put it on. We were listening to it together and I went, 'Now I know why people were excited!'"

However deep the desire for musical perfection got on the Deadhead side of the stage, and no matter the intensity of the taping contingent, those passions never approached the level of exquisitely maddening perfectionism sought after by the Grateful Dead crew. To those in the know, the names of the crew members responsible for the Dead's sound systems and sound-board recordings are spoken with nearly as much reverence as those of the band members themselves. The first in that line, the one who set the gold standard for "searching for the sound," was undoubtedly Owsley "Bear" Stanley.

Born on January 19, 1935, Augustus Owsley Stanley III was named after his grandfather, who was a U.S. senator from and governor of Kentucky. By his teens, Stanley had earned the nickname "Bear" because of his preternaturally hairy chest. The name stuck, and that is how Stanley is most often referred to within the Grateful Dead community. Fiercely intelligent, intellectually ravenous, pointedly opinionated, and at once reclusive and flamboyant, Owsley was a psychedelicized Renaissance man who had studied engineering at the University of Virginia and also—inspired by a 1958 performance by the Bolshoi Ballet—trained in ballet to the point that he could perform professionally. He became a mythical figure in the Bay Area, playing a key role in the Acid Tests during which the Grateful Dead were born. In her memoir, *Owsley and Me: My LSD Family*, Owsley's partner and frequent chemistry assistant, Rhoney Gissen Stanley, describes one of her first meetings with Bear, in January 1966, while in the thick of the San Francisco acid scene: "A few weeks later, dressed for a costume party in a paisley net dress, I was delighted to run into Owsley outside the Trips Festival at the venerable old Longshoreman's Hall. He looked like a troubadour in his colorful ribboned shirt and tight jeans. A Merry Prankster in a Day-Glo skeleton suit and painted face danced before Bear and opened his mouth. Owsley took out his Murine bottle of pure liquid LSD. Drop, drop into his mouth. I opened my mouth. Drop, drop—yum!"

Once initiated by the ingestion of the Owsley-created LSD sacrament, Rhoney Stanley embarked on a mind-expanding and life-changing night. "Inside was a party as the Grateful Dead played," she recounted. "Owsley took me by the hand and danced with me across the floor where he introduced me to his friend Richard Alpert, the renowned Harvard associate of Timothy Leary and coauthor of *The Psychedelic Experience*, the definitive psychedelic textbook of the time. . . . We merged with the crowd, and Richard and I danced. . . . In the phantasmagorical lights, my LSD vision was clear and sharp." Owsley and Rhoney touched and twirled. "How many times could I spin without stopping—one hundred and eight?" she asked herself. "Somehow I knew there was a magic number, and the dance was an ancient ritual of devotion." Owsley had clearly enchanted Rhoney, in much the same way as his charisma and forceful personality would enchant so many others over the years.

Although Bear would become well known for his association with the Grateful Dead, his 1960s day job was what made him infamous. Owsley was the counterculture's most celebrated LSD chemist. Between 1965 and 1968, he manufactured enough acid to turn on an entire generation of hippies in the Bay Area and well beyond, including the Grateful Dead and Ken Kesey and the Merry Pranksters. Among those who had been turned on and tuned in, Owsley's acid brands were as familiar as Pepsi, Clorox, or Little Debbie. Owsley's first batch of acid was called Blue Cheer. It came in large, rather cumbersome pills shaped like barrels. Blue Cheer established Owsley in the acid marketplace and was so well received that a popular Bay Area rock act—in what would be the first of many rock music crossovers with Bear's high-quality product—used it as the name of their band. After creating another batch called White Lightning—his first acid to be produced using a tabbing machine—Owsley cooked up one named Purple Haze, which inspired Jimi Hendrix's song of the same name.

While it is impossible to know exactly how many doses Owsley produced, educated guesses put the number in the millions. In fact, he was so prolific and his product so consistent that *Newsweek* magazine compared his manufacturing output to that of the Ford Motor Company. The Grateful Dead wrote their own musical homage to Bear's exploits as well. The title of their barely played song "Alice D. Millionaire" was taken from a *San Francisco Chronicle* story about Owsley that identified him as "the LSD millionaire." Owsley was as famous and public as one could be, given (and perhaps because of) the fact that his business involved the production of an illegal substance that put him, as a manufacturer and trafficker, at risk of jail time. He would, in fact, be arrested several times for possession and trafficking and did time in Terminal Island Federal Prison.

Despite all the hoopla around his exploits, in 2007 Bear insisted, "I never set out to 'turn on the world,' as has been claimed by many. And I certainly never made $1 million from drugs. I just wanted to know the dose and purity of what I took into my own body. Almost before I realized what was happening, the whole affair had gotten completely out of hand. I was riding a magic stallion. A Pegasus. I was not responsible for his wings, but they did carry me to all kinds of places."

Ultimately, the amount of money Bear made or the number of doses he manufactured is far less important than what he did with his money. He would serve as the band's benefactor in the early days, helping them pay for equipment, and even food and shelter. However, particularly to subsequent generations of the Deadhead community, the importance of his LSD career pales in comparison to his legacy of live music recording. Bear truly was the patron saint of the Grateful Dead taping community. Like some sonic ouroboros, he is both the source of that river of music and the place to which it ultimately returns.

In a rare, in-depth interview with Owsley conducted in Oakland, California, on January 13, 1991, David Gans took the opportunity to get Bear on record about his background, philosophies, and techniques with regard to music production and recording, starting with his early days with the band in 1966. "A few months before I met the Grateful Dead, I had bought a hi-fi," Bear recalled. "It had a cabinet on the bottom with a fifteen-inch speaker in it, and it was in a large box about the size of a small fridge. It had a little horn mounted on the top. The driver was maybe four inches in diameter; it was a relatively small horn. It looked like something that someone had rescued out from behind a screen at the local small movie theater. . . . When I started out with the Grateful Dead that became the Grateful Dead's PA system."

With his stereo serving as the PA for the Grateful Dead, the technical and sonic experiments began. "It had a McIntosh amp, two channels, forty watts per channel," Owsley said. "I knew we had to do something, because the technology was so primitive that it seemed like it was holding the music back, that we could go to another level if we had better instruments." From those humble beginnings, the Grateful Dead's sound systems evolved and advanced until they set the bar for all other rock bands. With Owsley in the lead, a dedicated Dead crew of technicians and audiophiles—including Betty Cantor, Jim Furman, Dennis Leonard, and Bob Matthews—sought after sonic perfection. When Owsley left the scene to do time at Terminal Island, this crew "stepped in for months at a stretch" and ran the operation on their own. As Nick Paumgarten noted in his *New Yorker* article, it was also around this time that "a taping regimen took root, even as the band members stopped paying attention."

As with the early hi-fi PA systems, Bear led the charge into those new frontiers. In addition to his work with the Dead in the late 1960s, he alternated fighting a legal case for his most recent bust (a 1967 raid on his lab in Orinda, California, had netted the police 350,000 doses of LSD and 1,500 doses of STP) and working as the house sound man for the Carousel Ballroom in San Francisco. In addition to hosting the era's top rock bands, the Carousel was co-owned for a short period in 1968 by the Grateful Dead, the Jefferson Airplane, Quicksilver Messenger Service, and Big Brother and the Holding Company. However, in short order, it became clear that the bands were better suited to perform on the stage than manage it, and the venue was taken over by storied rock music impresario Bill Graham. Meanwhile, alternating jail time and time spent mastering live music production, Bear continued his work with the Grateful Dead and their ever-evolving quest for the just exactly perfect sound. That quest—spearheaded by Bear—culminated in a monstrously large, incredibly sophisticated sound system that was dubbed the Wall of Sound.

The Wall of Sound made its live public debut at the Roscoe Maples Pavilion at Stanford University on February 9, 1973. As the band played the first notes of Chuck Berry's "Promised Land," all the tweeters blew. Subsequently, the system went back for more tweaks and made its official touring debut at the Cow Palace on March 23, 1974. This time the band tested the system with "U.S. Blues" before launching into its second song, "Promised Land." From that point on the Wall of Sound was the sonic centerpiece of all Dead shows until they took a long break from touring in October 1974.

In a Grateful Dead newsletter from 1975, the system's co-developer, Ron Wickersham of Alembic Sound Company, described the nitty-gritty of the system's origins and evolution: "The Grateful Dead's sound system has evolved over the last eight years as a technical and group enterprise, a sort of logical accumulation of speakers and people. Changes have been made continuously in all directions which aid in improving the quality of the sound, both which the audience hears and which the band has to work with on stage." The key personnel behind the concept and design of the system were Bear, Dan Healy, and Mark Raizene of the Dead's sound and equipment crew, Rick Turner of Alembic, and Wickersham himself. "The construction and regular maintenance is done at the Dead's technical workshops by the people responsible for managing and transporting the system on the road. The design and construction of some special electronic components was done at Alembic, where John Curl is a consultant to the project."

The specifics of the system were an audiophile's dream and a layman's nightmare. In the 1975 newsletter, Wickersham acknowledged Bear, "whose intuition we have followed and who is the essential catalyst for the system's development," and then launched into acutely technical details, on, for example, the vocal sounds: "The signals from each of the vocal microphones are brought together by a differential summing amp, where phase purity can be regulated and hence the transparency of sound maintained. From there the combined signal goes to a crossover which divides the frequency range into four bands (High, Upper Mid, Lower Mid, Low). The signal in each band is then separately amplified by MacIntosh 2300 amps fed to JBL 15 inch, 12 inch, 5 inch or Electrovoice tweeters." It was this plurality of speakers that allowed each sound to have its own channel and point of emission that made all the difference. "The center cluster of the vocal system, consisting of high and midrange speakers, is curved so as to disperse sound cylindrically; there is not much vertical dispersion, and horizontal dispersion is ideally between 140 and 180 degrees," Wickersham continued. "The vocal low range speakers are arranged in a column. Each type of speaker is designed to have the same horizontal and vertical dispersion so that all frequencies are heard equally well." Throughout the report, each instrument and array is broken down in similar detail, creating an in-depth portrait of not only the technical aspects of the sound system but also the intense consideration that went into its creation.

When Wickersham writes that "intermodulation distortion between instruments is of course non-existent," you can practically hear the countless hours of intense debate, discussion, and trial and error that went into the development of the Wall of Sound. Silberman has an interesting insight into what might have been behind some of Bear's obsessive drive for sonic perfection: "Owsley was a classic expression of autistic intelligence. Having spent a couple of days with Owsley, I would say that he either had a tremendous amount of autistic traits, or he would've been diagnosed as having Asperger's syndrome had he been born in a later generation. He had all the virtues of autistic intelligence in that he was absolutely single-minded. He had relentless insistence on quality, which expressed itself in everything from designing the first stereo system for concert amplification that would deliver a three-dimensional sonic image to the audience [to] the high quality of the tapes that he made, his insistence on taping every show, the high quality of his LSD, the fact that he was attracted to this very elaborate but beautifully precise process for synthesizing LSD in a purer form than the labs were making it." Silberman calls Bear "a process geek," and at that time in the early 1970s Bear was the leader of a crew of such geeks whose exacting attention to the Wall of Sound, acoustics, and the soundboard was the rigorous counterpart to the band's laid-back demeanor onstage.

Silberman also speculates that Owsley's often prickly demeanor could be indicative of what we now call autism spectrum disorder: "Owsley was not an easy man to get along with. He seemed to care little for how other people felt. What mattered to him was his own conception of what was really right. That's a very traditional autistic trait." In clinical language, people describe those on the autistic spectrum as thinking in binary terms. "I think Owsley thought in binary terms as well," Silberman says. "He had such a strong sense of what was right that he couldn't possibly be swayed from that view just because he happened to be hurting someone's feelings. He wouldn't care." Band historian Dennis McNally concurs: "Bear was into creating a mythos that didn't involve a lot of personal contact. Asperger's syndrome is on the mild end of the autism spectrum. Frequently it comes with savant qualities.

People with phenomenal memories, photographic memories, so forth and so on. But at the same time, extreme difficulty in relating to other people." McNally is less diffident than Silberman in offering a retroactive diagnosis. "You have to understand that Bear was clearly on the spectrum. Brilliant, but real great difficulty in communicating with other people, or having any kind of human relationship that didn't involve simply telling everybody around him what to think," McNally says. "Human relationships were not his strength."

Whatever the underlying internal fire was that drove Bear and everyone who worked on the Wall of Sound toward perfection, it is undeniable that the sophistication of the sound system was nothing short of revolutionary. What damned the Wall to a short—less than two years—touring life is best summed up in the final paragraph of Wickersham's newsletter essay: "The number of people going on the road to handle all the sound equipment, lights, scaffolding and staging varies, but a typical configuration is: band—6, sound—10, lights—4, staging and trucking—7, road management—3. The sound system travels in a 40 foot semi, staging and scaffolding on two flatbed semis and the lights in a 24-foot van. All this weighs about 75 tons." Simply put, the Wall of Sound was just too unwieldy and expensive to have a long life with a band that toured as heavily as the Grateful Dead. The gas costs alone would have buried most bands.

Struggling under the weight of too many expenses, too many employees, too many drugs, and too much interorganizational drama, the band not only shelved the Wall of Sound but took a complete hiatus from touring between October 1974 and June 1976, less than a year before the vaunted Barton Hall show. As Bear recounted, "Eventually it just became too much, and it collapsed on itself and the band just backed away from it suddenly, just like with the system that Tim Scully and I built back in '66: finally one day they came out and said, 'Hey, we can't handle it anymore,' so it changed. In this case they couldn't fire anybody—they always felt like *that* kind of family. They didn't know what to do, so they just stopped playing, hoping that the people would go off because they had to make a living, that they'd go off and somehow do something."

While Bear would be affiliated with the Grateful Dead in some way for the rest of his life, he would never be as intimately involved with the band as he was before the touring hiatus. However, the legacy of the sound he helped produce, the live recordings he made, and the meticulousness with which he approached his efforts, set standards for and provided inspiration to the early Grateful Dead taping community. As prolific as many Grateful Dead tapers were, none ever equaled Bear's contribution to the legacy of live Grateful Dead recordings. In 1973, the band released its fourth live album, *History of the Grateful Dead, Volume One (Bear's Choice)*, which featured the band's celebrated performances from February 13 and 14, 1970, at the Fillmore East in New York City. Bear is credited on the album as both producer and compiler. The album peaked at number 60 on the *Billboard* 200, and it remains required listening for Deadheads—new and old—today.

On March 12, 2011, Bear died in a car accident. Five months later, the Owsley Stanley Foundation was incorporated, with a mission to arrange for the preservation and eventual production and public distribution of "Bear's Sonic Journals," an archive of more than thirteen hundred live concert sound-board recordings from the 1960s and 1970s. According to the foundation website, those tapes are approaching the end of their "shelf life" and need to be digitally preserved. Costs are estimated at between $20,000 and $30,000, and the labor could involve as much as four years of studio time. These figures are evidence of Bear's perfectionism in the studio and on the concert hall floor.

The touring hiatus the Dead took between 1974 and 1976 put an indelible time stamp on the life of the band. When the band emerged in 1976, the Wall of Sound was gone, the entire operation was lighter on its feet, and the musicians were on a mission to reestablish their hard-forged musical and personal connections with each other. They were working on the music that would fill *Terrapin Station* and *Shakedown Street*. More than a few accounts of the band from this time used tropes about death and possible rebirth, either in headlines or in the articles themselves, in order to underscore the questions that fans and music critics had in 1976 and 1977. When the Dead got back on the road in June 1976, at the Paramount Theatre in Portland, Oregon, those questions began to be answered.

By the spring of 1977 it was clear that the Grateful Dead had been revitalized and hit their stride. And then some. The band came east in March and began with a show at the Spectrum, in Philadelphia, on April 22, riding the high of three great nights at the Winterland Arena in San Francisco. In Philly they tried out the new "Scarlet Begonias" > "Fire on the Mountain," and it cast a spell on the crowd. The band ended the show with slightly more than thirteen minutes of "Terrapin Station" and left the crowd, begging for more, with no encore. In what might seem to be literary foreshadowing, the masses of Deadheads leaving the arena found that snow had fallen during the concert. As fans got into cars and made their way home or just sacked out in the back of their vehicles, the Dead were already on Interstate 95 and headed to Springfield, Massachusetts, for the next night's show.

Just the Right Night

If you don't try to profit personally from it in a monetary sense, the whole community looks after itself. If you put out the good, it will come back to you.   —Peter Angwin, 2015

Stephen Burke loved live music. That's why he had joined the Cornell Concert Commission in the first place. The CCC was filled with bright college kids who wanted to be around live music, if not work in the music industry as a career one day. Of all of them, Mike "Mac" McEvoy—the Selection Committee chairman who worked with John Scher to figure out which bands were available and how to book them into Cornell—was the one who went the farthest in the business. Mike would eventually work for the big daddy of concert promoters—Bill Graham—at Bill Graham Productions in San Francisco.

But Burke wasn't a muckety-muck in the CCC. He was working on the blue-collar end of the spectrum. When Robert Horowitz was president of the CCC, he worked so closely with John Scher on producing Cornell concerts that for the September 1977 Dead show at Englishtown, New Jersey, Scher flew "Hor" (as he was known among friends) and his sister to the backstage artists' area in a helicopter. Considering that roughly 150,000 people were in front of that stage to hear the Grateful Dead along with the Marshall Tucker Band and the New Riders of the Purple Sage, it was pretty heady for a self-described "nice Jewish kid from New Rochelle" to be choppered over their heads like rock 'n' roll royalty.

Burke, on the other hand, had none of those inside connections. In truth, CCC leaders like McEvoy, Horowitz, and treasurer Eve Prouty barely even registered Burke's presence. When the CCC leaders met at the Nines on Friday nights, drinking and planning from happy hour until late at night when Robert Palmer music was played to mark last call, Burke and his buddies were not around. They weren't in on planning to produce the "Cheap Thrills" coupon book that would help bail the CCC out of debt by selling tickets to multiple Cornell events for one single price. They weren't in on figuring out how to persuade the administration to hold rock 'n' roll concerts despite the Deep Purple debacle or the fact that Ian Anderson of Jethro Tull had taken a piss onstage at Barton Hall and declared that he'd never return. Hor was such a mover and shaker that while he was chairman of the CCC, he sat on the University Unions Program Board at the same time, thus simultaneously overseeing which events were booked, and also where they would be hosted. It was a lot of responsibility. But Hor wore it well.

Burke was a mere worker bee by comparison. He joined the CCC with five other guys when he was a freshman and was still wet behind the ears when the Dead came to campus. But Burke and his fellow newbies attended meetings, showed up on time, worked hard, and proved themselves reliable enough that when May 8, 1977, rolled around, they were tapped to be in charge of ticket taking, with a little ushering and security detail thrown in on the side. It was a hodgepodge of relatively low-level responsibilities that he and his fellow CCC members were happy to assume. Burke wasn't even involved in the backstage security, where he could have rubbed elbows with a band member or some exalted, crusty member of the Dead's entourage. For a bunch of Deadheads that night, though, Burke and his crew were extremely important. They were like Ivy League Willy Wonkas, dispensing magic tickets with knowing smiles on their faces. Given the fact that the CCC proper would have, by necessity, frowned on their activities, their lack of visibility among the CCC elite would serve Burke, and roughly 250 Deadheads, quite well.

Burke grew up in New York City. He went to high school in Manhattan. In the summers, he'd pay a couple bucks to see major musicians—Miles Davis, for example—playing outdoors in Central Park. There was the Academy of Music, the Felt Forum, and any number of smaller music clubs readily available where Burke could drench his ears in live performances and get an understanding of how music crowds worked. When he was assigned to the ticket-taking detail at Barton Hall, he had a pretty good idea of what the Dead crowd would be like. That understanding included the awareness that a bunch of fans would be showing up without tickets but still hoping to see the show. With a touch of glee, he and the other ticket takers came up with a plan for how to manage these ticketless fans. As Sandy Kohler List wrote in Ithaca's own *Good Times Gazette*, "I reckon we owe our musicians at least as much as we expect from them, especially when they have done as much good for us as the Grateful Dead have done in the past." Maybe some of the staff led by Burke were inspired by her next lines exhorting Ithacans and visitors to "cross your fingers and do your best to contribute to the spirit of a high time for all concerned."

Burke didn't want anyone taking cash bribes for entry into the show. If that ever happened, he didn't know about it. His plan for easing the burden of fans who were shut out of the show was much more benevolent and in keeping with the Grateful Dead ethos. To his thinking, the show was already sold out. Nobody—not the band, the promoter, the CCC, or Cornell—was going to make any more money on ticket sales. Why not help some people out, and also avoid potential problems on campus caused by fans who were shut out with nowhere to go and nothing to do?

The plan that Burke and his fellow ticket takers hatched was a prankster masterpiece of which the Grateful Dead—had they known about it—may have very well approved. Once all the fans with tickets were let into the show, Burke's plan was to start easing some non-ticket-holders in the doors. People trying to immediately scam their way through the doors without tickets were told to wait. "We need to take care of people with tickets," Burke told them. "Come back when they're done. Come back and we'll see what we can do."

It was not a brief process. Eighty-five hundred ticket holders had to be let in the doors first. That process was not without wrinkles of its own. Barton Hall attendee and Deadhead Matt Adler feared that he would be crushed when the doors first opened. He was one of many caught in the initial crowd surge that night. Adler and others would recall the harrowing scene two years later when eleven fans were crushed to death trying to get into a Who concert at Riverfront Coliseum in Cincinnati. For those who waited to get into the show, entry was a smooth breeze through the doors. But for those eager to be the first into the venue, the experience was potentially dangerous and certainly claustrophobic.

And then there was Louis Gross, a Cornell University PhD candidate in applied math, who was manning the Super Trouper spotlight that night. To Gross, the initial surge of fans was just plain surreal. Seated on rickety scaffolding high above the crowd, Gross was reminded of the classes on population ecology he had recently taken with Professor Lamont Cole—one of the founders of the field—and also the lectures he had attended about voles and lemmings, given by a young professor named Peter Brussard. Looking down below, it was as if a magical transition had occurred, as a "whoosh of multicolored people simply flowed all around the Barton Hall floor and in seconds the scaffold was surrounded by flowered shirts and what appeared to be hundreds of small 'trees' holding mics." The crowd was robust, yet once inside the venue they were peaceful. They didn't disturb or attempt to climb the unguarded scaffolding on which Gross was precariously perched. Gross sniffed the air and considered that perhaps the pungent, organic smell drifting up to his nose was part of what kept the crowd so passive and relaxed.

Meanwhile, back down on terra firma, Burke and his fellow ticket takers were done letting the paying customers in the door. It was time to have some fun. Burke instructed everyone, "Absolutely under no circumstances do you take money from anybody. Absolutely none. You don't take anything from them. If they offer you a joint, you don't take it. If they offer you a beer, you don't take it. You don't take anything. It's absolutely not quid pro quo."

Rather than accept bribes, the ticket takers had something more playful in mind. If people didn't have tickets, they would have to contribute something else to get in the door. They could sing. They could dance. They could do chin-ups, push-ups, or tell a corny joke. Don't have a ticket to the show? You're in luck! You can get in with a speeding ticket, a laundry ticket, or a ticket to see *Creature from the Black Lagoon*! One guy got in with a guitar pick. Another dude—a gnarled older hippie who had traveled all the way from Tennessee to see the show—got in with a peanut butter sandwich wrapped in tin foil. Holding the sandwich up to his fellow ticket takers, Burke proclaimed, "Hey, look at this! It's a peanut butter sandwich! I've never seen a sandwich from Tennessee before. This guy is beautiful! You're in!"

Overall, Burke estimates that 250 attendees gained entrance to Barton Hall that night simply by playing along with good spirit. It took some people a minute to catch on to what was going on. Some of the more jaded concertgoers were wary that it was some kind of scam. Some flat out scowled and yelled, "Aw, come on, man!" But eventually, as more and more fans were admitted with a hearty chuckle and a wave-through, everyone who had the chance got in the door with some small, pleasant contribution to the night's festivities. Burke was thrilled. It wasn't something he—or anyone else working the doors that night—had ever tried before or would ever try again. To his thinking, a stunt like that could work only at a Grateful Dead concert.

Looking back on the show nearly forty years later, Burke doesn't want to inflate the importance of the ticket takers' playful prank. But he is also aware of how such small acts of kindness can serve to elevate everyone in attendance, including the band, to be just a little bit happier about the night's proceedings. We may recall Bill Kreutzmann's thoughts about the influential and powerful connection between the band and the audience: "They're really the seventh band member. There is some great power, be it God or whatever, that enters the Grateful Dead on certain nights, and it has to do with us being open and getting together with the audience. If we can do that, then it comes . . . and spreads everywhere." Social scientist Shaun C. Sutton puts the connection in terms that are more academic, but equally supernatural: "This achievement of communitas and the mystical transformation from individual to group consciousness formed the heart of the Deadhead ritual process." Burke sees it this way: "It could definitely be that those 250 people and their energy and surprise and their delight made it to the other 8,500 people and made it up to the stage. To tell you the truth, I really believe that. I really do."

The good vibes of that night's show started well before the doors opened. The band had arrived in the late morning riding high spirits from the show in the Boston Garden the night before, which had also been Kreutzmann's birthday show. The drummer had just turned 31. Like many concerts in the East, the night in Boston was high-energy; the Garden performance, beginning with "Bertha" and concluding with an encore of "U.S. Blues," propelled the band forward as they rode the Massachusetts Turnpike westward and into New York.

The two early May shows in New England—Boston on May 7 and New Haven on May 5—had been strong, inspired. The New Haven show featured "Scarlet Begonias" > "Fire on the Mountain," and the last chords of "Fire on the Mountain" jumped into "Good Lovin'" with a pulsing tempo change initiated by Phil. Mark Mattson, who attended that show—at the end of a four-night Dead run that included shows in Springfield, Passaic, and New York City—calls the New Haven show "one of the top ten concerts of my life (so far), and my favorite of the five spring 1977 Dead shows I went to." Mattson would also catch the May 28 concert in Hartford, Connecticut, on the eve of the band's return to California. There was "a lot of song overlap with the infamous Cornell show three days later," Mattson observes about the New Haven performance. "This is when I started to love 'Pretty Peggy-O.' I thought this was the best 'Music Never Stopped' ever, until I heard the one from two nights later in Boston." For Mattson, the New Haven show peaked, as it has for so many others on numerous other nights, with the jam on "St. Stephen."

Mattson missed the Boston Garden show—though he was in the loop among tapers in the region and heard it right away—and if he has any regrets, he keeps them to himself. But he might have a few. On just about any Dead listserv you can find a string of comments making a case that New Haven–Boston–Ithaca–Buffalo is a stellar run of shows. Perhaps, some venture, the best. Even if you forget the superlatives though, it did often seem that Dead shows sprang to life in thematic and sonic clusters. Shows spoke to one another, Nicholas Meriwether offers, the same way individual short stories may reflect a thematic whole and create a yoking effect when read side-by-side across a collection. Something was going on with the band all of spring 1977, and early May was a pinnacle of the artistic collaboration and community they had rediscovered on the road.

So it is no surprise that, by and large, the band members had been jovial and chatty during sound check at Barton. In Ithaca, unlike Boston, the crew did not need to deal with the stagehands union. By manager Rock Scully's account, the loading in and setting up at the Garden had been chaotic; set up on May 8, with the eager help of the CCC staff, had to be, by comparison, a pleasure. It had been a long trip from Boston, through the night, but moods were good, and the crew were seasoned veterans who were prepared to deal with any circumstance that might arise. For students who worked the concert, the sound check served as both a perk and a consolation for the fact that they wouldn't be able to enjoy the show like their nonworking peers. As staff members, they tried to maintain a professional demeanor around the band, but they were all giddy as hell. They were a small audience to a private Grateful Dead set! That said, they didn't want to let on how thrilled they were and blow the whole scene either. They were professionals, after all. Kind of. However, with the three o'clock daylight, made less bright and more moody by the wintry clouds, seeping through the glass of Barton Hall's hundreds of feet of windows at the eastern and western ends of the building, the setting felt magical—more like an intimate block party than a rock concert. It was almost more joy than Burke could stand.

As he recalls, the band was curious about the Cornell students too. Burke remembers the band members calling them up to the stage and asking them questions about school and their lives as college students. They seemed particularly appreciative of how hard the kids were working considering they weren't even being paid. Along with other questions, Jerry Garcia asked the students if they had any musical requests. One Cornell student stepped up and cheekily requested "Funiculì, Funiculà." Given that the song was written in Italy in 1880 to commemorate the first funicular cable car on Mount Vesuvius, it was a strange request, to say the least. Garcia thought the musical suggestion was a hoot. He and the band had a good laugh and then proceeded to find their way through the playful tune.

Lo and behold, the first known version of the Grateful Dead playing "Funiculì, Funiculà" live in concert happened just two weeks later, on May 22, 1977, at the Sportatorium in Pembroke Pines, Florida. The band played a few bars of the song to start that show and then launched into the proper show opener, "The Music Never Stopped." They also played "Funiculì, Funiculà," two weeks after the Pembroke Pines show, twice, on June 7 and June 9, during a three-night run at the Winterland in San Francisco. Throughout the rest of their career, the Dead would dip into "Funiculì, Funiculà" whenever the mood struck them—always to great cheers of approval from the crowd. For hard-core fans, there was always something a little special about hearing a few notes of that song—a minor tradition that began in Ithaca.

Amid the sound check, the conversations, and the playful exploration with the melody of "Funiculì, Funiculà," the last-minute details of the show fell into place. Barton Hall was the standard venue for big shows at Cornell, and there was a routine for stage setup, security, concession stands, and all the rest. The stage was situated roughly in the middle of the floor (with more than eight thousand tickets sold, the space, which holds upward of twenty-three thousand if you allow for people standing and sitting, would still not be filled) and faced to the north of the hall to create a more intimate environment. The band's door, to the southwest side of the building and leading to the small road separating Barton Hall from the Statler Hotel, was secured and allowed band members, the crew of roughly fifteen roadies, and the rest of the entourage to come and go without much stress. Security staffing, all drawn from the Cornell Concert Commission, increased in number as the hours passed, with some arriving at noon, many others arriving around 4 p.m., and then more in place at 6 p.m. There were lots of details, and what Cornell security did not demand, the Grateful Dead certainly did. Their multipage contract rider specified all the needs of the band, ranging from the printing of tickets to the handling of the Super Trouper lights to the provision of five cases of Heineken and two bottles of red Bordeaux wine. The pleasant anarchy that prevailed on campus and in Ithaca, as more and more fans arrived far above Cayuga's waters, was contrasted by the careful planning carried out by the CCC.

For Pete Angwin, born and raised in Palo Alto, the Dead were always special, but also omnipresent. His neighbors across the street were Kreutzmann's aunt and uncle, and Bill's cousins also went to school with Angwin. There was no such thing as getting turned on to the Grateful Dead. The Dead were simply threaded through the fabric of his days. By the time Angwin was swept along with the flow of the crowd into Barton Hall on May 8, he had already been to numerous Grateful Dead shows. He had also seen individual band members play in their side-project bands more times that he could recall. The truth was, those shows happened with such regularity in the Bay Area that Angwin barely registered them as special events at all. It wasn't until he started seeing more East Coast shows as a student at Colgate University in Hamilton, New York, that he noticed a difference between Dead shows on the East Coast and those on the West. As Angwin says, "Audiences were a little more fervent on the East Coast just because there were fewer times that [the Dead] would come through. They were there pretty much all the time on the West Coast. . . . It was just a little different feel is all I can say. On the East Coast it tended to be more of an event, and on the West Coast it tended to be more of a celebration."

As with so many other fans, Angwin's initiation into the concert ritual came through an older sibling. Angwin's brother, Tim, had caught the tail end of the Dead's Haight Street heyday. As a teenager kicking around the Bay Area in the late 1960s and then as a college student at Stanford, Tim had managed to catch some amazing performances. He was certainly tuned in enough to show his little brother the ropes at his first Dead concert.

It was 1973. The Winterland. Angwin was a freshman in high school. Together with a bunch of friends who dubbed themselves "the Bong Family," Angwin and his brother headed over to Golden Gate Park to hang out before the show. At the peak of their early Haight-Ashbury days, the Dead would bop down the street—instruments in hand—to play free shows in the area of the park known as the Panhandle, among other places. As photographer and early Grateful Dead "family member" Rosie McGee recalled, "When weather permitted, we pulled together wonderful free concerts in the Panhandle of Golden Gate Park. All it took was a flatbed truck, makeshift electricity, food, wine, friends, sunshine and wonderful bands that hadn't hit the big time yet." Indeed, on January 14, 1967, a watershed event called the Human Be-In was held in Golden Gate Park, featuring the Grateful Dead along with dozens of other hippie, spiritual, poetic, rock 'n' roll, and revolutionary luminaries including Ram Dass (then Richard Alpert), Timothy Leary (who took the opportunity to debut his new slogan "Turn on, tune in, drop out"), Allen Ginsberg, Gary Snyder, Lawrence Ferlinghetti, Dick Gregory, Jerry Rubin, the Jefferson Airplane, Big Brother and the Holding Company, and many others. Owsley even cooked up a special batch of "White Lightning" LSD for the event, which he personally helped circulate for free through the crowd.

The Be-In was a precursor to San Francisco's upcoming 1967 Summer of Love. Some mark it as the pinnacle of hippie culture. Others remember it as the beginning of the end, when the true underground got their cover blown, and the doors were thrown open for thousands of kids from across America to stick flowers in their hair and come to San Francisco. Not long after that, tour buses were cruising up and down the Haight-Ashbury district pointing out street freaks to visiting squares and stopping at hippie landmarks like the Grateful Dead's house at 710 Ashbury.

Regardless of your take on the Human Be-In, Golden Gate Park holds a special, almost magical place in Grateful Dead lore. "Panhandle Park" was the perfect place for Angwin and the Bong Family to play Frisbee, hang out near a drum circle, and soak in the Dead vibe before they headed over to the Winterland for

Angwin's first show. After that show, yet another Angwin—yet another "little brother"—was hooked.

Once Angwin started college, traveling from central New York to Palo Alto during school breaks also meant catching a bunch of Dead shows at places like the Frost Amphitheater and the Greek Theatre, along with casual club shows with Dead off-shoots like Bob Weir's Kingfish or Jerry Garcia jamming with Merl Saunders at the Keystone. As Angwin fondly recalls, "They weren't a big deal at all. They'd be small. There would be maybe a couple hundred people there. It was just not the big deal that it grew into."

One notable exception to the low-key vibe was a much larger-scale concert, "Day on the Green," that Angwin caught at the Oakland Coliseum. Such Bill Graham–produced West Coast concerts were clearly "events" as well as "celebrations." Featuring multiple, and often diverse, groupings of bands in a single day—something Graham loved to do from his earliest days as a promoter—between 1973 and 1992, "Day on the Green" would host such acts as the Beach Boys, Peter Frampton, Led Zeppelin, Marvin Gaye, Judas Priest, Natalie Cole, and Parliament-Funkadelic. In October 1976, Angwin saw the Who and the Grateful Dead share a double billing there. Far from the intimate vibe at the small clubs where Garcia and Weir played, "Day on the Green" featuring the Who and the Dead felt like a "big, open-air celebration."

For Angwin, the Barton Hall show was a good midsize show. To his thinking, it wasn't as personally memorable as the show the Dead played on his own campus of Colgate University on November 4 that year. As he recalls, "That was during my senior year at Colgate. The place had two thousand, three thousand capacity and didn't sell out. It was just an amazing show. We didn't know that they were going to play until the Monday before the show, and the show was a Friday night, so it was like a pickup date from something they dropped out of earlier in the week." He remembers the Colgate campus being abuzz for the whole week anticipating the show. "Certainly all that Friday, it was like, 'Yeah, the Dead's coming, they're playing down in our gym tonight.' For '77, that was the prime show for me."

For the Grateful Dead, these East Coast tours of college campuses were a key part of an early business plan that they maintained until they outgrew the venues. Their efforts in these seemingly insignificant areas would pay off throughout their entire career. Dennis McNally recalls, "There's a guy named Ron Rainey who began booking them in 1970. He booked them in every flippin' SUNY campus upstate. Oneonta, Delhi, just everywhere. Syracuse, Buffalo, Rochester, also New England and Pennsylvania. Until 1970, until *Workingman's Dead* and *American Beauty* and the college booking pattern, they could play in San Francisco and Manhattan, and that's it in terms of selling tickets. They went out and expanded their audience." McNally concludes, "Generally in a giant triangle, Boston to D.C. to Buffalo, within that triangle, approximately, is where they made their living the rest of their lives."

But on May 8, 1977, Angwin had no sense that he was part of a larger business plan. At one point during his entry into the venue, his only focus was on pure survival. The unseasonably cold weather and the threat of snow made Angwin and the fans around him eager to get inside, where it was warm and dry. They were amassed in a crowd out front, and when the hall opened, this blob of humanity began squeezing itself through the doors. Angwin was literally picked up and swept inside. For fifteen or twenty feet, it felt like he was swimming through the crowd. Although the memory is fuzzy now, he recalls a series of doors opening, so that it felt like being pushed through succeeding chambers. (Quite a few tickets would never be torn in two, as the crowds pushed and CCC staff at the doors could not check everyone's ticket.) Stu Zimmerman, a student in Cornell's School of Industrial and Labor Relations, confirms the flood of humanity that rolled into Barton. He rode that wave, lifted off his feet, until he was deposited right at the rail at the front of the stage. From that vantage he was able to watch Jerry's eyes, looking out from under his glasses, as Jerry chased the music through two highlight-filled sets.

Zimmerman's recollection is now tinged with the knowledge that the force of the crowd resulted in his having a prime place in the hall. But when Angwin heard the tragic news of the eleven fans killed during the Who concert in Cincinnati in 1979, his mind immediately went back to Barton Hall in 1977. "I've never been so scared in my life," he says. "If I had fallen down I could've easily been trampled. Years later when they had those fatalities in Cincinnati at the Who concert, I got to thinking back to the show in Ithaca, and going, 'Oh man, I know exactly what that feels like.'"

Angwin's moment of fear did not color his overall experience of the show at Barton. It was a great show, but he didn't walk out of Barton Hall that night feeling blown away by what he had experienced. His historical memory of the Cornell show has also been tempered by the pure rapture he remembers at having the Dead play Colgate later that year. That was clearly a high point of his college career, if not his life. Yet his appreciation of Cornell '77 has grown as he's listened to the recordings over the years. He began collecting bootlegs once he started school in New York. As with everything else Grateful Dead–related, it was something he quickly caught the bug for. One of his prized early tapes was the 7/18/76 show at the Orpheum Theatre in San Francisco.

The show was broadcast on KSAN–San Francisco, thus allowing Angwin and many other budding tape collectors to add a high-quality Dead recording to their stash.

Along with amassing a larger tape collection, Angwin learned the etiquette for sharing tapes within the Dead community. A real Deadhead never sold a bootleg. Trade, yes. Sell, no. As Angwin says, "It's just plain bad form to try to make a buck off of it, because in the end the music was something that was freely given from the band, they didn't have to do that, and then to try and capitalize on it was just totally against the spirit of the whole thing." Angwin took this righteous principle to the next stage and applied it to concert tickets as well. If you had an extra ticket for the show, it was bad form to sell it for more than it originally cost. Deadheads aren't scalpers looking to make a fast buck off a Dead show. Deadheads sell extra tickets for face value, and sometimes they may even "miracle" a fellow Head with a free ticket.

During his years of seeing shows, both before and after Cornell, Angwin experienced both sides of that equation—being the one in need, and being the one who could help out a fellow Deadhead. In the end, it all seemed to sort itself out.

If Pete Angwin had turned around or just moved a few yards to his left or right at Barton Hall in 1977, he might have run into another member of the Deadhead community with an equally faithful and deep connection to the scene's modes of operation. Bill Wasson's entry into the Grateful Dead scene was as dramatic as Angwin's was gradual. When you drop a thirteen-year-old kid into a Dead show at the Fillmore East in 1970, it's likely going to change the direction of his life one way or another. While you're at it, you can also blast "Also sprach Zarathustra" through the PA system before the band takes the stage. For good measure, you can give the kid some good strong acid. Then you can have the band close the show with more than an hour of "Dark Star" > "St. Stephen" > "The Eleven" > "Turn on Your Lovelight" that psychedelically caps off a full day and night (early and late shows) of Grateful Dead. On January 2, 1970, that was Wasson's initiation into the scene. As he puts it, his "mind was blown."

But those were different days. Wasson was a different person. He was a self-described "New York kid and crazy and wild and into drugs and did the things that kids into drugs in New York in the '70s did." Those things included seeing Frank Zappa live in concert at eleven years old—an experience that undoubtedly softened the blow of his first Dead show a little bit. As Wasson says, "That ruined me for life."

The Dead took a huge bite out of young Wasson's consciousness. By the time he started his freshman year at Cornell he'd seen the Dead at least twenty times, along with other bands like Pink Floyd, Yes, and Emerson, Lake & Palmer. Now, twenty-eight years after stepping away from that life, sober and a successful professional, Wasson isn't eager to have his name associated with all the drug stories of his youth. ("Bill Wasson" is a pseudonym created to protect his identity.) The road that led him to Barton Hall on May 8, 1977, was harrowing, and the memories are hazy. But still there are recollections from those days that Wasson holds close to his heart.

Wasson went to other Dead shows besides Cornell on their 1977 East Coast tour. He also followed Hot Tuna around the country. As he freely admits, "I would disappear from Cornell for three weeks and sometimes even fly out to California." To this day, he's amazed that he graduated from Cornell at all.

As Wasson recalls, back in those early days, there was no real Grateful Dead "scene." To him, being a Deadhead simply meant that you got the free Dead Heads newsletter the band sent out sporadically to people on their mailing list. Between 1971 and 1980, Grateful Dead employee and band friend Eileen Law oversaw twenty-five such mailings. Wasson was on her mailing list. In later years, he felt turned off by Deadheads showing up to hang out in the parking lot before the shows. It seemed to him that they were prioritizing the partying over the music. Still, Wasson's activities at Cornell on May 8 were surprisingly similar to the parking lot shenanigans that turned him off in the 1980s and 1990s.

"It was a great week," he remembers. "The tour was pretty amazing." When fans arrived in Ithaca that Sunday, the weather had turned, and rain and then snow were in the air. So he and others decided to make themselves comfortable in a warmer spot. "When it started to snow we broke into the—there was a hall right next to Barton Hall that was sort of empty, I think it was owned by the hotel school—and it was so cold we somehow got in there. I remember sitting in the lobby smoking pot. . . . We were up there all day, but just to party and to have a good time, not because we needed to be first in line."

In addition to going to the venue early to hang out, smoke pot, and trip on acid, Wasson had made a stack of Grateful Dead bumper stickers to sell. They were crude, he admits. "Really bad, really amateur." He was working as the arts editor at a small local newspaper and had access to their printing equipment. It was a good job overall. He got lots of free records and was able to write articles promoting his favorite bands like Hot Tuna, the Jefferson Airplane, and, of course, the Dead. The stickers Wasson made had the image of the Dead's iconic "Jester" character that was designed in 1972 by Stanley Mouse and Alton Kelley for the cover of *The Grateful Dead Songbook*. Printed along with the Jester was the venue name and show date: Barton Hall, May 8, 1977.

It wasn't that Wasson was hoping to make a bunch of money off the stickers. It was just a fun way to commemorate a local show. The truth of the matter is that he got too high to sell them anyway. He got so high, in fact, that he forgot he even made the stickers. Wasson never sold a single one. The stickers ended up among the other piles of rock 'n' roll memorabilia that he gathered in his home after nearly fifty years of concerts. He found a stack of them a few years ago and threw them all away.

To Wasson, despite his drug-addled brain, Cornell '77 was clearly a great show. The numerous times he has listened back to it on cassette and now on computer have borne out that original judgment. "I'll say this—years later as it became apparent that everybody had this on their top-ten, if not their top-one list, and it developed this legendary status, I'd go back and listen and go, 'Yeah, holy shit!' That version of 'Not Fade Away' was pretty amazing. The whole thing flowed so nicely. It's all about the chemistry—and I'm not talking about the psychedelics—but just the band and the crowd, it was just the right night." Wasson has moved on from the Grateful Dead scene now. Although he regularly sees 150 concerts a year, only ten of those have involved Dead band members since Jerry passed away. The truth is that he had already moved on by the time the 1980s hit. Still, he's clearly passionate about the shows that he saw in the '70s. Cornell in particular. "For me, it definitely holds up. I still listen to the show. Now, clean and sober and thirty-nine years later—holy shit!—you listen to a show like that that someone recorded on cassette thirty-nine years ago and you're still blown away. You know there's something special about it."

First Set

If I told you all that went down / it would burn off both your ears.
—Robert Hunter, "Deal"

I f you were a Deadhead fortunate enough to be inside Barton Hall when the concert started on May 8, 1977, and not one of the unlucky few stranded in the swirling snow outside, you may have found yourself speculating what song the band was going to play next. Sometimes on nights like this, they busted out a raucous "Cold Rain and Snow" to bring the audience together by acknowledging, through their music, the weather everyone was dealing with around the show. "Bertha" was unlikely, as the band had unleashed a ripping version in Boston the previous night. They had also "wave[d] that flag wide and high," encoring with "U.S. Blues" on May 7, 1977, as Jerry soldiered through guitar problems at the end of the show. Then again, with the Dead, you never knew.

Listening to recordings of Cornell '77, it is almost possible to feel the giddy waves of anticipation that undulated through the crowd when the house lights dimmed and the band took the stage in the cavernous barn of a building. Whether they had driven six hours straight to Ithaca after skipping merrily out of Boston Garden or it had been several months or even years since their last show, Deadheads knew the thrills that awaited them—and newcomers were easily swept up in the torrent of their excitement. Perhaps, oddly enough, concertgoers gave fleeting thoughts to their mothers as whoops and cat-calls echoed through Barton Hall. It was Mother's Day after all. Maybe some moms would even get a phone call after the show. Depending on how the night went, however, some mothers might wait until the following morning to get that phone call, or even the late afternoon.

Jerry sported his trademark black t-shirt, and Donna Jean was dressed more like a William Smith madrigal singer than a seasoned rock star. Bob's beard was as thick as Jerry's, but Bob still looked young enough to be the lead guitarist's kid brother, which was psychically true, if not biologically accurate. Inside the hall, guitars were tuned and the crowd clapped rhythmically, signaling that it was time to strap in for the long, strange haul. The show was about to begin. Then the music hit. Wait, what was that? "New Minglewood Blues"? They must not have dug deep enough into it at Boston Garden, because there it was again, sure enough, with Jerry flying across his fret board, sending out a flurry of notes urging Bob forward into the rapscallion's origin story.

Outside in the rain and snow, fans surged toward the doors as they strained to hear the muted thump of Phil's bass on the first-set opener. Inside the hall, the dance party was underway.

The hopeful fan who can be heard on audience recordings calling out for "America's favorite song, 'Truckin'!" did not get his wish on May 8, 1977. But many other Deadheads in attendance did have their set-list wishes fulfilled. For some, the show illustrates the astonishing musical range available at the band's fingertips: cowboy songs, dance songs, tear-jerkers, love songs, anthems, and raving rockers all follow one another with that inimitable Grateful Dead seamlessness. To others, the Cornell show will never deserve its oft-debated status of "best ever," owing to omissions from the set list. As one example, because band and fans alike agree that "Dark Star" was a vehicle for the group's most inspired, artistic, evocative, and, frankly, Grateful Dead–like playing, many argue that a show with no "Dark Star" could never be considered for the title of "best ever." No ifs, ands, or buts. No "Dark Star," no dice.

But, as the saying goes (and as the Dead seem to twistedly reference in their song "U.S. Blues"), there's more than one way to skin a cat (or a goat, as it were). For many young East Coast fans in attendance at Cornell, hearing a live "St. Stephen" would truly be a dream come true. The crowd would have to wait until the second set to hear the first notes of "St. Stephen," but it was hovering on the horizon. Some of the fun of Dead shows was anticipating a favorite or seldom-heard tune, or guessing what would be played based on the set lists of other shows on the tour. But, above all, being at a Dead show was about being in the moment. And *the moment* that evening at Barton Hall began with the band shooting their way into "New Minglewood Blues" like tragic heroes in a Clint Eastwood spaghetti western. It initiated a night of music that, while it might not have evolved out of some people's ideal set list, featured a depth and breadth of material that underscores the deep-reaching roots of the Grateful Dead's rich musical and storytelling influences.

"New Minglewood Blues"

From its first appearance at the Avalon Ballroom in San Francisco on May 19, 1966, until its final appearance at the Palace in Auburn Hills, Michigan, on June 27, 1995, just twelve days prior to the band's last gig, "New Minglewood Blues" was one of the sturdiest, most dependable songs in the Grateful Dead's catalog. With the exception of 1968, and the years 1972–1975, it was constantly in rotation—often heavily—and was a great choice for getting Deadhead boots stomping, dancing, and embracing the promise of the devilishly good times conveyed by the outlaw lyrics and the music's riff-heavy rock rhythms.

Altogether, "New Minglewood Blues" was played by the Grateful Dead 435 times, including 35 times in 1977 alone. Originally written by Noah Lewis and first recorded as "Minglewood Blues" by his band, Cannon's Jug Stompers, in Memphis, Tennessee, on January 30, 1928, the song was inspired by a Tennessee mill village named Menglewood. The rough-and-tumble village was built by the Menglewood Box Company and was rife with booze, gambling, and prostitution.

Aside from the title of their song, the Dead took almost no cues from Lewis's original version other than finding inspiration in the old company town and bragging about canoodling with a married woman. In Noah Lewis's original version, the infidelity is portrayed thusly: "Don't you wish your fairer was li'l and cute like mine / She's a married woman / But she comes to see me all the time." However, by the time Lewis recorded the freshly titled and revamped "New Minglewood Blues" on November 26, 1930, with his ensemble, the Noah Lewis Jug Band, the song's lyrics had morphed and taken on the edgier, darkly humorous flavors that would capture the Grateful Dead's imagination. In this version,

Lewis's sly sexual brag becomes more overt: "I was born in a desert / raised in a lion's den / My number one occupation / stealin' women from their monkey men."

Lewis's second version inspired the Dead's reimagining of the song. Because the Dead altered it so greatly, it was only fair of them to also change the title—twice. When the song was released on the self-titled 1967 album *Grateful Dead* it was listed as "New New Minglewood Blues." When it appeared on the 1978 album *Shakedown Street* it was listed as "All New Minglewood Blues." For the purposes of making their own set lists, Deadheads were most likely to shorten it back to the original title "New Minglewood Blues" or the shorthand "Minglewood Blues."

As Pablo Picasso famously said, "Good artists borrow. Great artists steal." Creative people working in every medium have used different words to come to the same conclusion: that they are shaped by the artists who came before them, and it is inevitable that those influences will be absorbed into their own work. In the case of the Grateful Dead, we often see lyrics, Bible verses, even nursery rhymes appropriated and reshaped. Musical artists have been begging, borrowing, and stealing lines from each other since well before recordings even existed. In the case of "New Minglewood Blues," there is lyrical spillover at every step of the way. Thus we find "Water Bound Blues," which was recorded by Texas Anderson on June 15, 1929, containing the lines, "I was raised in the desert / born in a lion's den / Says my chief occupation takin' monkey men's women"; or "It Won't Be Long," recorded by Charley Patton on June 14, 1929, containing the lines, "If you ever go down to Memphis / stop by Menglewood / You Memphis women don't mean no man no good"; or, even before those recordings, "Blue Yodel #1," recorded by Jimmie Rodgers on November 30, 1927, and containing lines that will echo familiarly in Dead fans' ears, "It's T for Texas, and it's T for Tennessee / It's T for Thelma, the girl who made a wreck of me."

By the time the Dead busted out "New Minglewood Blues" to kick off the Barton Hall show, the song had been honed down to its rock 'n' roll essence and could be fired off like a bullet whenever the band wanted to pull the trigger. Because it was played so often, it was certainly not considered a rare appearance, or a "breakout" tune, which so many Deadheads covet, but it was a consistent gem of a Grateful Dead song and a top-notch way to get the party started.

"Loser"

In comparing the Grateful Dead to the next generation of "jam bands" playing improvisational rock music, David Gans said of the newer bands, "They'll make you laugh, they'll make you dance, but they'll never make you cry." Indeed, the Dead never shied away from portraying the full range of human emotion and experience—the good, the bad, and the devastating—in their music. Thus it's fitting that they would follow a good-time party song like "New Minglewood Blues" with "Loser," portraying the dark side of the lifestyle they had just glorified. Indeed, attending a Grateful Dead concert could sometimes feel like sitting at the feet of a captivating storyteller with endless yarns to spin. With "Loser," Robert Hunter created lyrics and Jerry Garcia created music that wove a mournful tale about the sad desperation that can stalk a hustler's existence.

In 1971, the year the song debuted, the Grateful Dead played "Loser" a record fifty-two times. The first live appearance of the song was at the Capitol Theatre in Port Chester, New York, on February 18 that year. Because the show was intended to be a live release, it featured five new songs. Every song that debuted that night—"Bertha," "Greatest Story Ever Told," "Loser," "Playing in the Band," and "Wharf Rat"—would go on to become a Grateful Dead staple. Two of them, "Loser" and "Wharf Rat," boldly plumbed the darker depths of humanity. Both told the story of the outsider, the outcast, and, yes, the loser. Presenting both songs in the first person also meant that whoever sang them had to be able to portray this bleak existence believably, with the necessary gravitas and empathy. While Jerry Garcia may not have had a voice that crooners would envy, the pathos in his vocals was nonpareil, and he often shone brightest when the storytelling stakes were highest. Garcia's descending guitar line both swaggers and stumbles its way through the song, perfectly complementing the gambler's plea to his girl "Sweet Suzy" to loan him "ten gold dollars" to stake him back into the poker game. The narrator is both cocky ("I've got no chance of losing") and desperate ("Don't you push me, baby / because I'm moaning low"). Because we are aware of the title of the song, we know that the story won't end well. In part because of that foreknowledge, Garcia's blistering solos on "Loser" can feel like death by a thousand cuts. At Barton Hall, Garcia solos so high up on his fret board that he is, literally, at the end of the line. There are no more high notes left to play and nowhere to go but down. Jerry's solo whimpers, begs, postures, flails, and slices through the music like a knife plunged into the back of a sorry cheat who just ran out of luck. The game is over, the gambler lost, and he's about to learn what everyone else has known all along: once a loser, always a loser.

"El Paso"

While it may not be a forty-five-minute "Alligator," country and western artist Marty Robbins's "El Paso" was considered excessively long when it was first released as a single off his 1959 album *Gunfighter Ballads and Trail Songs.* Clocking in at four minutes and thirty-eight seconds, it was nearly double the length of most songs being played on the radio at that time. However, Robbins had a compelling story to tell in "El Paso," and although an edited three-minute version was also released, most listeners preferred the longer cut. It was so popular that it reached number one on the *Billboard* chart for both pop and country and western categories and won Robbins a Grammy for best country and western recording.

Among Deadheads, "El Paso" was known as a "Cowboy Bob" song. In later years, it was typical for Bob Weir to group two Cowboy Bob songs together in the first set. Among those were "Me and My Uncle," "Mexicali Blues," and "El Paso." All were highly narrative, first-person songs that allowed Weir to slip into rogue personas of western drinkers, fighters, gamblers, cocksmen, liars, scoundrels, murderers, and low-down dirty cheats. In other words, they were boot-stomping fun songs, and Weir knew how to deliver them with a rakish wink, nod, and tip of his hat. Of course, it didn't hurt that Weir's public persona was essentially a more playful, benign version of the characters he portrayed in these songs.

In "El Paso" the narrator falls in love with a Mexican woman named Felina who would whirl and dance (much like the Deadheads listening to Weir's singing) at Rosa's cantina. The narrator encounters another cowboy who also fancies Felina. A gunfight ensues, and our narrator kills his rival. He flees the scene out the

By 1977 the Grateful Dead had returned to a robust touring schedule, with shows across the country. Dedicated Deadheads made as many shows as they could and sometimes followed the band for entire tours. Ticket stubs courtesy of Dean Heiser.

The Cornell Concert Commission, founded in 1971, is a student organization with the mission "to select, promote, and produce all aspects of popular concerts at Cornell." This early logo, featuring a winged figure, was emblazoned on T-shirts and made into patches to be stitched onto jackets so that commission members would be identifiable among the crowds at concerts. Logo master for reproductions courtesy of the Rare and Manuscript Collections, Kroch Library, Cornell University, Ithaca, New York.

Mike McEvoy, Selection Committee chairman (*standing*), and Robert Horowitz, president (*seated*), were leaders at the Cornell Concert Commission at the time. Known as "Mac" and "Hor," they were instrumental in bringing the Grateful Dead to campus. They are shown here at a desk in the Department of University Unions, in Willard Straight Hall. Photograph courtesy of the Rare and Manuscript Collections, Kroch Library, Cornell University, Ithaca, New York.

The master copy of the black-and-white handbill announcing the May 8, 1977, concert features corrected information pertaining to ticket prices and sales outlets pasted over earlier information because details of the show were revised at the last minute. These were posted all around campus and the city of Ithaca. Handbill courtesy of the Rare and Manuscript Collections, Kroch Library, Cornell University, Ithaca, New York.

cornell concert commission

The 1977-1978 Cornell Concert Commission continued to improve on its ability to present the best in popular music in Ithaca. After last year's Grateful Dead show it looked as if the Commission might be pressed to one up itself. However, Linda Ronstadt proved to be one of the finest performances heard in Barton Hall in years. Miss Ronstadt had the capacity crowd totally captivated and received roses and Oreo cookies (her favorite) along with a standing ovation for such crowd pleasers as: "Tumbling Dice," "Will ing' ", "When Will I Be Loved", "You're No Good", and "It's So Easy." The concert found Linda at the peak of her popularity, off on her biggest concert tour ever and with her most successful album to date. The Commission surprised the Barton Hall crowd when it announced the return of Renaissance to Bailey Hall. Although the Commission was operating on a week and a half's notice, they pulled off another fine show. Renaissance sold out Bailey Hall in one day and the audience gave the group a ten minute standing ovation for their sensational "Ashes Are Burning" encore.

A Marshall Tucker show had been scheduled for December on the Sunday after classes ended, but it was cancelled due to an injury to the group's bass player. Shortly after the cancellation of what was expected to be the Commission's fourth sold out concert in a row, Emerson, Lake and Palmer were announced as the first act of spring semester.

During the past year, the Commission has greatly improved its working relationship with its promoter, John Scher, which should enable it to continue to draw top name acts. This past year also saw the advent of the Commission's Cheap Thrills activity discount book, which provided book holders with $1.50 discount on five concerts and an exclusive twenty-four hour advance ticket sale, in addition to discounts on movies, program board events, pool and ping-pong, drinks in the pubs and other items.

The Commission is always looking for new members and any Cornell student is eligible to join.

Members of the Cornell Concert Commission from 1977–1978, the front row all wearing their CCC uniform shirts with logo, are shown in this image from the *Cornellian*, Cornell's yearbook. (No photograph of the CCC appears in the 1976–1977 edition.) Eve Prouty, treasurer, is at the left of the front row holding a pen; Toni Riccardi, corporate liaison, is immediately to Prouty's left; and Robert Horowitz, president, is at the right of the front row with hands in pockets. Among others in the second row, from the left, are Andy Seiden, Ben Liemer (just over Prouty's head), Jon Ackerman, Kate Schnare (hospitality; looking to her right), and Doug Foulke (production manager; in sunglasses). Scan of photograph courtesy of the Rare and Manuscript Collections, Kroch Library, Cornell University, Ithaca, New York.

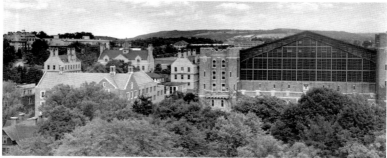

Before it became, in 1940, Barton Hall—named after Colonel Frank A. Barton, Cornell class of 1891, who for decades led Cornell's Cadet Corps and ROTC programs—the building was known as the New York State Drill Hall. Constructed at the time of World War I, the massive structure in the collegiate gothic style, situated just east of the Arts Quadrangle, was meant for military training and civilian exercise. These images from the 1940s provide a good sense of the size of the building. Photographs courtesy of the Rare and Manuscript Collections, Kroch Library, Cornell University, Ithaca, New York.

By the 1960s, the uses of Barton Hall varied significantly from those articulated by the New York State Legislature when it funded construction of the drill hall earlier in the twentieth century. These images show Barton at maximum capacity—with students filling the floor and packing the stands used for basketball games—on three occasions, ranging from collegiate athletics to political upheaval. The campus-wide meeting on April 22, 1969, in the wake of the occupation of Willard Straight Hall by members of the Afro-American Society who were protesting racism at Cornell is shown above. In the middle is a moment from a Cornell-Princeton basketball game from the mid-1960s. A scene from the Bread and Puppet Theater performance that was part of the weekend-long protest of the Vietnam War, referred to as the "Berrigan Weekend" or "America Is Hard to Find," on April 17–19, 1970, is shown below. Photographs courtesy of the Rare and Manuscript Collections, Kroch Library, Cornell University, Ithaca, New York.

Two tickets to the May 8, 1977, show at Barton Hall—the one in orange was for sale to the general public, and the other, in blue, was for sale to Cornell students. The crowd at the door was large and the urgency to get near the stage so widespread that many people were swept through the doors and into the hall. Many tickets were never inspected or torn by the Cornell Concert Commission staff. Tickets courtesy of Dean Heiser.

The Collegetown neighborhood, just south of the Cornell campus, was the residential locale for upperclassmen living off campus and the commercial shopping and dining district for all Cornell students. Here an Ithaca city bus makes its way west along its Bryant Park route in 1975. Johnny's Big Red Grill and Johnny's Carryout, both on Dryden Road, can be seen in the background. Photograph © Jon Reis / www.jonreis.com.

The busy intersection of Dryden Road and College Avenue is at the heart of Ithaca's Collegetown neighborhood. Sam Gould's variety store, which proudly displayed a sign indicating that the shop was 893 feet above sea level (and some 488 feet above Cayuga Lake), was a retail mainstay for students. The Royal Palm Tavern, in the background of this 1975 scene, was a popular student watering hole at a time when the legal drinking age in New York State was eighteen. Photograph © Jon Reis / www.jonreis.com.

College students relax and swim in Fall Creek under the pedestrian suspension bridge in this 1970s scene. The bridge, which spans the 140-foot-deep gorge, connects the main Arts Quadrangle to Cornell's North Campus, known as the site of residence halls, fraternities, sororities, and family homes. Warmer May temperatures would have offered a chance of swimming to those who arrived earlier in the weekend of the Grateful Dead concert. On Saturday, May 7, temperatures in Ithaca reached into the high seventies. By Sunday, however, a cold wind blew, with rain and then snow in the air. Photograph © Jon Reis / www.jonreis.com.

In fine weather Cornell students sunbathe, play Frisbee, and sometimes try to study on the lawns that descend from the Arts Quadrangle to West Avenue and the Baker Dorms (also known as the Gothic Halls), visible in this image. On a Mother's Day weekend at the end of the semester in 1977, the scene would surely have been livelier than this quiet moment captured in May 1976. Photograph © Jon Reis / www.jonreis.com.

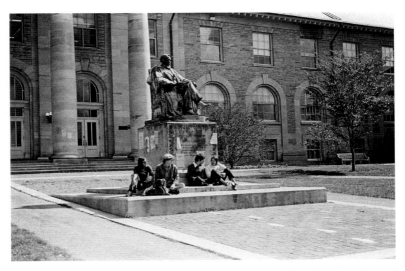

The statue of Andrew Dickson White, located on the Arts Quadrangle in front of Goldwin Smith Hall, honors the first president of Cornell University. Students, such as those in this 1975 image, tended to make the pedestal their own, both as a meeting place and as a surface to post handbills. Photograph © Jon Reis / www.jonreis.com.

View looking to the west from East Hill shows the one hundred block of East State Street in Ithaca after the completion of the Commons. Opened in 1975, the Commons was Ithaca's answer to urban renewal. The plan adapted two blocks of East State Street and one block of North Tioga Street into a commercial and public space closed to automobile traffic. Out-of-town Deadheads arriving early could have wandered downtown and taken in the scene. In this April 1977 view of the Commons and downtown Ithaca, Rothschild's Department Store is visible, as well as the Logos Bookstore, Schooley's Jewelers, and the White Mountain Ice Cream Parlor. Ithaca's West Hill is in the background. Photograph © Jon Reis / www.jonreis.com.

Department of
University Unions
Willard Straight Hall
Cornell University
Ithaca, New York 14853

Director's Office   Business Office   Program Office
607/256-7285   607/256-7287   607/256-7131

BUDGET-GRATEFUL DEAD

May 8, 1977

Security: Cornell Safety Division, 218 man-hours @10.00/hr.
      and one supervisor, 10 man-hours @ 12.00/hr.   2300.00

      NROTC, Building guards-3 men @3.00/hr. for 16 hrs.   144.00

Fire Safety: one man for 8 hrs. @ 8.00/hr.   64.00

Physical Plant Operations: 1 electrician for 16hrs. @ 19.00/hr.   304.00
         Custodian, 36 man hours @ 7.00/hr.   252.00
         Misc. clean up costs   50.00
         "Supers" scaffolding tower   88.00
         Raising lighting battens   150.00
         Damages to building   250.00
         Barricades for roadblock   30.00

Hospitality   600.00

Stage rental-Dome Arena   ~~850.00~~ *900.00*
Stage masking- Cooper Decoration   150.00 +*49.00*
"   "   Willard Straight Theater   40.00
Super Trooper Rental- APO   175.00
"   "   "   - Syracuse Scenery & Stage Lighting   200.00
Transportation- Ryder Truck Rentals   135.00
Sound Tower Scaffolding- South Central Scaffolding   183.00 +*15.00*
Gofer-petty cash   50.00
Misc. expenses   100.00
Plywood- Empire Building Supplies 10 sheets @ 13.00/ sheet   130.00

Tour Lights and Sound   5000.00

GRAND TOTAL   11245.00

Respectfully submitted,

      Member of Association of College Unions - International

At $11,245, the total projected budget for putting on the May 1977 Grateful Dead show looks meager by present-day standards. The Cornell Concert Commission was a tight operation, and efforts at cost savings were crucial at a time when the organization was running a deep operating deficit with Cornell University. Document courtesy of the Rare and Manuscript Collections, Kroch Library, Cornell University, Ithaca, New York.

Cornell University
Ithaca, New York 14853

Department of University Unions
Willard Straight Hall

Director's Office   Business Office   Program Office
607/256-7285   607/256-7287   607/256-7131

April 12, 1977

TO: Joe Paterson, Superintendent, Public Safety

FROM: Doug Foulke, Production Manager, Cornell Concert Commission

SUBJ: Security for the Grateful Dead Concert - May 8, 1977

Security will begin for the concert on Saturday. At 1800 the crash doors of Barton Hall are to be chained shut on the North, West and South sides of the building. If the Concert Commission personnel working in the hall on Saturday have left the building for the night then the East doors of the building will also be chained. The East crash doors are not to be chained if the Concert Commission personnel are still working or if the Production Manager of the Concert Commission has not informed Safety Division that we are through in the hall for the evening. The East crash doors should be opened by 0930 on May 8. The other crash doors should remain chained until 1800 on May 8.

PERSONNEL REQUIREMENTS: At 0900 on Sunday the Garden Avenue road block should be put up and manned. The positions are to be at the Garden Ave. and Tower Rd. closing traffic toward Barton Hall and at Campus Rd. and Garden Ave. just past he feed road to Lynah Rink and Teagle Hall. These posts are to be manned by Student Security Aids (SSA's). The SSA working this position is to turn away all traffic not directly related to the concert. The road between the road blocks is restricted during this period and no through traffic is permitted. A vehicle pass will be issued to all cars, trucks, etc., that will have access to the area.

It is to be realized that people associated with Monarch Entertainment and the Grateful Dead Productions may not have these passes when they first arrive. The SSA's should take this in to account when dealing with hassles that in all probability will occur. The road block is to be manned continually until that time at shich the two semi's have loaded and left. This should be approximately two hours after the end of the concert. Two shifts, 0900 to 1800, and 1800 to ? are suggested.

At 1200, four officers will begin external security. Their main assignment will be to police the perimeter of Barton Hall. They should discourage all loitering, except on the West (Statler) side of the hall, where the public will anxiously be awaiting admission to the hall.

A key budget expense for the Grateful Dead show was security. After the riot at the 1973 Deep Purple concert at Schoellkopf Field, the Cornell Concert Commission and Cornell University administrators were careful about managing large crowds. With more than eight thousand people expected to fill Barton Hall, Joe Patterson, the superintendent of public safety, circulated this memo detailing operations as they would unfold on May 8. Letter courtesy of the Rare and Manuscript Collections, Kroch Library, Cornell University, Ithaca, New York.

back door of Rosa's, steals a horse (a crime nearly equal to murder in the Old West), and rides from El Paso through New Mexico. After some time, as much as he tries to forget her, the narrator insists that he loves Felina more than he fears death, and he rides back into El Paso to be reunited with her. Unfortunately, he is met by a posse of cowboys who shoot him as soon as he rides into town. Our narrator manages to survive with bullets in his body just long enough to make it to Felina, who gives him one last kiss before he dies in her arms. End scene.

Between the outlaw narrative of the song, the bouncy, danceable rhythm the Dead gave it, and Weir's convincing delivery, "El Paso" was an excellent first-set song that also acknowledged the wide-ranging influences that helped shape the Grateful Dead's music. While most people wouldn't hear the term "country and western music" and immediately think "Grateful Dead," the leap was made by the band on a regular basis. When they wanted to, they nailed country and western, particularly the Bakersfield sound of the late 1950s, with the best of them, adding just enough psychedelic special sauce to put their indelible Grateful Dead stamp on the genre.

"They Love Each Other"

Do you remember that show at Roscoe Maples Pavilion at Stanford University on February 9, 1973, where the Wall of Sound was unveiled and all the tweeters blew out on the band's first song? Along with the Wall of Sound, the band also debuted some soon-to-be Grateful Dead staple songs that night, including "China Doll," "Eyes of the World," "Loose Lucy," "Here Comes Sunshine," "Row Jimmy," "Wave That Flag" (which would evolve into

"U.S. Blues"), and the fourth tune that the band played at Cornell on May 8, 1977: "They Love Each Other."

A Garcia/Hunter composition, "They Love Each Other" appeared on the Garcia solo album *Reflections* and on the Grateful Dead album *Steal Your Face*, both in 1976. Among Garcia/Hunter songs, it is most noteworthy for its seeming lack of an overt dark side. On the surface, "They Love Each Other" reads like a straightforward love song, describing the dizzying, breathless experience of falling head over heels in love: "got it from the top / it's nothing you can stop / Lord, you know they / made a fine connection / They love each other / Lord, you can see that it's true." Quite simply, this is a song that would be absolutely required on any Dead fan mix tape meant to woo a romantic partner. It's a song to sway to, swoon to, and to dance to with someone you love—or hope to love in the near future. At Barton Hall, Garcia drops in at roughly the 4:20 mark with a perfectly woozy, wobbling guitar solo that mimics the off-balance feeling of stumbling around drunk in love. At 5:50, Bob Weir hits a metallic sounding harmonic, right after Garcia sings "and when that train rolls in," that's so perfectly placed it seems inevitable, despite the fact that it's completely improvised. Again, we feel dizzy in love.

The American Book of the Dead: The Definitive Dead Encyclopedia points out that "They Love Each Other" is a low-key plaint by a jealous observer of young lovers in the rush of romance, but I don't imagine anyone listening to the song hears any of that. I'd venture to say that very few people ever thought of "They Love Each Other" as anything other than a pretty, lilting love song—jealous observers be damned. At Barton Hall, it's an early sign that the band is connecting with each other on a higher musical plane. They synch-up magically throughout the song with Weir's chakra-opening harmonics melting ears and hearts across the night. Their voices blend in gorgeous four-part harmony on the chorus, with Donna's vocals ringing beside Garcia's, inserting the perfect amount of female energy into the romantic mix. At the 3:00 mark, her real-life husband, Keith Godchaux, meanders into a solo that delivers a roomy minute of near ragtime rationale for including a provision in the contract rider for a "nine foot (9') Steinway piano and piano tuner" to be provided by the venue. Garcia's solo takes over from there, starting with a climb up to the stars before dropping back down to "merry run around" through the grassy fields of love for a while. Throughout the song, the band "makes a fine connection," so much so that when the tune ends at just below 9 minutes, it feels as though a vacuum is left that, for a moment, pulses with an unsettling, mournful silence.

Ah, love.

"Jack Straw"

In abstract experiential terms, first sets were made for the Grateful Dead audience to listen to stories, while second sets were for the audience to participate in them. And of all the first-set "stories" the Grateful Dead told, "Jack Straw" is among the most majestic, fully formed, and rich with Americana.

First performed on October 9, 1971, "Jack Straw" spent its first seven months as a Weir-only vocal number. By the time the band hit Paris on May 3, 1972, the vocal duties were split between Weir and Garcia. That's how they stayed until the song's final performance—the second-to-last performance ever by the band—at Chicago's Soldier Field on July 8, 1995. That show opened with "Jack Straw" featuring Weir on acoustic guitar.

In a 2004 interview, Weir commented on the literary inspiration behind "Jack Straw": "I had just read *Of Mice and Men* for about the tenth time. I was completely smitten by that story. I took a step back in time into the Depression, and that era, and this story emerged between me and Hunter about these two guys on the lam . . . ne'er-do-wells . . . victims of the Depression." With Steinbeck's classic Depression-era novel in mind, it's hard not to see the two primary characters in "Jack Straw"—Shannon (Garcia) and Jack Straw (Weir)—as a duo like George and Lennie, but with a dastardly outlaw bent. As with all great characters, though, even while they're robbing and killing we can't help but feel sympathy for them, even kinship with them, as they scramble for survival beneath the bleak existential awareness that "there ain't no winner in this game / Who don't go home with all / Not with all."

In addition to Shannon and Jack Straw, there is a third perspective given in the song—call it a narrator, or a "chorus" in the classical Greek sense—that comments on the goings-on of the duo and sets the scene for the characters' dialogue. This character is voiced by all the members of the band who care to contribute and also large swaths of the audience at any given show.

The pacing of "Jack Straw" was sped up and slowed down over the years. At Cornell, the pace is molasses slow on the chorus parts, with a swinging uptick during the conversations between Shannon and Jack Straw. The tempo push and pull between sections catapults the audience through the song, opening up into a particularly slow, lush vista for the chorus that sets a gorgeous visual scene midway through the song: "Leaving Texas / Fourth day of July / sun so hot, clouds so low / The eagles filled the sky / Catch the Detroit Lightning / Out of Santa Fe / Great Northern out of Cheyenne / from sea to shining sea." The musical vista created is expansive, wide open; and between the Fourth of July date, the sky being filled with eagles, the "sea to shining sea" quote from "America the Beautiful," and the pure Americana reverence for railroads that we find in numerous classic folk and blues numbers, the song all but waves an American flag across the audience before it launches into the inevitably sorrowful conclusion to the story.

Eventually, "Jack Straw from Wichita / Cut his buddy down / Dug for him a shallow grave / And laid his body down." And that's all she wrote for dearly departed Shannon.

"Deal"

On May 8, 1977, scoundrels and scalawags were everywhere at Barton Hall. Much as "Loser" commented on the dark side of "New Minglewood Blues" to start the set, roughly forty minutes into the show, "Deal" carried through the outlaw theme of "Jack Straw" but with a more whimsical, rollicking mood. "Deal" falls squarely into the "gambler" category of Grateful Dead song themes—and has a damn good time doing it.

Part of the beauty of "Deal"—and the lyrical reason the mood is kept light—is that it doesn't go into detail about any of the negative gambling experiences the narrator has had. In fact, those experiences are glossed over with a perfectly presented couplet of Robert Hunter lyrics, "If I told you all that went down / it would burn off both your ears." 'Nuff said, apparently. The overall impact of "Deal" is one of sitting at the feet of a proudly defiant lifelong gambler, pouring him a drink, "tighten[ing] up his shoes," and listening while he makes sweeping admonishments that amount to: *Do as I say, not as I do.*

At Barton Hall, "Deal" is pure Garcia from start to finish. It's as close to a strut as he comes, and he does it with style—offering sage advice with a wink and nod, peeling off a few choice rocking solos, and blending back into the harmonies with just a hint of lilt to his voice. It's fitting that the song is a Garcia showcase, considering that it debuted on his 1972 solo album, titled, fittingly, *Garcia*. Within the show's set, "Deal" acts as a gambler's palate cleanser of sorts. It is a straightforward, rocking, first-set song, and it was performed well at Cornell. The band would return to their beloved scoundrels and scalawags again before the set was over, but first it was off to Bobby-land with a mid-'70s song that, like "Deal" for Garcia, started from his own solo project.

"Lazy Lightning" / "Supplication"

Among Deadheads, certain lyrics resonate with particular power because of the way they comment directly on the fans' relationship to the band and the lifestyle choices being a Deadhead can engender. Of those sacred lyrics, "It's an obsession but it's pleasin'" stands as the clearest, most direct answer to the question most Deadheads face at one time or another: *Why?* Why travel hundreds of miles to see the same band night after night after night? Why collect yet another recording of the Grateful Dead playing a one-off gig in some random town in middle America? Why spend hours listening to different performances of the same song in order to better appreciate the subtle differences between them? Why listen to a forty-two-minute version of any song at all?

It's an obsession but it's pleasin'. That's why.

Along with those choice lyrics, "Lazy Lightning" packed a hell of a mid-'70s jazz fusion punch. For all intents and purposes, "Supplication" is a coda to "Lazy Lightning" and thus discussed as part of the same song. "Lazy Lightning" was never played without

"Supplication," and "Supplication" was played only twice without "Lazy Lightning," once in 1976 and once in 1993. Among the original songs played at Barton Hall on May 8, "Lazy Lightning" / "Supplication" is the one that time-stamps the show most clearly as a product of the 1970s.

With music by Bob Weir and lyrics by John Perry Barlow, "Lazy Lightning" / "Supplication" was written in Mill Valley in October 1975 and made its recorded debut on an eponymously titled album by Kingfish, Bob Weir's side band, in March 1976. Roughly three months later, on June 3, 1976, the Grateful Dead performed "Lazy Lightning" at the Paramount Theatre in Portland, Oregon, a show that also saw the debut of "Might as Well," "Sampson and Delilah," and "The Wheel."

In its relatively short life, "Lazy Lightning" was played 111 times, with 89 of those taking place between 1976 and 1980. In 1984 the song was played only three times and then retired forever. Of any Grateful Dead song, this one is late 1970s all the way. Particularly the Barton Hall version. There's a rhythmically light yet musically ornate feel to the jam section that echoes the 1970s jazz fusion that members of the Dead had undoubtedly absorbed through their finely tuned ears. At Barton Hall, Garcia in particular showcases his jazzy Mixolydian chops in ways that are more typically reserved for his side projects with organist Merl Saunders. It would seem that playing roughly sixty shows with Saunders between December 1974 and July 1975 in their stellar albeit short-lived band, Legion of Mary, had honed Garcia's jazz runs to a fluid perfection of tension and release. Although he had laughed when first presented with the aluminum-necked Custom Travis Bean TB500 guitar he played at Cornell, Garcia quickly embraced its sound and would eventually use it to record the *Terrapin Station* album. Altogether, he would play the Travis Bean at more than ninety concerts, including thirty-five Dead shows. At Cornell, a sticker affixed to the body of the guitar read "The Enemy is Listening"—a World War II slogan meant to keep Americans on the alert for Axis spies. Bill Kreutzmann provides one explanation for the sticker's meaning to Jerry: "Early pot heads were always ducking low because in those daze [*sic*] you could go to jail for a long time for holding just one joint. So the enemy was watching or thought to be. It was an inside joke amongst us hippies." While Garcia never made a public statement himself about why he chose to affix this sticker front and center on his guitar, it's crystal clear that he made nothing but friends while wielding it through "Lazy Lightning" and every other song at Cornell.

The highlight of the Barton Hall "Lazy Lightning," the part that seems to slow time and coaxes the song wide open for musical exploration, takes place at the 3:43 mark. The vocals—led by Weir and Donna Jean Godchaux—had already made their way through several rounds of the collective chant "My lightnin' too." The song had built to a lyrical crescendo that highlights the obsessive love under discussion, and Weir's voice in particular had risen to ever more histrionic levels. With the instruments and vocals at a peak, the song hits the 3:40 mark and suddenly the music evaporates, leaving only a solitary high hat and a subtly off-kilter Phil Lesh bass line to keep us going. The 3:40 minute mark would be the end of the line for most bands. But not the Grateful Dead. At 3:43, Jerry Garcia hits a Cb5/E chord, slides it down a half step, and then slides it back up to resolve. It is only one chord and one fret, but the effect is uncanny. It's as if Garcia has opened a slanted doorway into the song that is just large enough for all the other players to slip through before it slams shut, leaving them huddled together on the other side in a shag-carpeted conference room labeled "Jam."

It is at that point—3:43 into "Lazy Lightning" / "Supplication"—that 1977 Grateful Dead steps fully into Barton Hall, puts one hand on its cocked hip, and peers over its rose-colored shades to better dig the scene. For the next three minutes, the band slides through the jam like quaaludes through the bloodstream until Weir finally jumps back onto the microphone at 6:48 to launch into the "Supplication" coda with the apt vocals, "Dizzy ain't the word for the way you're making me feel now / I need some indication, girl, if all of this is real now / I've heard it said there's something wrong in my head now / Could it be infatuation or am I just being misled now." As if delivering a magical incantation for heartsick lovers, Weir chants out the words, "Supplication . . . infatuation . . . inspiration . . . imagination . . . excitation . . . hallucination" until finally the full-tilt rave-up comes to a hard stop with one last primal outcry: "Whoo!"

"Brown-Eyed Women"

Out of the 1970s and into the Prohibition era. The band comes flying out of the gate for this ripping version of "Brown-Eyed Women," with Garcia telling Bakersfield-sound-type tales about a good-hearted bootlegger Daddy and a tough Mama who raised eight sons while living in a "tumbledown shack in Bigfoot County." The energy from "Lazy Lightning" is still flowing through the band, particularly Weir, who chops away at the song's rhythm like he's cutting "hick'ry just to fire the still," while still finding chord inversions that bridge the gap between the 1970s and the 1930s. Garcia hardly wants to slow down either, extending his guitar solo for a second go-round in an otherwise tight and tidy version of this Grateful Dead classic. With the song clocking in at barely over five minutes, the band gets in and out of this one with muscle and agility. It's a lovely story, well told.

On the audience recordings of Cornell '77, the whoops of the audience during the chorus are infectious and speak to the band's ability to tell an otherwise maudlin tale that's almost impossible not to tap your foot to. After all, at the heart of "Brown-Eyed Women" is the story of a man who did what he needed to do to support a large family in rural America, but was ultimately broken by the death of his beloved wife, Delilah. As the narrator says, "the old man never was the same again." But no matter, when the chorus comes around with Garcia's buttery lilt leading the charge, the lyrics "Brown-eyed women and red grenadine / the bottle was dusty but the liquor was clean," feel like a celebration of the good things in life trumping the sorrows of mortality. With the echoes of "The Last Waltz" concert by the Band (which had taken place on Thanksgiving 1976 on the Dead's home turf of the Winterland Ballroom in San Francisco) still ringing through the rock 'n' roll territories, "Brown-Eyed Women" is delivered like the best song Robbie Robertson never wrote. Garcia offers it up as if he was born beside a whiskey still, destined to be a boy "turned bad" and determined to burn through the world like moonshine through a farmer's belly.

"Mama Tried"

It is only right that Weir closes out the scoundrel section of the night's festivities with this Merle Haggard classic tale of yet another mother's son gone wrong. Once again—this time directly—the straight-shooting Bakersfield-sound style of country and western music gets the Grateful Dead treatment, staying true to its earthy roots yet somehow always slightly psychedelic. Why is it only right? Because, among other things, May 8 was Mother's Day. The performance of "Mama Tried" at Cornell is fun and functional, but the playing is secondary in importance to the fact that it is played at all. This is a great example of the Grateful Dead being in on the joke, and also flexible enough to allow their set list to reflect the gig at hand. The Dead performed "Mama Tried" 302 times throughout their career, and—much like "Mexicali Blues" or "Me and My Uncle"—it always served as a playful vehicle for Cowboy Bob to strut his spurs.

Haggard's inspiration for writing "Mama Tried" was hard-won. He had indeed done time in prison for robbery, although he didn't receive a life sentence with no hope for parole, as the song goes. He had also felt guilt that his mother, who had supported her children as a bookkeeper after Merle's father died of a brain hemorrhage, was forced to watch as her son turned into a criminal. The story goes that while Haggard was doing time at San Quentin, Johnny Cash played a concert there, thus inspiring the young convict to join the prison's country music band. The rest, as they say, is outlaw history.

"Mama Tried" was released in July 1968 as the first single and title track of Haggard's seventh album. In a testament to its staying power, the song was awarded a Grammy Hall of Fame award in 1999. The Grateful Dead began performing "Mama Tried" in 1969, only a year after it was released, and—with the exception of 1972 and 1973—played it every year they toured until its final performance at RFK stadium in Washington, D.C., on June 25, 1995. In short, "Mama Tried" was a Grateful Dead workhorse.

The best thing about the Barton Hall version? A beat after it ends, Phil leans into his microphone and, tongue firmly in cheek, says, "Thanks, Mom."

"Row Jimmy"

The long, slow, evocative version of "Row Jimmy" played at Barton Hall brings out all the subtleties and nuances in this shape-shifting beauty by Jerry Garcia and Robert Hunter. "Row Jimmy" is a tone poem of sorts, evoking the imagery and sounds of time-less fairy tales told in vignettes that are tidily contained in couplet flashes sprinkled through the song. As Hunter said in a November 1977 interview, "I like the setups in that, the characters. I like 'Julie catch a rabbit by his hair / come back step like to walk on air'—that's a whole song by itself. Then there's another song: 'Here's a half a dollar if you dare / double twist when you hit the air.'"

Indeed, you can follow the lyrics right through the song, each couplet containing just enough hint of character, setting, and conflict to contain a world in only a handful of words: "Don't hang your head let the two-time roll / Grass shack nailed to a pine wood floor"; "Broken heart don't feel so bad / Ain't got half of what you thought you had"; "That's the way it's been in town / ever since they tore the jukebox down." The fact that these lines all contain a simple end-rhyme structure only adds to the fairy tale vibe, making it possible to absorb each discrete lyrical unit without digesting the song as a whole. This structure is perfect for children who might enjoy language play and the chewy roll of vowels that Hunter gorges on throughout the song. It's also per-fect for people on acid who might flash on individual images but not follow the song as an entire composition. Quite frankly, with "Row Jimmy" you don't need to. In that sense, it is the perfect psychedelic fairy tale. Using a smartly goofy pun to start off the song ("hair" playing off "hare" as a synonym for rabbit), which is slightly disturbing ("catch a rabbit by his hair"), also keeps us in mind of the best fairy tales.

At Barton Hall, the band unfurls "Row Jimmy" nice and slow, taking time to add vivid splashes of color to each and every vignette and allowing each band member to paint an artistic flourish into the landscape. The most standout parts occur as the indulgently slow rise and fall of Jerry's lush slide guitar plays against Keith's subtle yet insistent organ rhythm. Ultimately, though, Jerry's sound is buried one layer below the surface. It's Keith's organ playing that brings us to the edge of the carnival grounds where the woozy, slightly nauseating sound of a merry-go-round winding down makes us feel pleasantly dizzy and otherworldly. It's Keith who keeps this rendition of the song in the realm of off-kilter fairy tale where "Row Jimmy" belongs.

"Dancin' in the Streets"

"I didn't care for the 'Dancin' in the Streets,'" says one person who attended the Barton Hall show. Even forty years after the fact, he adds, "I still don't care for it. I don't like that disco version." David Gans observes of the song, "I don't really think of that as disco Dead. 'Shakedown Street' is pure disco, four-on-the-floor, straight relentless beat. I think of this version of 'Dancin' in the Streets' as more of a funk groove than disco." And Gary Lambert offers this comment on how the song was done live and in the studio: "The rather fey treatment it got on the *Terrapin Station* album felt more like disco than the live versions they were doing. The live versions had that really interesting time signature thing they did in the middle of the jam, and it was more of a funk groove in the live shows for sure. . . . If it was disco, it was kind of a weak attempt at it, but it was pretty good funk, and real good live dance music." Say what you want about disco Dead or whether you prefer the late-'60s style of "Dancin'" to the late-'70s versions: as far as I'm concerned, resistance to this fifteen-minute "Dancin' in the Streets" is futile. Mary Suma, who covered the show for the *Ithaca Journal*, called it the "highlight of the evening," and she has a good point.

This is the Grateful Dead at their god-almighty funkiest. In fact, you can take out every other instrument in the band and listen exclusively to Phil Lesh's bass on this tune, and it would still be one of the funkiest songs the band ever played. Throughout the Cornell version of "Dancin'," Phil alternates fat and sassy bass runs with huge, sliding glissandos up and down his fret board that defy you not to shake your ass. Lesh may be the polar opposite of funk bass legend Bootsy Collins in every way, but when push comes to shove, he can also get nasty with the best of them.

While Phil manhandled his bass, Jerry gave his Mu-Tron III an energetic workout. The Mu-Tron III is the guitar effect behind one of the signature sounds in Garcia's sonic arsenal. Among other things, it's the effect behind the iconic sound of "Fire on the Mountain," which had made its debut less than two months before Cornell at the Winterland Arena on March 18, 1977. Steve Silberman describes the Mu-Tron III as giving Garcia's guitar "a huge, fat sound with a distinctive *thwack* that resembled a steel drum turned up to 11."

At Cornell, Jerry runs his Mu-Tron III lead lines into the land of funk and back out the other side, smack into Bobby and Donna's vocals at the 13-minute mark. Aside from a gaping vocal miscue to start off, Bobby and Donna keep it together for the duration of the song. According to Donna, that was no small feat. She says, "I don't know whose idea [the new arrangement of 'Dancin' in the Street' was], but disco was very happening. Mickey was so into *Saturday Night Fever.* Oh, my God—what the band would have to put up with in the hotel room; Mickey had his tape player going full blast with the door open, playing *Saturday Night Fever*. But also, Garcia, God bless him, was into all kinds of music, provided it was really good. Bobby and I had to really concentrate to get the phrasing [on that song] really sharp and staccato."

Bobby and Donna do keep their vocals sharp and staccato throughout the song, with Bobby doing double duty by matching Jerry's beefy Mu-Tron runs with rhythmic riffs that bite and shimmer like the finest pink Peruvian crystals. "Dancin' in the Streets" was one of the first songs the Dead played and was an anthem across urban America (first as a party anthem and later as a civil rights anthem) from the time Martha and the Vandellas released it in the summer of 1964. At Cornell, the Dead give the song a full workout. It is an incredibly upbeat and perfectly sweaty way to end the first set, and a harbinger of the mind-blowing second set that was about to occur.

At the close of "Dancin' in the Streets," when Bobby leaned into the microphone and said "We're gonna take a short break, we'll be right back," you get the sense that everyone in the room could probably use a breather. In fact, Bobby spoke these words even as Donna's and Jerry's backup vocals were still echoing through the hall. If nothing else, it's clear that Bob needed a breather after the pulsating life force he just breathed into "Dancin'." He gave it everything he had. It's time to recharge backstage and perhaps refuel with some of the food and drink that was stipulated in the concert rider: five cases of Heineken, twelve large bottles of Perrier, cheese, fruit, nuts, crackers, and "any other creative snacks" the CCC might provide. Second sets tend to be long, strenuous journeys; Bob and the band would need all the energy they could gather.

In the hall, the crowd howled, clapped, whistled, and screamed their approval as the band members set down their instruments and sauntered offstage. On audience recordings, the environment sounds electric with excitement drenching every caterwaul spilling through the crowd. The fans at Barton Hall had just gotten the Grateful Dead at their best; a "band beyond description" at the peak of their late-70s game. Perhaps some even sensed that they were at the midpoint of what would be considered a historically significant show in Grateful Dead history.

Outside of Barton Hall, the snow was falling, and Cornellians were buttoning up against the cold, but one can imagine that, inside, sweaty layers of clothes were peeled off and discarded in random piles around the edges of Barton Hall. They would still be there after the show. Or they wouldn't. Who cared? Everyone was wondering what song they'd open second set with. . . .

Second Set

Takes a whole pail of water just to cool him down.
—Robert Hunter, "Fire on the Mountain"

B etween first and second sets, Cornell student Rick Koh found himself at the front of the crowd at Barton Hall. Although it was an excellent vantage from which to watch the musicians, Koh found it harrowing being pressed between the mass of bodies behind him and the metal barrier in front of him. He recalls, "I was on the rail right in front of Jerry. It was really packed in there." The precarious situation for those on the rail was never lost on the Dead. They knew that many fans wanted to be as close as possible to the stage, but that it was often the least comfortable—and least safe—place in the venue. As Cornell '77 attendee Stu Zimmerman recalls, he was willing to withstand such discomfort in order to "catch a glimpse of Garcia's eyes." But the problem was that the people behind them also wanted to be up front, and throughout the show the mass of humanity would press forward. The steel rail in front of the stage was not forgiving. Rick Koh remembers,

"I only made it to the front 'cause two or three people in front of me passed out. I remember pulling people out over the rail, taking them out the front way. We truly were horribly smashed and bug-eyed."

Mark Nathanson, a recent high school grad, had driven in from Sylvania, Ohio, to catch the show. He was not on the rail, but he recalls the show being exceptional and the atmosphere semitropical: "During the intermission, I became really hot, and we were in the coolest spot in the gym. I had an Indian embroidered shirt made of fine white cotton that was drenched." As Garcia sings in "Althea," inside Barton Hall the "space was getting hot," despite the snow falling steadily outside. The crowd was so densely packed that before the second set started Jerry felt moved to remark, "All these people in front are getting horribly smashed here. So that means all you people in the back have to move back . . . just move back *some*."

The trademark Grateful Dead maneuver that spared Koh, and everyone on the rail, at least a measure of discomfort is called "Take a Step Back." Spearheaded by Bob Weir, "Take a Step Back" is, in Weir's comical description, "everyone's favorite fun game," wherein the band tries to help the people in the first rows not get crushed by the people in back. "Take a Step Back" made its first appearance in the 1970s as the band dealt with their swelling fan base and remained a band option for crowd control at general admission concerts for the duration of their career.

Cornell is a typical example of "Take a Step Back," but with the addition of Jerry Garcia pitching in to support Weir's efforts. As always, the band played little riffs and runs to help keep the mood light and add some fun to an otherwise potentially dangerous crowd-control issue. Weir started off the "game" at Cornell with an announcement from the stage: "All right, now we're gonna play everybody's favorite fun game, 'Take a Step Back.' When

I tell you 'take a step back,' everybody take a step back. Right? Right." The directions explained, he launched immediately into the activity. "Okay, take a step back. And take another step back. And take yet another step back. And another, take a step back." Then, like a grudging camp counselor, he immediately took stock of how the game went for the participants. "Everyone feel better?" He paused for the crowd to respond, but not hearing the positive response he desired, Weir playfully groused, "What do you mean 'no'?" At that point, Jerry stepped in to back him up with his own mild plea for everyone to "just move back *some.*" Lastly, Weir put a capper on the duo's routine: "Then all your friends up front won't be real bug-eyed."

After doing their part to help the "bug-eyed" masses, the band settled back into their preferred role as musicians. The crowd was less densely packed up front, but Barton Hall was still sweltering. Smoke from cigarettes and joints wafted up into the immense space under the steel-frame roof. Beers were passed around and held aloft in celebration. The Barton family, descendants of Colonel Frank A. Barton, Cornell class of 1891 and longtime head of Cornell's Cadet Corps and ROTC, might have been shocked to see the old "drill hall" the scene of such a stupendous party. A loud swarm of conversation filled the space. Poised on the stage just feet above the mayhem, the "Take a Step Back" game over, the band eased into an up-tempo bounce that marked the proper start of the second set: a legendary "Scarlet Begonias."

"Scarlet Begonias"

For many people, the magic of Cornell '77 starts with "Scarlet Begonias." More specifically, it starts with "Scarlet Begonias" played into "Fire on the Mountain" ("Scar-Fire" in Deadhead parlance). Even more specifically, it often focuses on the transitional jam between "Scarlet Begonias" and "Fire on the Mountain." It is in this passage—between two songs that loom large in the Grateful Dead's songbook—that the band demonstrates how it has channeled the energies of the long experimental jams of its psychedelic past to find new paths between songs. Throughout the band's career, some of their most exciting, creative playing could be found in those transitional passages, gently easing from one song to another, neither fish nor fowl, but rather something more thrilling than any one song could contain. Jerry Garcia described his particular affinity for those musical transitions: "I love it when it's possible to do that. That's something that I'm better at than I am at other things. That's one of the things I'm good at. Eventually—like, if I have a place to go, eventually, I can get there and make it pretty seamless. Because for me, the relationship between one thing and the other is always obvious. You know what I mean? Even if it's completely invisible to everybody else, to me, it's always really obvious, and all I need to do is know both halves and eventually I'll find the place that works. The walk between the two. Like Weir sometimes does it, but he has sort of a blockier notion, you know? Which is okay; but for me, I like that invisible thing. I like that sort of sleight-of-hand approach."

The heartbeat of the Grateful Dead can be located in those "sleight-of-hand" passages that Jerry describes. At Cornell '77, the heartbeat between "Scarlet Begonias" and "Fire on the Mountain" is strong enough to live (and, as early Grateful Dead fan Allen Ginsberg might say, "to eat") a thousand years.

As a stand-alone song, "Scarlet Begonias" has a little of everything you want in an upbeat Grateful Dead song. It's bouncy, danceable, rhythmically alluring, and—particularly when we begin to catch glimpses of "Fire on the Mountain" on the horizon—it turns sultry and provocative in the way of all dangerously memorable seductions. Lyrically, it's one of Robert Hunter's master creations, sprinkled with all of his major influences and infatuations: flowers, girls, gambling, fairy tales, nursery rhymes, dancing, fellowship, hallucinations. . . . It also contains some of the most iconic and image-defining lines in Deadhead cosmology, such as "strangers stopping strangers / just to shake their hand"; "Once in a while / you get shown the light / in the strangest of places / if you look at it right"; "I ain't often right / but I've never been wrong / it seldom turns out the way / it does in the song"; and, of course, "Everybody's playing in the heart of gold band / heart of gold band." It is those lines that create the biggest lifts—and the most sense of communion—in the audience when they are delivered with gusto by Garcia. It's such lines that provided the homegrown bumper sticker and T-shirt industry, whose sales kept many a Deadhead on the road from show to show, with pithy lines to help attract saucer-eyed buyers.

Indeed, musically and lyrically, "Scarlet Begonias" is the complete package. Perhaps that's why, from its debut at the Cow Palace in Daly City, California, on March 23, 1974, until its final performance on July 2, 1995, at Deer Creek Music Center in Noblesville, Indiana, the Dead played the song a total of 316 times. The song was never out of rotation, and, outside of its debut year of 1974, 1977 was the year they played it the most. Twenty-five times. It seems the Dead were just having too much fun with the song to leave it alone, particularly because they now had its perfect counterpoint with the 1977 debut of "Fire on the Mountain." In a poll conducted by the compilers of *Deadbase*, the "Scarlet Begonias" from Cornell '77 was named by participants as their all-time favorite version of the song.

Their favorite version of "Fire on the Mountain"? Also Cornell '77.

"Fire on the Mountain"

Why mess with perfection? When you have the perfect two-song combination, it's wise to explore that combination every way possible until two distinct songs merge into one sublime suite of music. Such was the case with "Scarlet Begonias" > "Fire on the Mountain." With a handful of exceptions, "Fire on the Mountain" was consistently paired with "Scarlet Begonias" for twenty-one years. While some fans who "got on the bus" with the Dead back in the 1960s lamented the loss of forty-minute jams on single songs, others understood that those occasionally aimless jams had migrated into two- or four-song clusters that allowed more focused but equally creative play and interplay by the band. "Scarlet" > "Fire" was a classic Grateful Dead pairing. And if not *the* best, Cornell '77 was certainly among the best of them.

"Fire on the Mountain" is a slinky, sexy song. It is the musical equivalent of indulging in one last hot, grinding fuck before Armageddon descends and the world melts into flames; all the passion, abandon, and remorse for things not done channeled through the sacral chakra while desperate flames of desire lick the sky. It's also notable for its cowbell. That's as it should be, considering drummer Mickey Hart is credited for writing the song's music. Mickey first recorded a rap-style version of the song for an unreleased album called "Area Code 415" in 1972. An instrumental version called "Happiness Is Drumming" was included on Mickey's 1976 studio album *Diga*. "Fire on the Mountain," as we know it, made its first appearance in the Dead's live repertoire at the Winterland on March 18, 1977, where it followed "Scarlet

Begonias" and closed the first set. It was played twenty-two times that first year in rotation.

Along with prominently featured and rhythmically intricate drum parts, it's Jerry's trusty Mu-Tron III effect that gives "Fire" its sultry vibe. The Mu-Tron III defines "Fire on the Mountain" so distinctly that it's hard to imagine the melody of the song without it. The overall impact of the tune is almost tropical in feel, with the bells of the cymbals and the cowbell taking the place of steel drums, and Phil's meaty tone, in classic Lesh style, playing more a lead and melody role than a traditional bass line. Also, once again, Robert Hunter's lyrics provide the perfect accompaniment to the music, featuring "dragons with matches," flames from the stage that "spread to the floor," and this little blessing wrapped in a sage warning: "If mercy's in business I wish it for you / More than just ashes when your dreams come true."

Hunter tells the apocryphal origin story that the lyrics to "Fire on the Mountain" were "written at Mickey Hart's ranch in heated inspiration as the surrounding hills blazed and the fire approached the recording studio where we were working." It is an image so powerful and apt it's almost too good to be true. It also sets the stage for such memorable moments of musical synchronicity as when the Grateful Dead played the song in Portland, Oregon, on June 12, 1980, as Mount St. Helens erupted in Washington State. The crowd exited the show to a rain of gray ashes. Some stories, some songs, are just too good to bother fretting about the blurry lines "beyond which you really can't fake."

"Estimated Prophet"

Rarely do we get such specific insight into the original meaning of a song as we do with "Estimated Prophet." Bob Weir says,

"The basis of it is this guy I see at nearly every backstage door. There's always some guy who's taken a lot of dope and he's really bug-eyed, and he's having some kind of vision. He's got a rave he's got to deliver." In excellent postmodern fashion, the song is about members of the audience, to whom it is delivered in a borderline hysterical rant that Weir uses to mimic the frenzy that his music drives them to. Of course, the beauty of delivering the ravings of a messianic madman is that it allows Weir to rave like a messianic madman—and have a hell of a lot of fun doing it. In Cornell, as per his usual delivery, Weir sinks deep into this role, howling on about angels in shafts of light rising up to heaven; parting the sea like Moses; using his words to fill the sky with flame; and all the sundry voices that have been giving him secret instructions while "you've all been asleep." With perfect paranoid symmetry, the speaker is also aware that "you would not believe me." Nevertheless, the message must be delivered.

"Estimated Prophet" is played in 7/4 time, which creates a rhythm that is slightly off-kilter to rock music listeners' ears but also perfect to groove your body back and forth to while dancing. At its best, the tempo is relaxed, perhaps even a little slow, with each instrument contributing one note at a time. In Cornell, the start of "Estimated" sounds like a long-dormant robot being rebooted: various components come online as the robot tests one leg, one arm, flexes its fingers, turns its head one way, then the other. . . . As the song goes forward, the robot gets looser, more lubricated, until it is finally marching forward at a steady pace with small billows of steam puffing out its ears, its eyes glowing fire red. All the while, Jerry's Mu-Tron III acts as the mechanical lubricant. It slides in and out of the groove, wrapping around Lesh's ivy-climbing bass lines, softening Weir's madman words, and bouncing off the drummers as they toss beats back and forth.

It's Jerry's guitar that takes us on the trip. It's Jerry's guitar that delivers us back to the alley where the wacked-out robot madman finally throws up his hands and meanders off muttering, "My time coming any day, don't worry about me, no, don't worry about me, no, no, don't worry about me, no, no, no, no, no."

"St. Stephen"

"St. Stephen" was a fan favorite from the time of its first appearance. At the beginning of its life, it was a staple of the band's live performances. The song's debut show on May 24, 1968, in Festus, Missouri, represents a quintessential late-1960s fantasy set list. Except for a musical break after the opening tune and one before the closing number, each song bleeds into the next. In the Dead community, musical passages that yoke songs together are visually symbolized on set lists with a right-facing arrow pointing from one song to the next. At Festus, the entire show is one long, psychedelic right-facing arrow: "Lovelight," "Cryptical Envelopment" > "The Other One" > "Cryptical Envelopment" > "Dark Star" > "St. Stephen" > "The Eleven" > "Caution (Do Not Stop on the Tracks)" > "Feedback," "We Bid You Goodnight." At only three dollars per ticket, including a performance by the band Iron Butterfly and "Visuals by Lights for the Blind and High," the whole long, strange night was quite a bargain, too.

From May 1968 through 1969, "St. Stephen" was usually paired with "The Eleven" in much the same way that it appeared at Festus. In 1970, the band began experimenting with different combinations around the song, and a version of Buddy Holly's "Not Fade Away" became the predominant follow-up number. However, on Halloween of 1971 the band played "St. Stephen" followed by "Not

Fade Away" and then put "St. Stephen" on hiatus for nearly five years. It made its epic reappearance as the second-set opener on June 9, 1976, at Boston Music Hall.

Because of its half-decade absence from the Dead's live shows, many fans at Barton Hall in 1977 had heard "St. Stephen" only on bootleg recordings or on the album *Live Dead*. Robert Wagner—who had been seeing shows for five years at that point—was among those who were thrilled when the band launched into the tune. "I was very excited to hear 'St. Stephen,' for sure. That was something I didn't hear when I went to the two shows in September '76, the Duke 9/23, and William and Mary the next night. I knew 'St. Stephen' was back in the repertoire, but they didn't happen to play it those two shows. So I was very, very excited to hear it." As they had done often in the last year of the song's pre-hiatus performances, at Cornell the Dead shifted from "St. Stephen" directly into "Not Fade Away" and then, after a stunning transitional jam, returned to close out "St. Stephen" and cap off nearly twenty-five minutes' worth of uninterrupted music.

"St. Stephen" is truly a song that only the Grateful Dead could write. Regardless of what, if any, specific Stephen is under discussion here (there are options, but the most likely answer is no specific Stephen at all), it's about a saint of some kind. And what does the saint do? He goes in and out of a garden carrying a rose and, more or less, prospering. Where are the chicks, the muscle cars, the good times? What the hell kind of rock song hits its climax with the lyrics, "One man gathers what another man spills"? Is this a rock concert or Bible school? Frankly, there is no reason for this song to be as good as it is, other than the fact that it is a pure, uncut Grateful Dead song.

Not only did the Dead pull off "St. Stephen," but they turned it into an anthem for Deadheads. Why? Because, for many

Deadheads who just didn't fit into mainstream society, it seemed that "wherever they go the people all complain." But these were good people, peaceful people, people who liked to sing and dance and possessed an unshakable faith in the transformative experiences they gathered at Grateful Dead shows. In short, they were saintly and persecuted and given to taking comfort in notions of supernatural retribution delivered by spiritual forces outside themselves.

Make no mistake, whoever or whatever provided the initial lyrical inspiration to Robert Hunter, Deadheads who took this song as an anthem saw themselves in the Saint Stephen role. There was comfort there. There was comfort in thinking, "All he lost he shall regain." There was enough comfort that it made you want to return again and again (to the song and to the Grateful Dead scene as a whole) until you'd been there so long you got to "calling it home."

At Cornell, the band paused for several minutes between "Estimated Prophet" and "Saint Stephen" to tune up, and, most likely, smoke a cigarette and decide what song to play next. The preceding silence makes those first notes of "Saint Stephen" sound even more majestic than usual. They are filled with import, regal almost, a "Hail to the Chief" moment suitable for announcing the entry of a saint into the arena. The East Coast crowd, many of whom had probably never experienced "St. Stephen" outside the confines of their record player spinning the *Aoxomoxoa* or *Live Dead* albums, went nuts.

At Cornell, the band played "St. Stephen" directly into "Not Fade Away" and then returned to finish "St. Stephen." Although not coupled to the extent of "Scarlet Begonias" and "Fire on the Mountain," this two-song combination popped up with some regularity once the band dropped its unwieldy original partner,

"The Eleven," from their repertoire after 1970. With its straight-up rockin' Bo Diddley beat, "Not Fade Away" was about as far from the eleven-beats-to-the-bar song "The Eleven" (see what they did with the title there?) as you can get. With the unified two songs stretching to roughly twenty-five minutes, the Cornell audience was treated to an extended roller-coaster ride of music, leaving off with the deliciously ambiguous last line, "But what would be the answer to the answer man?"

During the exquisite "Morning Dew" that would end the second set, Garcia would provide an equally koan-like answer of sorts, "I guess it doesn't matter anyway."

"Not Fade Away"

Ah yes, that Bo Diddley beat. The second stress occurring on the second, rather than the third, beat of the first measure. The beat that street-corner musicians once called "hambone" and hammered out on their arms, legs, chest, and cheeks. The "patted Jumba" beat that came to rock 'n' roll via West Africa. The beat that, when Dead crowds swelled to their largest, was executed with near-perfect synchronization by tens of thousands of fans clapping in unison to show the Grateful Dead how much their music was appreciated and to beg them to come back out to play just one more.

The Grateful Dead debuted their take on "Not Fade Away" at the Carousel Ballroom (which predated the Fillmore West at the same San Francisco location) on June 19, 1969. They played it only once that year, then three times in 1969, before hitting the tune with full commitment a total of forty-nine times in 1970. Although that would be the most they ever played "Not Fade Away" in a single year, the song remained a staple until the end of the band's career, including twenty-six performances in 1977. When the dust cleared in 1995 they had performed the song a total of 531 times, and fans had all but commandeered the end of the song to turn it into a massive group chant, accompanied by clapping the Bo Diddley beat, to display their gratitude for the Grateful Dead. To be in an arena filled with thousands of blissed-out music fans clapping in unison and singing a profession of their undying love for the band was to know the true meaning of rock 'n' roll devotion.

In 1977, the Dead took a smooth, laid-back approach to "Not Fade Away." In Cornell, the song is light and bouncy (instead of the straightforward rock 'n' roll rave-up it would become) and opens into long jam sections with Garcia exploring the upper regions of his fret board. It is a shimmeringly good version, but perhaps the unique part of Cornell's "Not Fade Away" is the part that almost occurs, but then doesn't. The drum solo.

By 1977, with Mickey Hart back in the band, it was de rigueur to have an extended drum solo at the mid-to-late part of the second set. Eventually, a drum solo followed by a free-form jam section—known to fans as "Drums" > "Space"—midway through the second set became sacrosanct. As Grateful Dead archivist David Lemieux says, "You look at Cornell where there was no 'Drums and Space.' 'Space' wasn't really quite as standard as it would become later in the year, and more particularly in '78 and '79, but generally most shows would have a drum break, a drum duet for Billy and Mickey that would usually come out of 'Estimated' > 'Eyes' or 'Playing in the Band' or something like that. And then you get a show like Cornell that doesn't have a 'Drums and Space,' nor does it have 'Terrapin Station,' a song they were playing a lot of times. So Cornell falls into a bit of a strange place in that it isn't necessarily like the other shows on the tour, in terms of the sequence and format of the show."

But a "Drums" section almost does occur. Toward the end of "Not Fade Away"—at around the 14-minute mark—the jam falls apart and the drums become more prominent. There's a driving cymbal beat that rattles above the jam, pulling everyone forward and through the murk, to where they momentarily regroup. Once everyone is back on track, it sounds as if we're heading back into the meat of "Not Fade Away"—all instruments playing full-steam ahead—but then something happens, the jam disintegrates again, and you can hear a musical debate about what will happen next. The drums become steadily more prominent. The drums begin to take over. They begin to break away. There is, in fact, the start of a "Drums" section happening. But then it doesn't. The "Drums" section never takes off. Cornell became a 1977 show with no "Drums."

One attendee, Brad Krakow, a Deadhead who, as a member of the Cornell Concert Commission, also worked the show, believes he knows the reason why. "You may notice that this is one of the few shows that does not have a drum solo. I know why. Bill the drummer had a bum hand. He approached me sometime before the show to ask if I had any —— (some drug I had never heard of) as his wrist was killing him. There was my chance to be a hero of rock 'n' roll, and turns out I didn't speak the language, much less have the stuff. I mean, I could barely afford beer back then, much less exotic painkillers. I mumbled something about looking for aspirin, and he went looking for a more supportive local." While a potentially injured wrist didn't seem to affect the show otherwise, it does seem to be a plausible explanation for an aborted "Drums" section. In any event, the band played on, skipping "Drums" and putting a cap on "St. Stephen" instead, before launching into what many consider to be the finest "Morning Dew" the band ever played.

"St. Stephen" (coda)

While lasting only a couple of minutes, the return to finish the last two verses of "St. Stephen" before shifting seamlessly into "Morning Dew" is classic Grateful Dead. With this deft move, they combine two songs—"St. Stephen" and "Not Fade Away"—into a suite of sorts, with each song commenting on the other, undeniably connected by a musical tether that begs dual interpretation as a thematic tether. No, their love will not fade away. In fact, "St. Stephen" will remain. All he's lost he shall regain. Then, with another deft shift executed by flowing without pause into "Morning Dew," the final lyric of "St. Stephen": "But what would be the answer to the answer man?" is answered by Jerry Garcia's mournful-wail-of-a-Zen response: "I guess it doesn't matter anyway."

"Morning Dew"

Dick Latvala, Dead archivist from 1985 to 1999, made this notebook entry about Cornell '77: "'Morning Dew' was possibly the best version yet, with a burning finish." There were dozens of seat-of-the-pants thrilling moments at Cornell, but no song couples that adrenaline thrill with pure heart-wrenching poignancy more than the "Morning Dew"—always a mournful, deep song—that closes the second set. This version finds Garcia's vocals driving down to the core sadness of the song's tale and then soaring to the highest peaks of frenzied ecstasy to bring it to conclusion.

Canadian singer-songwriter Bonnie Dobson wrote "Morning Dew" in 1961 after a discussion with friends about the potential outcomes of a nuclear war. Dobson said of the song: "I wrote 'Morning Dew' during my second or third engagement at the Ash Grove in 1961. When I'd go to Los Angeles I'd usually stay with my friend Joyce Naftulin, and it was in her apartment that I wrote 'Morning Dew.' I can't give you specific dates, but I do remember the circumstances. There had been a gathering of friends, and toward the end of the evening a discussion had ensued about the possibilities and the outcome of a nuclear war. It was all very depressing and upsetting. The following day I sat down and started putting together the song. I had never written or even attempted to write a song before. It took the form of a conversation between the last man and woman—postapocalypse—one trying to comfort the other while knowing there's absolutely nothing left. When I'd finished, I recall phoning another friend and singing it to her over the phone. She said it was good, but maybe that's just ancient fancy at work."

I can't think of a better description of the Cornell version of "Morning Dew" than "ancient fancy at work." Garcia's vocals are so haunted and filled with ancient pathos that he does indeed sound like a man crying at the end of the world. The Dead first played "Morning Dew" at the Human Be-In at Golden Gate Park on January 14, 1967. Early on, Garcia affected a strong southern drawl when he sang the song. At times the mimicry was so pronounced as to be a distraction from the beauty of the song. By 1977 he had buried the southern affect just far enough below the surface that it provided a slightly dusty gravitas to his delivery without drawing (or drawling) too much attention to itself.

The "fancy" (in all senses of the word) and thrilling part of Cornell's "ancient fancy" takes place at the end of the song. Having led his intrepid troop of survivors through a desolated landscape filled with sadness and fear, Garcia uses his guitar like a torch to guide them forward with just one more step into the postapocalyptic dawn. His voice calls out that nothing in life truly matters, but we hear in his aching moan that this is less a statement than a question: *Does it matter? Do any of us matter? Does any of this matter at all?* The lyrics leave off there, but Garcia answers with some of the most exciting guitar playing of an already stellar night. He digs deep into his fret board, deeper than ever before, wailing against his strings as if frantically broadcasting an SOS across a wasted universe. The band follows suit, giving everything they have, hammering, banging, crashing, flailing, howling, exhaustedly clamoring for the attention of an unseen hand that might reach down and elevate them above the fray. The conclusion to the Cornell "Morning Dew" is the sound of the last band of humans clinging to tattered shreds of hope as they struggle to rise above the chaos humankind has wrought upon itself.

Do they succeed? Does it matter?

Because encores were generally a given at Grateful Dead shows (more notable when absent than when present) they functioned almost like mini-set breaks. Everyone expected that the band was going to reappear from the wings to play music again (albeit for only one song . . . or, on special occasions, perhaps for a "double encore" with two songs), so speculation would have been lively about what song might be played. Often those discussions revolved around the tempo of the song—would the band go out rocking, or would they cool things down with a ballad and send everyone out of the hall on a more mellow vibe? At Barton Hall, the steam that was already rising in the audience between sets would have been thick, practically visible, by encore time. The smells of pot smoke, cigarette smoke, sweaty bodies, and more exotic scents like patchouli, or other body oils favored by scent-conscious hippies, would have been strong enough to nearly overpower anyone who encountered them—a bit nauseating, more than a little intoxicating. Perhaps friends who got separated during the show began a half-hearted search to reconnect. Hugs would have been exchanged. Hoots and howls would have flown across the spacious hall. A few extra glances would be given to the walls where sweaty clothes had been discarded in the hopes they would still be there. Post-show plans would be solidified, rides home (or even to Buffalo for the next show) lined up, numbers swapped so that connections could be made down the line. But, mostly, people would have been keeping one eye on the side of the stage looking out for Bob or Phil or Jerry—any one of the Grateful Dead—shambling back out, giving a small, unassuming wave, and plugging back in for one more go-round.

"One More Saturday Night"

Can it matter?

Does it now?

Hell yes it matters! Wipe off those tears, crank up that old Victrola, put on your rocking shoes—it's time for one last hurrah, the big encore, hey now it's Saturday night!

In describing some of the special beauty of the Dead's spring 1977 tour, Steve Silberman says, "Gone were the half-hour 'vista cruiser' versions of 'Playing in the Band' and 'Dark Star' that defined second sets in the pre-hiatus era. Instead, the band seemed to be aiming for punchier, more focused sets that were less *discursive* but more *narrative*. Within this tighter framework, each song became a chapter in a two-part story that unfolded every night—that familiar 'waveform' of shows that prevailed, more or less intact, from 1977 on." If Cornell was indeed a story, the ending would read: And they all lived happily ever after—rock on!

The Dead had just taken their audience on an epic journey filled with gamblers, cowboys, murderers, ill-fated lovers, wayward saints, crazy-eyed prophets . . . they had traversed scorching deserts, snow-filled backcountry, country gardens, fiery mountains . . . they had loved, lost, suffered, celebrated, danced, sang, laughed, cried. . . . Together, the audience had played out the full scope of the human experience under the skilled guidance of seven intrepid travelers, and now it was time to send everyone home with one last full-blast rock 'n' roll song: "One More Saturday Night." Often times the band reserved this number for Saturday night performances (just as "Samson and Delilah" would become associated with Sunday night performances), but, clearly, not exclusively. At Cornell, they used the song to bust open the heavy mood left by "Morning Dew" and reassure the crowd that, when all else failed, rock 'n' roll would survive to save us all:

> I went down to the mountain, I was drinking some wine,
> I looked up into heaven, Lord, I saw a mighty sign,
> Writ in fire across the heaven, plain as black and white,
> Get prepared, there's gonna be a party tonight.

With the entire band going full-tilt boogie, Bob and Donna wail their way to the end of the song while Keith acts like a third percussionist hammering away at his piano keys. By the time the song reaches its apex, the energy ricocheting through the music is palpable and one can imagine the spirit of the night lifting through the rafters of Barton Hall and filling the gorges around Ithaca with song and dance. And then it is over. With disarming casualness, Bob Weir leans into the microphone and says, "Thank you all. Good night."

The house lights blazed to life, washing away the red and orange spots left behind by Candace Brightman's light show. The crowd on the floor of Barton Hall lingered and loitered, half not wanting to let go of the moment and half anticipating the arctic blasts that awaited them outdoors. Above the din of conversation, icy snow could have been heard striking the vast windows of Barton Hall.

When they pushed out the doors of the hall and headed back to dorm rooms, homes in town, and parked cars and vans scattered across Ithaca, sweaty and satisfied fans were pelted with ice and snow. Temperatures that night were on their way to a low of twenty-seven degrees. Worried about hypothermia and another concert debacle (memories of the 1973 Deep Purple riot still lingering), the staff of the Cornell Concert Commission made arrangements during the show to have a load of hospital blankets sent over to Barton Hall in order to warm up all those people who had not dressed for the unseasonable weather. So the cozy, protected-in-a-bubble glow of the show persisted perhaps a little longer than it might have on other nights of the tour that spring. A last joint was shared; final slugs of beer were knocked back. Friends held on to friends, all a bit bleary-eyed and buzzed on gratitude or whatever else they'd imbibed that night. Snatches of lyrics were sung, and early questions were asked about the overall quality of the show and when the first bootlegs might surface. Staff of the CCC watched people move along, a little worried about the weather, but thankful for a safe and successful night at Barton Hall. Dead fans one and all headed out into the snowy night.

Once the hall cleared, the Dead's crew began breakdown, and Betty Cantor-Jackson and other technicians began the work of spooling up hundreds of yards of cable. Tapes from the night's show were secured. Cigarettes were smoked. Backs slapped. Thoughts turned to the road and the next night in Buffalo, about 150 miles west of Ithaca.

The Memorial Auditorium, in downtown Buffalo, was the band's next destination. It was a big space that could accommodate, seated and standing, more than twelve thousand people and was used for NHL hockey games by the Buffalo Sabres, NBA basketball games by the Buffalo Braves, and major events like political conventions. (The Memorial Auditorium, also known as the War Memorial Auditorium or just the Aud, was torn down in 2009 after years of vacancy when the city's sports teams moved to more modern facilities.) The Dead performed their first show in Buffalo at the Kleinhans Music Hall in 1970—an intimate venue that is home to the Buffalo Philharmonic Orchestra. That show was played as a benefit for the Buffalo Philharmonic, and the mini-set—"Dark Star" > "Drums," "Lovelight"—featured the orchestra jamming along with the band. The Dead returned to Buffalo and played the Memorial Auditorium twice in 1973. Buffalo, and, indeed, all of upstate New York, was a career-long, well-cultivated stronghold for the Grateful Dead.

The show at the Aud promised to be a good one with a bigger crowd than could be accommodated at Barton Hall. As the band traveled west on rural routes before getting to the highway, echoes of the Cornell crowd faded and light snow continued to fall. The force of the storm waned with every mile, and in Buffalo there was only light rain with temperatures in the mid-thirties to high forties. (Ithaca would see just more than a quarter inch of snow.) Back east, though, folks were just starting to realize that a spring storm for the record books was in the works. The Catskill Mountain peaks would see as much as twenty-seven inches of snow, and seventy-mile-an-hour winds were registered in coastal Maryland, with the cities of New York, New Haven, and Boston (all recent stops on the East Coast tour) each getting inches of snow.

In the run of four shows early in May—New Haven, Boston, Ithaca, and Buffalo—the May 9 concert was full of the most surprises. There were renditions of "Ship of Fools," "Comes a Time," and "The Other One," all from the second set—all songs that were making only occasional appearances on set lists since the April 22 show at the Spectrum. "Mexicali Blues" was also given a twirl around the room—another highlight of the Bakersfield sound— for the folks in western New York. Even the opening "Help On the Way" seemed to take the crowd by surprise, with a full four seconds elapsing between the first note and the crowd's knowing cheer of recognition. (Contrast that with the immediate, delighted reaction of the crowd at the very first notes as "Slipknot" transitions into "Franklin's Tower.") And staples of the tour like "The Music Never Stopped" were played with a unique, even ferocious, energy. The "Drums" section that was absent the night before in Ithaca makes a robust appearance between "The Other One" and "Not Fade Away."

Much as with Cornell '77, the Memorial Auditorium set list has some notable absences that must be taken into account when considering both the spring '77 tour and the Dead's larger repertoire. No "Dark Star." No "Terrapin Station." And, having been knocked out of the park in Cornell, no version of "Scarlet Begonias" > "Fire on the Mountain," which was an oft-appearing duo that spring tour. No matter. The sound was great, and the band was in excellent form, still riding the high that began at the Boston Garden. Or was it at the Palladium in New York City? Or did it begin all the way back in Philly, the night when another snowstorm welcomed the Dead to the East Coast? Each of those special nights was captured on Cantor-Jackson's dynamic mix, and as versions of her tapes and several bootlegs made their way around the Dead community, the conversation about which show was the best on this amazing tour began to flourish. It continues to be a lively debate among Deadheads even today.

the cornell concert commission & john scher proudly present the

GRATEFUL DEAD

TICKETS:
6.50 *CORNELL STUDENTS*
ADVANCE SALE ONLY

ALL OTHERS AND
AT THE DOOR **7.50**

OUTLETS:

SUN., MAY 8,
BARTON
8:00 P.M.

W.S.H., NOYES CENTER, N.C.U., DISCOUNT RECORDS, RECORD PEOPLE,
I.C. RECORD STORE, RECORD THEATRE – SYRACUSE, CHRISTENSON –
GENEVA, RECORD PEOPLE & COREY UNION – CORTLAND,
HI-FI RECORD & TAPE CENTER – JOHNSON CITY

This large, full-color promotional poster was seen all over the Cornell University campus and across the central New York region. The Cornell Concert Commission logo, with the winged figure, shares the space with the famous Grateful Dead logo—which came to be known as the Stealie, after the album *Steal Your Face*—first conceptualized and drafted in 1969 by Owsley "Bear" Stanley and Bob Thomas. In homage to the Dead, the head of the figure in the CCC logo has been rendered as a skull. Poster courtesy of Jay Mabrey.

▌Concert Preview▐
Resurrecting the Dead

By JAYNE LIPMAN

THE GRATEFUL DEAD.
Sunday, May 8 in Barton Hall.

Before you read this, I have one confession to make. I am an extreme Grateful Dead loyalist. I have travelled many hours, many times to see them perform, and will continue to do so as long as they do. Appraisals of art and music are largely a matter of personal taste. Trying to write an unbiased article about them is difficult.

With this note of caution, the fact remains; the Grateful Dead are undisputedly one of the most popular contemporary music acts in the country. What other group, aside from the legally tied-up Stones or the temporarily sedentary Joni Mitchell, could sell out concert halls in all major cities in a matter of hours, prior to any public notice of the dates? And, more pointedly, why? What is the magic behind the name which draws large crowds wherever it appears?

Anyone who's ever heard the Dead on a record can testify that their music is quite accessible, from renditions of country western tunes to Chuck Berry rockers. Equally appealing are their numerous original tunes, which combine the talents of all band members with a cryptic lyricist named Robert Hunter. Each band member contributes equally, although Jerry Garcia is said to be the leader of the band (a statement which he denies).

Garcia is almost legendary to guitar enthusiasts, and Bob Weir, Phil Lesh, Keith Godchaux, Mickey Hart, Bill Kreutzman and Donna Godchaux play rhythm guitar, bass, keyboards, vocals and drums, respectively, with a creativity and talent which few will dispute.

Yet there must be more to it than musical competence, although that is a feature which is becoming harder and harder to come by lately. Something else must cause people to offer up to fifty dollars a ticket to see them, despite their comparatively poor record sales. That something can be seen only at a Grateful Dead concert.

A live performance conveys what the vinyl just can't do. Contrary to the glitter which so often dominates today's live shows to the point of obscuring the music itself, the Dead make no pretensions. The Grateful Dead remain one of the few groups who have resisted the pressures of glamourizing their act.

What they do instead is to rely totally on the music, concentrating on the very sounds which emanate from each instrument. In letting the sounds flow, they create an almost jazz-oriented rock, a freeform composition which expands spontaneously, coming out different each time, and also serving as an interlude between any two songs.

The band has an expansive repertoire to choose from, and they always include a few extra surprises, even for the most seasoned veteran. With such room for variation, it is rare that one will witness two identical concerts. One piece may run from five minutes to forty, allowing the listener total involvement.

Hence we have the correlation between the music and the mind-expanding drugs so often associated with Dead concerts. In the sixties, they often played for over six hours, the music offering an auditory complement to the visual experience derived from drugs. Today, although the Haight is gone, the association remains.

The concert this Sunday will feature material from a forthcoming album. It is their fourteenth, excluding solo albums by Weir and Garcia. In spite of all the changes in music from the day of the Haight to the year of the Hype, the Dead have managed to survive.

Night of the Grateful Dead

===Jonathan D. Cohen===

Anyone who keeps an eye on American popular culture is going to have a field day on Sunday when the Grateful Dead give a concert at Cornell. Who are the 8,500 people who the Concert Commission plans to shoehorn into Barton Hall for the biggest party around here in years? Will they take drugs — and what kind of drugs will they take? What value do they assign to rock music, the United States of America, Western Civilization? In short, how is this spring celebration going to relate to the history and the point of view of the Grateful Dead?

Since San Francisco in the middle sixties, the Grateful Dead have been making music about kind women, nice weather, bumming around and getting stoned. They've come to represent the carefree, euphoric side of sixties insanity. While the Napoleans threw bricks, the Grateful Dead spoke for the satyrs and the Christs, the Don Quixotes and the vegetables. Jerry Garcia plays it sweetly enough to make a vegetable sway. His guitar solos could raise a smile in a Teagle Hall secretary.

Of course very few people in the sixties really got to be all that carefree. There was Ken Kesey, but he had such big forearms. Once Madison Avenue caught on to sweetness and light they sold the promise of being carefree to every youngster beset by terrible cares. The results were a terrible thing to see, particularly at gatherings where youngsters came to be carefree. The moods of such gatherings became dominated by drug-intensified thoughts like, "What would Ma think of this?" or "Why can't I remember what day it is?" or "Perhaps God is much like me, a fragile existential being, waging a losing battle with the forces of evil."

A lot of this bad panic has disappeared here in

what Tom Wolfe calls the "Me Decade." The interesting thing to judge on Sunday will be the influence of sixties craziness on all manifestations of "Me." Call it "The Greening of America" or call it mass psychopathology, but you have to admit that that sixties jumble of primitivism, politics, music, media and drugs has had a huge influence on the way you and me is.

We can thank (or blame) the sixties for a lot more than our coed dorms and our no-draft Army. The late sixties gave us our whole conception of "Me." For all young America seems to operate on the assumption that one changes the world by the way he looks at it. Who needs politics when you too can be a glowing brown child-God.

Out on tour in the big cities the Grateful Dead attract crowds that seem to still be attracted to late sixties styles. There are so many of these people out there that I'm surprised CBS doesn't do a special. Here at Cornell, however, the Grateful Dead will have to play to an audience that encompasses a wide variety of personal styles. It shouldn't be much of a problem for them. Their harmonies are pleasing to any ear, and they communicate a sense of unbounded joy that all kinds of "Me's" can relate to.

Things will be a little close in Barton Hall. If I was running the thing I'd put up signs like: LET SOMEONE ELSE SIT IN THE FRONT; or PARANOIDS YOU ARE ENTERING A HIGH PEER PRESSURE ZONE — REDUCE WEED!

If all we "Me's" can have such a big party together, then maybe there is hope for "us" after all.

The Friday, May 6, edition of the *Cornell Daily Sun* ran this preview of the Sunday concert. The article promises that concertgoers will hear music from the upcoming record, *Terrapin Station*, but also lets readers know that no studio recording can compare to a live Dead show. Image courtesy of the Rare and Manuscript Collections, Kroch Library, Cornell University, Ithaca, New York.

Sold Out

Tickets to the Grateful Dead concert have been sold out, according to Eve Prouty '79, concert commission finance chairman.

Ticket sales ended Friday at 4 p.m., Prouty said.

Of the 8,500 tickets sold, approximately 4,700 were sold to Cornell students and an additional 1,300 in the Ithaca area, Prouty said.

This represents the "largest gross sales ever, on any concert," Prouty said. She estimates this figure to be about $59,000.

This notice likely appeared in the *Cornell Daily Sun*, and it reported the show to be sold out, with all eighty-five hundred tickets purchased in three days. The gross sales of around $69,000, when set against the concert expenses of about $11,000, indicate that the May 8, 1977, event was a profitable one for the Cornell Concert Commission. Image courtesy of the Rare and Manuscript Collections, Kroch Library, Cornell University, Ithaca, New York.

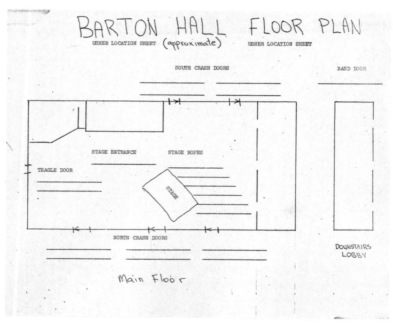

In the cavernous space of Barton Hall, the stage for the Grateful Dead concert was set to the north at the center of the floor. With massive floor space—enough to accommodate a two-hundred-meter running track—a crowd of more than eight thousand people could still appear to be modest. So the concert setup took that into account and used the hall to its advantage. Teagle Hall, to the east, houses the university recreation offices, and the Statler Hotel, to the west, is the university hotel. Floor plan courtesy of the Rare and Manuscript Collections, Kroch Library, Cornell University, Ithaca, New York.

The Grateful Dead traveled from the Boston Garden show, on May 7, to Ithaca and arrived at Barton Hall via limo. When they pulled up outside Barton on the afternoon of May 8, uniformed security was already in place. Danny Rifkin, the manager of the Dead, sporting a full beard and tweed sports jacket, is shown exiting one of the limos; he is accompanied by an unidentified person, in a leather jacket and carrying sound equipment, perhaps associated with the promoter John Scher. Photographs © Jon Reis / www.jonreis.com.

Cornell student and freelance photographer Larry Reichman was on the floor of Barton the afternoon of May 8 as the Grateful Dead crew worked with the staff of the Cornell Concert Commission to set up the stage, lights, and all the rest. A friend of his on the CCC secured a pass that allowed him to be in Barton Hall for the entire day. Photographs © Lawrence Reichman / www.GD BartonHall1977.com.

The Grateful Dead concert was, like all other shows at Barton Hall, general admission. For $6.50, if you were a Cornell student, or $7.50, as a member of the general public, you had a chance to stand near the stage. In these photos from the 1970s, early arrivals at a concert are shown staking claim to territory on the floor. Photographs courtesy of the Rare and Manuscript Collections, Kroch Library, Cornell University, Ithaca, New York.

The band jamming during the first set at Barton Hall. In this shot, *left to right*: Jerry Garcia on lead guitar, Bob Weir on rhythm guitar, Bill Kreutzmann on drums, Phil Lesh on bass, and Donna Jean Godchaux with backup vocals. (Drummer Mickey Hart is positioned behind Lesh and Donna Jean Godchaux.) This photograph accompanied the concert review that appeared in the *Ithaca Journal*. After shooting one roll, Jon Reis went downtown to the newspaper offices to process the film in order to make deadline. Photograph © Jon Reis / www.jonreis.com.

Three at the mics for the Dead: Jerry Garcia, Bob Weir, and Donna Jean Godchaux. The crowd, pressed to the rail, is visible, and this perspective shows how tight it was getting in Barton Hall. At the start of the second set Bob Weir would lead the crowd in a sorely needed "Take a Step Back" in order to relieve the pressure. Photograph © Jon Reis / www.jonreis.com.

Jerry Garcia with his Custom Travis Bean TB500 electric guitar, emblazoned with the enigmatic "The Enemy is Listening" sticker, is captured onstage at Barton Hall on May 8. Jon Reis took this shot and several others while working part time for the *Ithaca Journal*. All of his images, on a single contact sheet, are from the first set. Photograph © Jon Reis / www.jonreis.com.

As if delivering a magical incantation for heartsick lovers, Bob Weir chants out the words, "Supplication . . . infatuation . . . inspiration . . . imagination . . . excitation . . . hallucination" until finally the full-tilt rave-up at Barton Hall comes to a hard stop with one last primal cry: "Whoo!" Photograph © Jon Reis / www.jonreis.com.

Larry Reichman attended the show and took these photographs, about ten rows back from the stage. These images highlight the drummers Bill Kreutzmann (at left) and Mickey Hart (at right). Photographs © Lawrence Reichman / www.GDBartonHall1977.com.

Snow was in the air when the show began at 8 p.m., and photographer Jon Reis remembers it falling steadily as he drove home after getting his photos in for the next day's edition of the *Ithaca Journal*. He took this shot, out in the hamlet of Forest Home on the edge of the Cornell campus, the morning of May 9. Photograph © Jon Reis / www.jonreis.com.

The *Ithaca Journal* review of the Barton show appeared on May 9 and featured one of Jon Reis's photos. Reporter Mary Suma, also working with a tight deadline, offered just a bit more than a set list with comments. She estimated the crowd at nine thousand, which suggests more than just 250 or so people got in without tickets. The *Good Times Gazette* gave the show the front page of its weekly paper that hit the newsstands on May 12. That review, from Richard Ellenson, was less positive and called the show pleasing but flawed. Images courtesy of the Rare and Manuscript Collections, Kroch Library, Cornell University, Ithaca, New York.

Good Times Gazette

ALIVE OR DEAD? Page 9

TV CROSSWORD PAGE 19

MAY 12, 1977 • ITHACA'S WEEKLY ENTERTAINMENT GUIDE • 25¢

FREE!

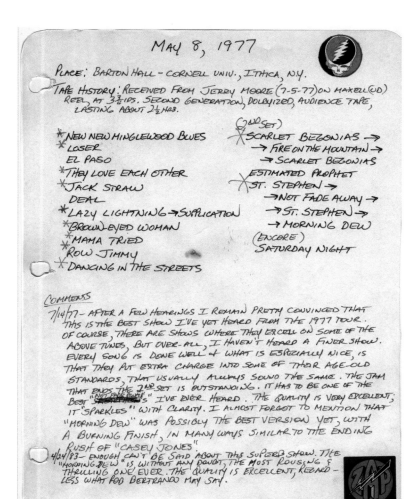

Dick Latvala was the Grateful Dead's archivist from 1986 through 1999, and he kept detailed listening notes on the master tapes made by and for the band. His July 14, 1977, assessment of Betty Cantor-Jackson's recording of the Barton Hall concert is superlative: "I remain pretty convinced that this is the best show I've yet heard from the 1977 tour." His critical listen to the same recording on April 24, 1983, confirms that earlier judgment. But in time his evaluation would change, and Latvala would identify a number of shows from 1977—including Boston the night before and Buffalo the night after—as better than Cornell '77. Listening notes courtesy of Carol Latvala and the Grateful Dead Archives at the University of California, Santa Cruz.

Betty Boards

In Deadhead circles, she was renowned for her ear.
—Nick Paumgarten, 2012

It was spring tour, May 1987. Heather Horsley was an eighteen-year-old freshman at the University of Utah. As a transplanted East Coast Deadhead, she felt like she had won the geographical lottery. She was a mere twelve hours from Marin County, the home of the Grateful Dead, and they played so often on the West Coast that she was able to hit a show once or twice a month while still staying in school. Every couple of weeks, she would load up her little Chevy Chevette with seasoned Deadheads and new converts alike and take a scenic drive to see her favorite band.

On this particular trip she had cajoled a new friend from Vermont who lived in the dorms to join her in the Chevette along with some guy who was, apparently, her long-lost distant cousin. Whatever. Together, they made the thirteen-hour trip to Laguna Seca Raceway in Monterey, California. Horsley mail-ordered her tickets and was confident that she could help her travel partners score tickets too. As they pulled into Laguna Seca and began their ascent up the winding entry road, she felt like she was coming home. Arriving at a Dead show always had that effect on her. They parked the Chevette and set up camp for what would be three days of daytime shows and Deadhead bliss.

It was after the second show, on their way back from a supply run into town, that they noticed a guy in a cowboy hat and blue mechanic's jumpsuit waving people back into the venue. He notified them, via megaphone, that people who wanted to come back inside were welcome to take part in the Grateful Dead's first video to be made specifically for MTV. As Horsley recalls, "Our teenage years were marked with long hours watching Howard Jones, or 'Safety Dance' and V.J. Martha Quinn, so this is something I would not pass up." So, around 9:30 p.m., they promptly headed in, along with some five thousand other fans. "My friends and I ended up near the front and in the middle of the crowd. For the next five hours we were asked to sit, stand, and sing while the Dead played 'Touch of Grey' three times and the skeleton puppets played 'Touch of Grey' twelve times. Between takes when the crowds got restless one or another member of the band would come out and jolly us up." The making of a video turned out to be a lot less entertaining that she had hoped. People took to amusing themselves to pass the time. "At one point the guy next to me, Jesse, who I never saw again, encouraged me to get on his shoulders, and being only five feet," Horsley says, "I gladly concurred."

Thus, in Deadhead-land, Horsley became known as the blond girl in a tank top with sunglasses on her head dancing on a young man's shoulders in the "Touch of Gray" video. Given the impact of that video on the Grateful Dead's popularity, it is a seminal piece of band history. (Interestingly enough, the day the video footage was recorded was May 9, 1987—ten years and one day after Cornell '77.) Spearheaded in part by the popularity of that video on MTV, *In the Dark* went double platinum and became the band's only album to reach the top 10 (peaking at number 6) on the *Billboard* 200 chart. The video, merging the staged live performance with shots of the band, portrayed by life-size marionettes playing the song, was directed by Gary Gutierrez. (Gutierrez had also created the animation sequences for the Grateful Dead movie that had been released in 1977.) If 1977 had witnessed the revival of the Dead, 1987 was its full-scale launch into popularity. The band that seemed always to have been out of time and existing on the fringes of popular culture was flirting with a truly mainstream audience.

The commercial success of *In the Dark* would net the band hard-won financial success but also swell the ranks of their concert audiences to sometimes unmanageable numbers. The irony is that, just ten months prior, thousands of hours of crisp live recordings of the Grateful Dead had been unceremoniously auctioned off. While Horsley and her friends were dancing at Laguna Seca, a high school chemistry teacher (and non-Deadhead) was trying to decide what to do with the contents of the three weathered road cases he had purchased for $100 at an auction in Marin County. The cases contained Grateful Dead gold, but the teacher didn't know that. He bought the items because he wanted to own the cases, emblazoned with Grateful Dead logos, that held the tapes. Who knows, they might be worth something someday, right? Other tapes that had been purchased at the same auction had already been transferred to digital format and circulated via tape-trading networks through the Deadhead community by the time *In the Dark* was released. However, the chemistry teacher had no idea of the rich bounty of live Grateful Dead recordings that he was sitting on. Those recordings—among others now referred to in Deadhead circles as "Betty Boards"—were recorded by former Grateful Dead sound engineer Betty Cantor-Jackson.

Betty Cantor began her association with the Grateful Dead shortly after the band formed. In the late 1960s, she pitched in working at the Avalon and Carousel Ballrooms in San Francisco, doing everything from selling food to helping record performances, often during Grateful Dead shows. Her first official job with the band was assisting sound engineer Bob Matthews during the recording of the Dead's second studio album, the 1968 release *Anthem of the Sun*. She also had a romantic relationship with Matthews at that time. Later, Betty became romantically involved with, and eventually married to, Grateful Dead crew member Rex Jackson, thus further solidifying her association with the band.

"My late husband started recording on the road when he was on the equipment crew," Cantor-Jackson recounts. "He and I purchased our own gear and tape. I recorded whenever I could get to the gigs. I recorded the Grateful Dead frequently when they were at home venues, I recorded any and all Jerry Garcia Band gigs I could get to for years, in all its configurations, as well as other bands I liked whenever I could. In those days, bands were cool and happy about me getting a feed."

It was during the Dead's 1975 touring hiatus that Betty's husband, Rex, sank deep into an alcohol and cocaine binge that he wouldn't survive. On September 5, 1976, in the midst of a long bender during which Rex drove both Mickey and Bear to the edges of their patience, the car that he was driving back from West Marin to his home in Mill Valley went off the road. Jackson was killed in the crash. At the time of his death, he had gone from being a crew member to being road manager for the Dead. In addition to the hole he left in the Dead scene, he also left behind a son,

Cole, with Cantor-Jackson, and a daughter, Cassidy, with Dead family member Eileen Law. The song "Cassidy" was inspired by the birth of Jackson's daughter, and the song "Sunrise" was written upon Jackson's death by Donna Jean Godchaux and the Grateful Dead. Jackson's family was embedded in the life and music of the band.

When the Dead resumed touring in 1977 after a successful second half of 1976, Cantor-Jackson was hired as part of the road crew. Her duties included helping with sound and wrangling Bob Weir's stage setup. "I'd been out on '76, and that was Rex and me doing it. We just wanted it to happen. In those days, the band, if they're out for more than two weeks, they got to take their old ladies, as it were," says Cantor-Jackson, describing the informal mix of family and professional life on the road with the Dead. "So that was my seat. If it was longer than two weeks, I got my travel fare. I brought my own gear, did my own thing, brought my own tape, everything, and just taped that road trip." After Rex was killed, though, she was left with practically nothing. The band invited her to join the crew, solo. "So they said, Okay, well you can come out and tape. Then I took over Bobby's stack. Each band member had an equipment person that took care of their gear, so I took care of Bobby's. A lot of that was because Bobby went wireless, and [Steve] Parish didn't want to do it."

On March 1, 1979, Dead keyboardist Keith Godchaux was replaced by Brent Mydland. Eventually Cantor-Jackson became romantically involved with this newest band member. Cantor-Jackson remembers Brent as a "monster player" and also Jerry's love of playing with him. Yet Mydland was often unsure about his role in the band. "Brent was very insecure. He'd say, 'They're all yelling for Keith.' I'd say, 'No they're not. Come on, Brent. They love you, Brent. Stop thinking you're just a substitute. You're not.' He had the 'new guy' syndrome." Band publicist Dennis Mc-Nally concurs. Despite seeing how much Jerry loved playing with Mydland, the keyboardist never felt secure in his role in the band. "Brent wasn't treated badly within the Grateful Dead, but it isn't like he got a lot of therapy. Nobody got therapy in the Grateful Dead! That was just not their social pattern. He came there with severe self-esteem issues. Obviously it came from a long time before he got to the Grateful Dead."

Mydland's insecurity within the band spilled into his romantic relationship as well. Cantor-Jackson portrays it as a contributing factor to their breakup. Ultimately, she believes that the dissolution of that relationship also led to her departure from the band's employment and inner circle. "Brent and I split up after a few years, with the last year spent in the studio working on his solo project. This put me in the category of the dreaded 'ex.' I didn't think that could apply to me, but he was a band member." Cantor-Jackson contends that with the bitter end of her relationship with Mydland, she lost all her connections to the band. "Everyone was paranoid of me being around, so I no longer had access to my studio or the vault."

While strained interpersonal relations may have played a role in Cantor-Jackson's dismissal and may have made the band wary of being too chummy with her—though one doubts to the point of paranoia—it should also be noted that during the same period there was a larger purge of others, within the Dead's inner circle, who were abusing drugs and alcohol. In the early to mid-'80s a wave of people got fired for addiction issues. Garcia's own addiction and health problems had pushed the organization to draw firmer lines around substance abusers within their ranks.

Although it may not seem so from the outside, the Dead did create formal guidelines for how to handle substance-abuse issues.

Nicholas Meriwether—founding archivist at the Grateful Dead Archives at UC Santa Cruz and organizer of the Grateful Dead Scholars Caucus—notes, "There was always a publicly stated rule that you can do whatever you want as long as it doesn't interfere with either the music or your job, depending on where you are." He adds that that rule "was true for everyone." It applied to Dick Latvala, who had problems with alcohol and cocaine in the late 1990s. Meriwether continues, "The band did the same thing for Dick. They just kinda looked at him and said, 'Okay, time for you to clean up,' and they shipped him off to rehab. That ostensibly is how Rock Scully leaves the band as well. He's not really kicked out of the band permanently. He's told to go off to rehab. But something goes wrong in all of that and he just never comes back." So these moments of crisis and response—sometimes temporary, sometimes permanent—were common at the time. The only exception to the rule was Garcia and his habits. "Nobody could really stand up to Garcia, although they tried," Meriwether states.

Regardless of the circumstances of Cantor-Jackson's departure from the Grateful Dead, even a quick scan of the band's road-crew personnel over the years confirms a heavily male-dominated culture. Roadies like Lawrence "Ram Rod" Shurtliff, Bill "Kidd" Candelario, Clifford Dale "Sonny Boy" Heard, and Steve Parish led a boys' club that was accused by many in the concert industry of having too much power. Given the fact that, in addition to being crew chief, Ram Rod was also president of the Grateful Dead's business operations, it's not a reach to say that, at the very least, the Grateful Dead's crew inhabited a singular space in rock 'n' roll culture whereby the crew had a voice equal to the musicians in the band. Cantor-Jackson remembers, "They were the world's most macho road crew. Oh god! Pretty much, trust me, I've been in a lot of them and been around a lot of them—they were definitely the most macho road crew." Their power within the Grateful Dead organization and their machismo made it hard on some women associated with the band. "I had to carry just the same weight as they did or I'd have been laughed off the road," Cantor-Jackson says. "I'll tell you that."

Following her dismissal from the Grateful Dead, Cantor-Jackson fell on hard financial times. By 1986 she could no longer afford to live in her home and was forced to put her possessions into a storage facility until she could sort out her living situation. However, before she could find an affordable place to live, she was overwhelmed by the storage fees. Unable to pay her back bills, her items were seized and sold to the highest bidder during a public auction in 1987. Among the items auctioned off were about a thousand reel-to-reel tapes, including many live shows by the Grateful Dead.

In this way, the "Betty Board" recordings passed from the inner circle of the Grateful Dead to the outside world. According to Cantor-Jackson, she notified the Grateful Dead's office about the auction prior to when it was held. Based on the fact that an eventual owner of many of the tapes was informed about the impending auction of rock 'n' roll memorabilia by a former employee of Bill Graham Productions—an organization closely aligned with the Grateful Dead's organization—it would seem that, however the news was spread, the Grateful Dead had an opportunity to reclaim the "Betty Board" recordings rather than have them fall into outside hands. No evidence suggests that anyone in the organization made that effort.

More than two hundred hours of "Betty Board" auctioned recordings surfaced in the late 1980s. It took until the mid-1990s for many more of them to surface. The non-Deadhead schoolteacher who had inadvertently purchased some of the tapes promptly put them into a barn he owned, where he left them to sit. When he finally realized that the true historical value of the cases were the reel-to-reel tapes contained inside, he decided that the recordings might be worth money. Given that the Grateful Dead had become a full-blown, highly visible pop culture presence— their concert grosses were regularly noted among the highest of any touring musical group—it would've been fair to assume that the tapes might even be worth millions. However, no one was willing to offer him the amount he was hoping to get. In fact, there were questions as to what exactly was contained on the tapes, and whether, given their decayed and filthy condition, they were even playable. Eventually, word of this new stash of Betty Boards filtered down to longtime taper, musician, and sound engineer Rob Eaton.

Given his knowledge of Dead bootleg taping and his expertise with studio work, Eaton was in a uniquely well-suited position to advise the teacher about the stash that he was sitting on. It turned out that Eaton's main role, however, would be to restore the recordings to playable condition before their contents were lost forever. At the time of purchase, the road cases were in such poor condition that no one else at the auction had even bid on them. When the teacher got the cases home, he discovered that one of them was filled with cookbooks, a second was filled with decaying seven-inch reel-to-reel tapes, and a third contained ten-inch reel-to-reel tapes in a similarly compromised condition. To a non-expert, the contents of the cases looked like a lot of garbage. To an expert like Eaton, the tapes, clearly of immense cultural value, would at first appear to be hopelessly compromised. Years of neglect seemed to have rendered Grateful Dead gold into muddy unlistenable goulash.

On a rainy night in December 1995, the teacher drove Eaton out to a barn in northern California where he had stored the road cases since their purchase. Most of the tapes were decayed and rotting. Eaton concluded that they had been in some sort of flood. Still, he persisted. He inspected the tapes and made extensive notes about their condition. While the teacher had invited Eaton to see the tapes to answer questions about their monetary value, Eaton's main concern was whether they could be restored for listening.

At that point, it was in both their interests for Eaton to take some of the reels back to New York to see if he could salvage them. He took five. If they weren't playable, they were worthless to everyone. With a meticulousness that Bear himself would have admired, Eaton set about his task. "I spent the entire flight back to New York transferring my handwritten notes into a database for reference. As soon as I got home late the next afternoon I immediately began the restoration process, which took a solid 36 hours to complete." What he discovered was remarkable, given the years of neglect. "I was amazed," he says, "that even the most damaged tapes were not only playable but sounded great." Eaton informed the teacher that his only hope for ever getting money for the recordings would be to have them restored. The teacher grudgingly conceded and began shipping Eaton new reels to clean and repair.

Eaton describes the process: "The shipments usually came in groups of thirty reels at a time about every week. It took over six weeks to complete the project. Each reel was restored by hand, one at a time. I then transferred the reels to DAT using studio-quality equipment. I listened to every inch of every tape completely and took detailed notes on everything. When it was all said and done I had invested more than 700 hours into the project." Eaton insists that after shipping the reels back to the chemistry teacher, he never saw them again.

Despite Eaton's loss of contact with the physical tapes and the legally contentious ownership of the entire stash of recordings, many of the shows that had been auctioned off following Cantor-Jackson's eviction from the storage unit began being dubbed and passed among the bootleg community. For certain, some of those were from collections purchased by auction buyers other than the teacher. However, the chain of ownership regarding who owned which of the recordings and who launched them into the Dead community is unclear, and a discussion of provenance, not to say ownership, can easily bog down in minutia and hearsay. It seems to be the case that those who know do not say, and those who say do not know. The introduction of many Betty Boards into general Deadhead circulation meant that, for the first time, outstanding recordings of many shows, including the four key nights of the fabled spring 1977 tour—New Haven, Boston, Ithaca, and Buffalo—were now available.

As with audience recordings, the lower the "generation" of a Betty Board recording (that is, the fewer times the recording you are listening to was recorded from previous sources), the better the sound quality. The ultimate goal as a collector is to make a copy from the master recording, thus making a "first generation" copy. Whether a huge record company preparing an official live release or a fan wanting the best sounding version of a given show, the closer to the master, the higher the quality. Naturally, record companies have more resources to "clean up" a recording and make it sound better, but still, the master recording is the gold standard.

These designations hold for both soundboard recordings (for example, Betty's or Bear's of any other recording straight from the

Dead's sound system) and for audience tapes made by fans recording the show on their own equipment. Particularly with audience tapes made by non-professionals, we must also take into account the equipment, microphone placement, and overall skill of the taper. Some tapers are just better than others—the quality of their recordings is higher, so their products are more desirable. A first generation soundboard or excellent audience recording is as good as it gets for a tape collector. Because audience recordings also include more ambient crowd noise, some listeners prefer those because they feel closer to the actual show environment. Others prefer soundboards because they are most purely the sound of the musicians playing. Nowadays, there is also the option of listening online to "matrix" versions of shows that combine elements of both audience and soundboard versions. The internet has tremendously expanded the number of listening options, and some fans have spent countless hours creating matrix versions of shows to perfectly suit their own tastes. Of course, official, cleaned-up versions of any show—including Cornell '77—are traditionally considered to be the crispest, the final word on any recording.

Because of the highly desirable quality and sound of Betty's recordings, once the Betty Boards started to surface, any collector worth his or her salt strived to get copies as close to the master source as possible. And everyone with any tape collection at all had to have at least one copy of the Cornell '77 Betty Board. Grateful Dead archivist David Lemieux recalls being a young Deadhead and getting his first high quality Betty Board copy of Cornell '77: "I was getting into tape trading around '85, '86, and I remember getting Cornell in '88 maybe. It was on a sound-quality level and on a performance level head and shoulders ahead of anything I had up until then." Lemieux continues, "I think Betty is a tremendous recording engineer. The Betty Boards are spectacular-sounding tapes. If you listen to her tapes from anytime on that tour you can't tell what show they're from—they all sound the same in a really good way. It's just very consistent sound. It's really remarkable what she was doing."

"I just dealt with the band. I made my own mix to make myself happy and to hear what I wanted to hear," Cantor-Jackson says, describing the motivations and the artistry of her process for recording Cornell '77 and other lauded Betty Board recordings. "I wanted to hear the whole band! I had every microphone, so I had my own control. I didn't have to put the same amount of guitar as somebody else does in the room. Or the same amount of vocal as they do in the vocal monitor. I can put whatever I feel is appropriate. That's one of the reasons my mixes are complete. Whereas a PA mix may not be quite as complete. It may be heavy on vocals and drums and a little lighter on instruments because the instruments are coming out of amps in the room, so it is sound reinforcement." The details are critical but can be lost on someone who is not an audiophile or has not run a sound board. But what becomes perfectly clear to anyone listening to her describe her work is that the whole process—from the setup, to the mix, to the perfecting of the masters—is incredibly personal. "I am not sound reinforcement," Cantor-Jackson says today. "I am sound."

As the band strived for perfection on stage, Cantor-Jackson perfected her own process for enshrining the moment for fans. She wanted to hear each member of the band performing within that greater "blesh-like" organism, and in so doing she approached her own elevated plane of creative transcendence. The Grateful Dead became the muse for Cantor-Jackson's sonic creations.

She also remembers well, and fondly, a typical "day at the office" for her concert recording process circa 1977. Again, the details are crucial to the quality of the tape or, now, audio file, that a fan listens to. "I went in, helped set up the PA, and ran my snake and splitter system, which would feed the PA, the monitor console, and mine," she recalls. "I was a hundred feet away, or a hundred-foot snake away somewhere in another room. I had speakers at that point, as well as headphones. Later onstage I was always just in headphones, isolation headphones onstage right next to the monitor mixer, right there on the side of the stage." As she recounts her work habits, one can imagine her setting up gear on the floor at Barton Hall. It might have taken the better part of the afternoon, as the sun faded low and snow flurries kicked up in Ithaca.

"I think in '77 I was still in a separate room doing it with speakers and with headphones. What I did was run a split—which means it divides the microphones—and there's microphones on-stage that are plugged into a phase box. That box then feeds three different places. Basically, that's what the split is about. One set of those same microphones goes to the PA mixer up front, one set of those microphones goes to the monitor mixer, and one set went to me. So I did my own mix separate from everybody else's mixes." The unique quality of the sound Cantor-Jackson captured hinged on her ability to control her mix in a way that pleased her ear; that meant separating her feed entirely from the sound of the room. "The PA, being sound reinforcement, is something in addition to the sound that you're hearing in the room already coming off the stage from their amplifiers. What I did was not that, because I didn't take the room into consideration, as far as what was coming out of the amps. My feed is how much control

I put and how much I put into the mix, which was really separate from anybody else's stuff."

"Basically," Cantor-Jackson says of all of her sound work from 1977, "it was an independent mix."

As routine as the recording process must have seemed to Cantor-Jackson back in 1977, the legal wrangling over the custody of those recordings has been anything but straightforward. Anyone remotely familiar with the discussion surrounding the legal chain of custody of Cantor-Jackson's recordings can testify that the path has been circuitous, treacherous, and, at times, litigious. Stanford Law School graduate and former touring Deadhead Stephen Robinson clarifies some of the issues that delayed the official release of Cornell '77: "There are two copyrights for a piece of recorded music. First, there is copyright for the underlying musical composition. That consists of the music and words. Second, there is copyright for the sound recording. That consists of the fixed sounds in a tangible medium that can be played back. The author of a fixed-sounds recording can be the performer or the producer/recorder that processes or fixes the sound into a recording."

Or, to put the crux of the problem in simpler terms: Betty argued that she owned the second copyright on all the recordings she made of the Grateful Dead because, according to her account, even when she was employed by the band, she purchased the blank reels herself, and she produced them independently and strictly for her own pleasure. On the other hand, with regard to the recordings made during her official employment, the band's position was that they owned all copyrights to the Betty Board reels because she made them while working as a sound engineer on their payroll, using their equipment—and, in any event, they indisputably owned the copyright to the music contained on them. Unfortunately, the dispute got even murkier due to the fact that the reels were sold in a legal auction and that many were no longer the possession of either Cantor-Jackson or the Grateful Dead.

As of this writing, all of the Betty Board reels that were acquired from different sources are now, undoubtedly, the possession of the Grateful Dead. Those reels are safely ensconced in the band's famous "vault" of recordings, located in Burbank, California, in a giant warehouse owned by Warner Music Group. Journalist Nick Paumgarten describes entering this hallowed hall of music for his first visit: "We passed through a door into a vast climate-controlled hangar of shelves loaded with boxes containing the reel-to-reel multitrack recordings of studio sessions and concerts of hundreds of artists. . . . The Dead's section was toward the back, surrounded by a chain-link fence. It was a vault within a vault—the Holy of Holies." The Cornell '77 Betty Board reels are now, finally, in the Dead's vault. At long last, the record label owns a suitably high-quality recording of the show to release. Mark Pinkus, general manager of Grateful Dead Properties at Warner Music Group's Rhino Entertainment, is thrilled that the record company took possession of those reels, particularly Cornell '77: "We got ahold of the master tape, we cleaned it up and it's a great event. It got Rhino-cized and it has beautiful packaging and liner notes. . . . It's a great release."

The legal and business stalemate around the Betty Boards of Cornell '77 has finally ended. Nearly forty years after the show was played, Cornell '77 has at last been issued as both a standalone show and as part of a four-show box set, *May 1977: Get Shown the Light*, that includes New Haven 5/5/77, Boston 5/7/77, and Buffalo 5/9/77. Cantor-Jackson is pleased to know that so many Deadheads have benefited from the recordings that she made both independently and as an employee of the Grateful Dead. "I'm glad they got out there for people to hear. It's wonderful having your work appreciated. I was really only doing this to capture the music. That's how I like it. I consider it 'the capturing of.' I just want to hang on to it for everybody. I mean, it's Jerry! Jerry's my buddy!" For Deadheads everywhere, the 2013 release of the *May 1977* box set and the 2017 release of *Get Shown the Light* are causes for celebration and chances to reconsider that stellar tour all over again. Now that all the Betty Boards are in the vault, reunited at last, the future looks bright for more releases from this golden age of Grateful Dead music.

The Show That Never Happened

Yo this show is great but not the best . . . the 76 run at the Beacon surpassed it.   —Anonymous

When sixteen-year-old Mark Pinkus walked into his girl-friend's bedroom in Sherman Oaks, California, in 1984, he didn't recognize the picture of Jerry Garcia hanging on her wall. Being a music fan, he was a little embarrassed when she goaded him, "You honestly don't know who that is?" But up until that point, Pinkus's bands were the Clash, the Rolling Stones, Bruce Springsteen, and the Who. The Dead hadn't crossed his radar yet. But they were about to.

After a few more challenges to his musical mastery—"Um, that's the Grateful Dead. You haven't heard them?"—Pinkus left her house and hightailed it down to Tower Records. He bought his first Grateful Dead album. It was the only one they had in stock: *Skeletons from the Closet: The Best of the Grateful Dead.* Since it said "Best of," Pinkus figured that was exactly what he'd be getting. As he says now, "It's the weirdest 'best of' ever made."

Skeletons from the Closet is a mishmash of Grateful Dead songs put together from various recording sessions and released in a quickie manner by Warner Bros. in February 1974. On the other hand, the album has achieved triple-platinum status (more than three million copies sold) and has introduced legions of would-be fans, like Pinkus, to their new favorite band.

The next day, Pinkus scooted down to another Tower Records store and picked up the Dead's *Europe '72*. As he says, "It took me forever to understand that record, but once I got into it, that's how it all began." Later that same year, Pinkus would attend his first Dead concert. It was an auspicious one. The Greek Theatre at Cal (to non-Californians, that is the University of California, Berkeley) has legendarily good vibes for a Dead show. The band has played some amazing sets there. Pinkus's first show—7/13/84—was no exception. It was a Friday the thirteenth, but nothing about the show was ill-fated.

An unusual combination of "Scarlet Begonias" > "Touch of Gray" > "Fire on the Mountain" started the second set. The band played without pause, one song bleeding into the next, until the ripping "Sugar Magnolia" set closer. But it was the encore that made this show one for the Deadhead record books. The Dead played their first "Dark Star" since 1981. It had been 167 shows since their last one. The drought had been broken. In one of those great examples of Grateful Dead magic, thousands of fans witnessed a shooting star in the night sky over the Greek just as the song started. As if the moment needed any more gravitas, the Dead flashed celestial images on huge projection screens behind them while they played.

Pinkus recalls saying to his friend: "I don't know what they just played or what the hell just happened, but we're going tomorrow night." They had played only one song off the two Dead albums Pinkus owned ("Sugar Magnolia," which appears on both), but that didn't make any difference. After that show at the Greek, Mark vowed to see the Dead as much as he could. "I was on the bus, and the rest is history." Pinkus would end up seeing seventy-three Grateful Dead shows before Jerry Garcia died. Even in the farthest outreaches of a stellar "Dark Star," though, the young man never could have predicted that one day he would sit in a conference room with the members of the Grateful Dead. He certainly couldn't have predicted that they would ask him to sing one of their songs back to them during that meeting. There was no way he could have known that his personal path down the "Golden Road to Unlimited Devotion" would lead to one of the coolest jobs a Deadhead could score. Mark would become general manager of Grateful Dead Properties at Warner Music Group's Rhino Entertainment. He would oversee all official Grateful Dead audio and video releases.

It was 2010, and Pinkus had already been at Rhino for almost twenty years. The label had been in business with the Grateful Dead since 2006. The president of Rhino at that time asked Pinkus to handle the Dead's catalog, but, first, introductions had to be made. Mark would have to pass a drug-free acid test of the band's devising. "The four of them [Bob Weir, Phil Lesh, Mickey Hart, and Bill Kreutzmann] got together with their representatives and myself and Kevin, the then-president of Rhino, and had a great meeting introducing me to the band. There were a couple of questions. It was clear that they liked the idea of the person in charge being a Grateful Dead fan. I said, 'I'm a terrible singer, but if you want me to sing a song let me know. It won't be pretty.'" Pinkus pauses. "I did indeed get asked to sing. I had to sing the opening lines to 'Victim or the Crime.'" He clears his throat and belts out those job-winning first lyrics, "Patience runs out on the junkie." Then chuckles, "Luckily, I stopped at that."

The vocal performance may have been rough, but Pinkus's business track record in handling the Grateful Dead's catalog has been stellar. One of his first projects was overseeing the release of the complete run of Europe 1972 shows. All twenty-two of them. The massive release had been one that official Grateful Dead audiovisual music archivist and CD/DVD producer David Lemieux had been wanting to do for years. They got together and made it happen.

With that impressive launch, the partnership between Pinkus and Lemieux was off and running. With their dedicated staffs, they have orchestrated some of the most exciting audio and video releases of live Dead in the band's history. Despite the legal complications delaying an official release of Cornell '77, both Pinkus and Lemieux remain huge fans of the show. Pinkus says of Cornell: "To me, the three standouts, and I don't feel unique in saying this, are the 'Scarlet-Fire' and the 'Morning Dew.' So much has been said about those three. The 'Scarlet-Fire' is so joyous and the jam between them is so sweet, and Donna just sounds so great in the pocket there. The 'Morning Dew' is as epic as ever." But for Pinkus, like a lot of Deadheads reveling in their appreciation of a great show, there is a lot to like, and the list of favorites goes on. "If I had to pick a sleeper hit out of the twenty songs they played that night, I'd go with 'Brown-Eyed Women.' It's a personal favorite song of mine." Always the record man, he can't help but add, "I've always felt that if that was on a studio album it could've been a real bona fide radio hit. I always felt like that was the hit that got away from the band. And this version is just as good as any."

Pinkus then sinks deeper into Cornell: "I'd be remiss if I didn't mention the 'St. Stephen' > 'Not Fade Away' > 'St. Stephen.' When I hear it in this setting . . . having seen shows through the '80s and '90s, we all saw a ton of 'Not Fade Away's, we did not see a ton of any 'St. Stephen's. It's just interesting to hear how well they were playing it. It's such that late-'60s song, and they brought it back in the '70s and it just sounded so good." He then muses on how and why this sequence of songs faded from the Dead's repertoire. "Why they couldn't bring it back a little bit more often in the '80s is just a shame, because this clearly shows they know how to play it."

Lemieux has a similar passion for Cornell '77. Like Pinkus and countless other Deadheads, he got his first Betty Board copy of the show in the 1980s. It became immediately clear to him that the Grateful Dead's playing that night was exceptional and that the recording quality paid a unique justice to the band's performance. As he says, "It's having been able to hear the performance and the quality—that we were lucky enough to hear it from starting at around '87 and '88 when the Bettys started circulating— that's when we figured out how very special the show is."

Like any expert in a field, Lemieux has a take on Cornell '77 that is both passionate and measured. "I think it's a great show. I think the first set is really good. I don't know how much more head and shoulders above the rest of the tour's first sets, because there were some magnificent first sets on that tour. I do think the 'Dancin' in the Streets' is really one of the most solid ones, just incredibly meaty. But I think the second set, in particular I'm thinking of 'Scarlet-Fire,' the 'Not Fade Away,' and the 'Morning Dew,' of course, those, to me, are the things that stand out as truly exceptional. Exceptional as pieces of music. A lot of shows will have that one song where you go, 'You've gotta hear the "Scarlet-Fire" from the show!' Cornell has got three or four of those moments. Aside from those moments, the rest of the show really is good. It's not a mediocre show with some highlights. It is an exceptional show. If it didn't even have those highlights, if the 'Scarlet-Fire' wasn't what it was, nor the 'Dew,' nor the 'Not Fade Away,' it would still be a ridiculously great show. But add to that—I hate to use superlatives—but some of the best moments in Grateful Dead history, it really just puts it head and shoulders."

Nicholas Meriwether—founding archivist at the Grateful Dead Archives at UC Santa Cruz and organizer of the Grateful Dead Scholars Caucus—has a similarly passionate yet scholarly take on Cornell '77. Like most of the people who have ended up working with the Grateful Dead's legacy in a professional capacity, Meriwether was a stone-cold Deadhead first.

Born and raised in South Carolina, Meriwether was steeped in all the musical traditions that the band drew on, with the exception of the Bakersfield sound (despite the fact that he grew up in the South, he had no ear for the unique sound of California country music from the Central Valley until he discovered the Grateful Dead). Meriwether's father was a classical music aficionado, so that music became a seminal soundtrack in Nicholas's formative years as well. Factor in a love for jazz and bluegrass improvisational music, and Meriwether went off to college with all his musical ducks in a row. Except for one. He had never gained an appreciation for the Grateful Dead.

"I went to college in the Northeast, and I had a good friend freshman year that was from California. He became my roommate sophomore year. Sophomore year he made a comment about the Grateful Dead, and I said something witless and idiotic, and he said, 'No, you should actually listen to them,'" Meriwether recounts. It was a fateful challenge. "He put on the eponymous live album from 1971, *Grateful Dead*, nicknamed Skullfuck. I remember listening with mounting disbelief to the album because I loved it. I was enamored with really pretty much everything on it. 'Playing in the Band,' everything, but the thing that absolutely blew me away was the song 'Wharf Rat.' I had never heard rock music, or popular music, in which the lyrics and the song structure had been so intelligently melded. I was hooked."

As was the path for many, Meriwether then started off down the Golden Road by collecting as many bootlegs as he could lay his hands on. Following his new passion, he quickly found a community of other Deadheads on campus, many of whom had already amassed their own tape collections. Finally, in November of '85, Meriwether walked into his first Dead show at Brendan Byrne Arena (now the Izod Center) in East Rutherford, New Jersey. As he recalls, "I was absolutely hooked by that show. I remember being absolutely dazzled by the parking lot scene, and that also harkened back to lots of things I had known in the South. I saw all of these modern twists on things like Appalachian folk crafts" out on the expanses of asphalt at the Meadowlands. "I found a vibe in the parking lot that was just magnificently different to what passed for mainstream yuppie Reagan misbehavior."

As a fan discovering the Grateful Dead in the 1980s, Meriwether was struck by the disconnect between the band's music and what passed for music on the radio. "For me and for the folks who came of age in the early-to-mid-1980s," he says, assessing his generation, "we tended to hate everything that was on the radio. Top 40 was pretty bad at that point, with a few exceptions." Alienated from the airwaves as well as an increasingly conservative political culture, Meriwether and his Deadhead compatriots found in the Dead "absolute incredible proof that what passed for the mainstream Reagan condemnation of the 1960s was just absolutely wrong. Here's this band that's absolutely the opposite of the glitz and glamour of showbiz, shambling onstage and turning in these breathtaking concerts that were far from Beach Boys golden oldies, but were just as exciting and valid and innovative and world-class as anything that I could have imagined." The Dead were not a nostalgia act, not by a long stretch, and for a band that hewed closely to the lines of apolitical subculture (and not counterculture), the political resonance of the music and the scene were evident.

"That's how I became a Deadhead; I was hooked at that point," says Meriwether. And in a spot-on premonition of what was to come, as Meriwether exited Brendan Byrne he turned to his friend and said, "I will spend the rest of my life thinking about this."

He has. As the first archivist to officially tackle the archives donated to UC Santa Cruz by the band in 2008, he was tasked with taming a massive quantity of papers, including business records, correspondence, and assorted memorabilia that the band gave to the college. It was Meriwether's job to organize the collection and facilitate its use with the public, scholars, journalists, fans, and anyone else with an interest and need to know more about the Grateful Dead.

Through his intense, scholarly study of the band, Meriwether has developed some unique perspectives on the band's history and body of music. In his estimation, what makes Cornell '77—and 1977 on the whole—shine as a high-water mark for the Grateful Dead comes down to the drummers. "What shakes out in '77 is especially what you hear so clearly in Cornell: that powerhouse sense of both drummers working in this inexorable union. You get a different kind of hypnotic event. It's what you hear centrally in Cornell. That's where that powerhouse entrainment takes on a very different cast and quality in the band's music," Meriwether says. "What you hear is a telepathic mesmerization that's an extension of what we heard develop in the late '60s and then after Mickey leaves, particularly in the early '70s. It takes on this new and interesting propulsive quality that it didn't have before."

Meriwether takes a big breath and then dives a little deeper. "Right now I'm reading William Vollmann's book on freight-train riding in the mid-2000s. He talks about this kind of mesmerizing, hypnotic quality to being on a freight train and hearing the clackety-clack of the ties and the rails. You get very much a sense of the same kind of hypnotic quality, but propulsive, regular quality in the drumming in 1977. Especially in Cornell. You see what the Dead are capable of doing with it," he says with a sense of summation. "It's very different from that light, floating jazzy feel with Kreutzmann as the sole drummer in the early '70s. But it's still animal. And it's still the same feeling that they're after."

In addition to the outstanding playing from Cornell '77, Meriwether credits the Betty Board recordings for bringing this noteworthy performance to wider attention. "The Betty Boards were such an absolute shocking revelation," he says. The shock had something to do with technology, with craft, and with money. "You have to remember that good, high-quality dubbing wouldn't really become common until the advent of the digital era—even though, for some tapers, the digital era has already begun by the mid-1980s. By then, there were some wealthy or committed Deadheads who were actually making DAT tapes, and preserving them and disseminating them," but Meriwether makes clear they were in a small minority. The rest of the community was trading and listening to recordings of lesser quality on inferior equipment. "But then when the Betty stuff comes out, what really happens is that people can listen to the caliber of Betty's mixes, which were simply stunning." By "people" Meriwether means a lot of people. Almost any and every Deadhead with a decent tape connection now had access to great recordings of key shows, including Cornell '77.

"When the Betty Boards first got released I remember listening to a tape of that and just saying, 'My god, I've never heard a bootleg that had this kind of ambience. That had this much haunting clarity to the instrumentation.'" Because of the uncannily high level of musicianship and the crystal-clear quality of Betty Cantor-Jackson's recordings, in Meriwether's opinion Cornell '77 rose to the topmost tiers of the mammoth mountain of bootlegs.

Another Cornell-appreciating expert, Dennis McNally, saw his first show at the Springfield, Massachusetts, Civic Center on October 2, 1972. At the time, he was working toward his PhD in American history at the University of Massachusetts. Because his dissertation was on Jack Kerouac and the Beat generation, McNally was already plugged into a deep-root inspiration for the Grateful Dead's ethos. In 1976 he moved out to San Francisco to get closer to the source and to whatever shows might occur during the band's touring hiatus.

In 1979, with McNally's doctorate completed, Random House published his first book, *Desolate Angel: Jack Kerouac, the Beat Generation, and America.* McNally had only a vague prayer that his book might reach Jerry Garcia's eyes when he mailed a copy off to the band's fan-club mailing address. The way the rest of the story unfolds is one for the good Dead karma record books. McNally positioned himself into being an extra in the filming of a skit that the Dead used during their 1980 run at Radio City Music Hall. The skit debuted during the Halloween show and was also shown via closed-circuit broadcast to theaters around the

East Coast. Jerry had also participated in the skit, and McNally got the chance to chat with him on set. It turns out, Garcia had read and loved McNally's book. Two months later, Rock Scully and Alan Trist approached McNally with a request that came directly from the top. Jerry wanted Dennis to write a history of the Grateful Dead.

Once McNally began his work as an independent scholar researching the history of the Grateful Dead, the leap to becoming a regular employee of the band followed shortly thereafter. McNally recalls, "By 1984, I was running out of money and looking for work, and Rock Scully had moved on and they needed a publicist—actually, what happened was that the receptionist complained because no one was responding to press calls, so Garcia just said, 'Get McNally to do it, he knows that shit.'" Garcia then gave McNally his crash course in how to be a publicist for the Grateful Dead. Summoned to Garcia's house, McNally was instructed by Jerry: "'First, we don't suck up to the press.' I said, OK, got that, no sucking up. Then he said, 'That about covers it—here, smoke this.'" Garcia handed McNally a joint and, with that, he was christened as the band's publicist. McNally would end up serving in that capacity during the most popular time in the Grateful Dead's thirty-year career.

Although McNally didn't attend Cornell '77, he did see the March and June '77 shows at the Winterland that sandwiched the epic East Coast run. He says of that year, "The band enjoyed their time off. They had the material for *Blues for Allah*, and it was still quite new, and quite good. Wonderful material. They had the material from *Terrapin*, which was still quite new. They had settled into their return, and they were playing at a peak," he adds, mournfully, "until Mickey had to fuck himself up with that car accident. Lord only knows what '77 could have been like, but that interrupted it, and by '78 something else was going on. But it was a particularly good moment; '77 is really one of the best years."

As the band's historian, and also as a Deadhead who saw shows throughout the '70s, McNally explains the power of Cornell '77 with two simple words: Morning Dew. In his words, "The whole point of 'Morning Dew' after that first solo is to bring the whole song to this point of absolute tension, and then it just stops and it's, 'I guess it doesn't matter anyway.' For whatever reason, on this day, Jerry forgot to stop. That tension goes on, twice as long, three times as long, as he ever did. To me, that's the legend of Barton Hall." After countless discussions and many formal interviews with Garcia, McNally also has a unique vantage from which to speculate about what the reluctant icon might make of the wide-spread reverence for Cornell '77. He says, "He'd shrug. He'd be bemused. I think he could understand it if you made him listen to the show."

Zeroing in on the one song that he feels justifies the reverence for Cornell '77, McNally further speculates on how Garcia would feel. "What he'd say about such things is that anytime you find a gimmick that really drives the audience wild, you have to get rid of it. This is the ultimate example of a gimmick, which is to say the closing frenzy of 'Morning Dew.' He'd immediately have to think of another way to do the song. One which would necessarily not generate the kind of excitement that this one did. In that way, he'd probably be a little embarrassed." McNally reflects on the impact that incessant touring had on the band's music. "If you figure out a gimmick, a trick, that you know is going to just set the audience wild, that's what it is, it's a trick. If you're going to play new every night, you have to get rid of those gimmicks."

McNally delves a little deeper into the connection between Garcia and gimmicks, and the difference between being a musician and an entertainer. "This was the Grateful Dead sharing their lives onstage musically," he says. "It wasn't theater, except in the inherent theater of music. It wasn't the idea that it's your job to get the audience to stand on its head and scream. They were musicians. They were performers only in a limited sense." That applied particularly to Jerry. There was no showbiz in him. "He could admire that in James Brown," McNally reflects, "but the whole shtick of the cape and the freaking out and the breaking back to the microphone . . . that was not him. That was not in Jerry's DNA."

Listening to author and lifelong Deadhead Steve Silberman speak about the band, it's as if the Grateful Dead actually are a part of his DNA. In fact, it's possible to believe that the band's music is as inevitable a part of human evolution as opposable thumbs and that attending a Dead show was a ceremony as worthy of anthropological study as any psychotropic rite taking place in the Amazon or a shaman's hut in Mexico. But, as Silberman points out, "Because it was happening in basketball arenas in Pittsburgh, nobody cared."

Silberman's initiation into the mysteries of the Grateful Dead began at a festival noted in the *Guinness Book of World Records* for being the "Largest Audience at a Pop Festival." It's estimated that six hundred thousand people attended the "Summer Jam" music festival at Watkins Glen, New York, in 1973. The bill was the Allman Brothers, the Band, and the Grateful Dead. Although the concert proper was held on July 28, it's the sound check that the Grateful Dead played the day before the concert that eventually made it onto the massive five-disc box set, *So Many Roads (1965–1995)*, from Rhino Records. As one of three Grateful Dead experts who selected tracks for that release, along with David Gans and Blair Jackson, Silberman made sure that the music played that day was included in the collection. As Silberman says, "The day before the official show, the Dead came out and did a sound check that turned out to be one of the most absolutely beautiful, completely improvised, and yet tightly thematic pieces of music that they ever played in their entire careers."

The mind-boggling eighteen-minute improvisational jam foreshadowed little of the next day's performance. You can hear faint inklings of "Dark Star," "Fire on the Mountain," and perhaps a few fleeting notes of "Eyes of the World"—which they did play the next day—but perhaps not. This funk-tinged jam is all about teasing the next move, stoking the interstices of their music and exploring new pathways. After a moody, even unsettling, beginning, the sound check takes off at the 2:30 mark and never looks back. This is a band setting out for territories unknown, uninterested in plying the crowd with their standard numbers, completely comfortable in a wordless space of sound and experience.

At the time of the Watkins Glen sound check, Silberman was just another sixteen-year-old kid who had lied to his parents about going to his first Dead show. It was a small lie, really, just something to enhance their sense of security about the concert Silberman was going to one way or another, come rain, flood, or mud. The friend he was supposed to go there with bailed out at the last minute, so Silberman told his parents that he was going with a different buddy. Again, he was going to the concert either way, so why not let them persist in the delusion that he'd be traveling with a friend?

The truth was that Silberman would be making the trip from New York City to Summer Jam and back by himself. He would travel by ferry and Greyhound bus, and by catching rides with strangers. It was Silberman's initiation into the Grateful Dead, and, in many ways, adulthood. Or, as Silberman puts it,

"Going to Watkins Glen was quite an ordeal for a little nerd from New York." That said, he is also aware of the larger ritualistic significance of his journey to see the Dead. "If you notice, a lot of the use of psychedelics in initiation rituals in cultures where psychedelics are used traditionally involves some sort of ordeal where the kid is dropped off in the wilderness and he has no food or water and he has to figure out how to survive. For millions of young suburban kids, the Grateful Dead circus was the ritual initiation wilderness in which they found their own competence and their own vision of the world with the help of the community."

Along with the difficulty of travel itself, Silberman ingested large quantities of LSD while also contending with challenges man-made (the porta-potties were so far away that he had to hold his excretions for twenty-four hours), natural (there was an unseasonable frost the morning of the concert), and again man-made (the porta-potty that he eventually used had been previously set on fire by concertgoers trying to stay warm against the frost). Silberman says, "I still remember, these guys gave me a ride all the way back from Watkins Glenn to Staten Island where they lived. I took the Staten Island Ferry. I still remember seeing people on the ferry reading the *New York Daily News*, and the headline on the front page was something like, '500,000 Hippies Drown in Sea of Mud.' I still had the mud on my pants!"

His airtight Grateful Dead bona fides are not known by many. Most people know Silberman primarily as a longtime journalist for *Wired* magazine, or as a social media presence so profound that he was named by *Time* magazine as having one of the best Twitter feeds in 2011. A onetime assistant to poet Allen Ginsberg, Silberman is active in the Buddhist community, the LGBT community, the autism community, the liberal political activist community, and the overall mensch community. It is clear, though, that winning a gold record for coproducing the Dead's career-spanning box set *So Many Roads (1965–1995)* is near the top of his list of proud accomplishments. Silberman may be many other things to many other people, but he is always a Deadhead to the end. As he says, "There is a feeling of homecoming and consolation to listening to live Grateful Dead tapes that is still absolutely present for me. There is nothing else like it in my life. I absolutely assume that if I live so long as to end up in a nursing home, that I will want to listen to a lot of Grateful Dead, because it is where I feel most comfortable and most alive in the world."

So the question is, what does Silberman—a card-carrying member of the Deadhead intelligentsia—think of Cornell '77? "If you listen to all the shows that were recorded around that time, Cornell still has a stature that is *sui generis*. It stands on its own. It's an exquisite show. It deserves its accolades." Does Silberman think it's the best Dead show ever? No. But mainly because he doesn't believe such a thing is possible. "I disagree with the notion that there could be a greatest Grateful Dead show. I would never say that Cornell is clearly the greatest Dead show. That's ridiculous. There are ten other shows that are as good. But as good in different ways. I would never pit the Dead against themselves and say, 'Well, this is clearly the best show.'"

But he will allow that there can be better and best recordings, and here again the Cantor-Jackson tapes figure in the assessment of Cornell '77. "It was clearly the best-quality recording of one of the very best performances of their career, and that's why it has this iconic status in history and deserves it."

For every Cornell '77 lover, an equally emphatic hater exists. As Abraham Lincoln said while adapting the wisdom of fifteenth-century English poet John Lydgate: "You can please some of the people all of the time, you can please all of the people some of the time, but you can't please all of the people all of the time." It is with this aphorism in mind that we must swallow, with a grain of salt, the words of such Internet commentators as Poo Face, whose blunt assessment of Cornell '77 reads in sum total: "Grossly overrated." Forty years ago, Richard Ellenson, writing for the aptly titled *Good Times Gazette* of Ithaca, agreed with Poo Face in his review of the show: "The Dead show was pleasing, but it also was flawed. There was enough energy in their music to keep the crowd on their feet, but they did not seem able to sustain their image." Ellenson then rolls out sweeping indictments pertaining to consistency, harmonics, and weak improvisations. His concluding judgment was that, in May 1977, the Dead's best days were behind them.

In the opinion of Poo Face (and Richard Ellenson), Cornell '77 is grossly overrated. Plenty of other Dead fans feel the same way about the Ithaca show. Discussion board comments regarding Cornell '77 run the gamut from "meh" to sounding more like a Barton Hall Hater's Convention:

Nothing against anyone who thinks this is like the greatest dead show of all time, but I have to firmly Disagree. If you have ever heard Hartford from this same month and year on some heady doses, this show isn't shit compared to that. Have to give [it to] this show and every other from May of '77, but Hartford just incapacitated me. Just my opinion.   —Murphy

Good show, but c'mon. Jerry is obviously struggling during the Scarlet Begonias solo. Tight, good energy, but hardly the show of shows.   —Anonymous

I don't know. I've listened to this show about ten times now and I don't see what the fuss is all about. It's not bad but I have yet to lose sleep thinking about this concert. I have heard Grateful Dead shows that have made me almost cry from the music and this one does not do it for me. Someone please explain why this show deserves to be up there along with The Field Trip, Dick's Picks 4, Dick's Picks 18 and The Winterland Shows?   —Will

Best show ever? Not even close. Get real. No show without Pig Pen and TC can be the best ever. Whoever says it's the best ever needs to have more than 5 shows in their collection. Give me a frickin break.   —wtf

This show is overrated, 1977 is overrated. The best music the Dead ever played is to be found in 1972, 1973 and 1974. 1977 has some great jams yes but there ain't no weirdness. 72–74 weirdness and great jamming transcends 1977 just jamming. The Dead without weirdness is like a jelly donut without jelly. The donut still tastes really good. But it doesn't have any jelly.   —The Truth

While never saying anything negative—or positive for that matter—even Bob Weir has had some fun at Cornell '77s expense. In a playful segment broadcast from his TRI studios, Weir, seated behind an interview desk and chatting with Dead roadie Steve Parish and archivist David Lemieux, addresses a nasty rumor that has been floating around the Dead community for years: "It's been a long time; I think it's unclassified." He looks around in a shifty, conspiratorial way, and then confides to the audience, "The deal is, that legendary Cornell show never happened."

Bob Weir built TRI Studios, his self-described "playpen for musicians," specifically for the purpose of broadcasting live performances on the Internet. Its official launch was Friday the thirteenth, May 2011. The facility uses the website tristudios.com as its online home base. In true Dead fashion, every aspect of the studio's sound quality is fine-tuned to within an inch of its life. It is clear to me, having spent time at the facility and spoken to its employees, that no expense was spared in making sure that—to paraphrase Weir's words on several recordings talking about the Grateful Dead's sound aspirations—everything was just exactly perfect.

In August 2012, I had the good fortune to spend a few days at TRI while musicians rehearsed and then performed for Jerry Garcia's seventieth birthday concert. The show was dubbed *Move Me Brightly* and featured Mike Gordon from Phish on bass, along with Jeff Chimenti, Joe Russo, Neal Cassal, and many others, including Donna Jean Godchaux and Phil Lesh. Eventually that show was released as a documentary concert film directed by Bill Kreutzmann's son, Justin.

TRI wasn't built for crowds. It was built to make you feel like you were sitting in a small, intimate club watching artists perform under relaxed and exquisitely orchestrated conditions. The whole time I was there, I was expecting to get kicked out. I had been invited there under the auspices of a combination book and documentary film project (titled *JAMerica*) that I was working on about the jam band scene. In fact, my *JAMerica* documentary project partners, Denver Miller and J. R. Kraus, filmed many of the interviews and much of the performance footage that appeared on the *Move Me Brightly* documentary. I had spent so many years watching Weir from a distance, though, that I felt certain someone would take issue with my hanging around this close to him for so long. But no one ever did. At one point, I found myself the only non-musician in the room while the band was running through a take of "He's Gone." I sat on a chair fifteen feet in front of the stage and sang along with every word. I couldn't help myself. At one point, Weir locked eyes with me and I froze, afraid that I had committed the faux pas that would get me tossed once and for all: undue reverence. Instead, he set down his guitar, pulled a stool over, and sat down next to me. No words were spoken. We just sat there, side by side, the singing done, as Weir listened to the band he had assembled playing the ending to "He's Gone" in tribute to his beloved, departed best friend. In a lifetime filled with many transcendent Grateful Dead moments, this was, by far, my most intimate. It is a musical memory that brings a warm glow of joy every time I recall it.

That's what it felt like to be in TRI. Warm. Familiar. Familial. Like you were a guest in Weir's home. So it was a fitting place for him to deliver a tongue-in-cheek revelation about Barton Hall during his equally tongue-in-cheek talk show, *Weir Here*, which he broadcast from TRI in 2013. Weir gleefully continued spinning out the details of one of the favorite conspiracy theories in an occasionally paranoid Deadhead universe: "A lot of folks think they were there. If you think you were there, just ask yourself: were you in a 7–11 or a Burger King or something like that, and somebody came up to you—somebody from 'the company'—and said, 'Hey, you look like just the kind of guy who might dig this hat!' It was sort of a well-made, sort of semi-elegant tin hat. We were playing over here in San Rafael at Front Street, our studio, and it was a very successful experiment. People still to this day think that concert actually happened. And they enjoyed themselves thoroughly! That's the great thing, man. Where's the downside there? We didn't even play that well!"

As hard as it may be to swallow, there are those who believe that Cornell '77 was actually part of a mind-control experiment conducted by the CIA (which, using insider slang, Weir refers to as "the company"). They believe that, in fact, the show never happened at all—that it was either played at an alternate location (in Bob's version, it's the Dead's Front Street studio space) or that the recording is spliced together from different shows and presented as a single show from 5/8/77. The "spliced-together" camp even circulated a list of the origin shows from which the Cornell '77 track list could have been fabricated:

"Barton Hall, Ithaca, NY 5/8/77"

Track Listing Actual Source

1. Minglewood Blues [4:47] Winterland 3/20/77
2. Loser [7:30] Springfield 4/23/77
3. El Paso [4:22] Chicago 5/13/77
4. They Love Each Other [6:59] Lakeland 5/21/77
5. Jack Straw [6:00] Tempe 10/6/77
6. Deal [5:43] St. Paul 5/11/77
7. Lazy Lightnin' [3:29] > St. Louis 5/15/77
8. Supplication [4:21]
9. Brown-Eyed Women [5:12] Winterland 6/8/77
10. Mama Tried [2:37] Seattle 9/29/77
11. Row Jimmy [10:52] Fox, Atlanta 5/19/77
12. Dancin' in the Streets [15:43] Pembroke Pines 5/22/77 (DP3)

Set II:

13. Scarlet Begonias [9:14] > ???
14. Fire on the Mountain [15:21] ???
15. Estimated Prophet [8:32] Passaic NJ 4/27/77
16. St. Stephen [4:43] > Mostly Passaic NJ 6/18/76
17. Not Fade Away [16:22] > with some tricky splicing of the
18. St. Stephen [1:53] > middle of an unidentified NFA
19. Morning Dew [13:36] Cow Palace 12/31/76
    Encore:
20. One More Saturday Night [4:54] Springfield 4/23/77

Because the conspiracy theory posits the hoax as a CIA "experiment," there is no need to explain why such an elaborate scheme would be orchestrated (other than the fact that the entire band were actually secret agents, duh). It was a mind-control experiment. That's just what the CIA does. After all, it is a well-documented (and actually true) fact that the CIA's MK-ULTRA program experimented with using LSD for the purposes of mind control in and around the Bay Area in the 1960s. So why not mess with the cream of San Francisco's hippie music scene too?

It would certainly not be the first "mind test" the Dead participated in. During a run of shows at the Capitol Theatre in Port Chester, 1971, the entire audience participated in long-distance ESP experiments being conducted by parapsychologists Montague Ullman, Stanley Krippner, and Charles Hornorton under the auspices of the Maimonides Hospital in Brooklyn. The experiment was focused on dream telepathy. The audience was shown slides that were being projected onto a large screen above the stage, one image per night over a six-night period. The audience—and band—were instructed to try to "send" the images with their minds to British psychic subject Malcolm Bessent, who—asleep each night by 11:30 in order to receive the transmissions—would then record what images had appeared in his dreams. There was also a second receiver in the experiment, a medical technician named Felicia Parise, whose participation was never mentioned to the audience. When the test was completed, out of the six nights the experiment was conducted, Bessent had reportedly dreamed on four of those nights about the picture the concert audience focused on, a result that is statistically greater than chance alone would allow for. Parise, on the other hand, reportedly dreamed about the picture only one out of six times. While the data didn't prove anything conclusively, the test was fascinating, and the results (including the possibility that Parise's score would have been higher if the images sent to her weren't "displaced in time") were published in the *Journal of the American Society of Psychosomatic Dentistry and Medicine* under the title "An Experiment in Dream Telepathy with the Grateful Dead."

As Weir says in his TRI broadcast, "Where's the downside there?"

While the CIA–Cornell '77 conspiracy theory is an outrageous tale, to be sure, it is also one that perfectly fits an old saying that came about during another set of tests that the Grateful Dead participated in: the Acid Tests. The saying goes, "Never trust a prankster." With such a large popular following, Cornell '77 was bound to become a target for Deadhead pranksters looking to stir up trouble. In the comments section of a website called "The Setlist Program"—a searchable database of Dead shows that also allows visitors to discuss them—a commenter using the name "clarson" writes,

> It isn't widely known but Cornell was actually the second test of these mind control procedures. The first occurred in mid-1975 and was a dismal failure. 2 major mistakes were

made. First, they picked the one time that the Dead were not touring. This created all sorts of problems with the subject audience. The more serious mistake was in not updating the criteria of the experiment. Due to typical government inefficiency, they used the 1969 version of the Dead that was playing when the program was conceived. The sudden appearance of Pigpen, who had died 2 years earlier, literally blew the minds of those in attendance. 6 months were spent erasing all traces of the "show" and carefully rebuilding as much of their minds as possible. The subjects were eventually released and most of them became evangelists, their only lingering memory of the whole experiment being an unshakeable belief that they'd witnessed a true miracle.

Yup, never trust a prankster.

For many Deadheads, though, Cornell '77 is neither a hoax nor a miracle. A good show, to be sure, but not worth all the hype around it. Even the original Grateful Dead vault archivist Dick Latvala changed his opinion about the status of Cornell '77 over the years. His posts on an Internet forum group known as "Dead-net Central" ranged from the benignly dismissive, in which he called Cornell '77 "the most over-rated show in G.D. history," to a full-blown and detailed list titled "About 20 Shows That Would Be Better Releases Than 5/8/77, from the Year 1977," that includes such thoughts as

(1) 2/26 & 2/27—The first 2 shows of the year, and together would make a much better and way more fulfilling listening experience than Ithaca.

(4) Both the night before and the night after (5/7 & 5/9) would be more pleasing as releases.

(12) Each of the next 5 nights [11/1/–11/6] rips Ithaca. But the 11/4>6 shows are difficult to choose between. If I had to pick one of the three, I would have to go with 11/6.

And the concluding note, "So maybe this doesn't total 20 shows, but it gives a pretty clear idea of where I place 5/8/77 amongst the meat from this year. I don't feel it's necessary to point out what is specifically lacking on the 5/8 show, since this would only further distance it from the shows listed above."

Ouch. Death don't have no mercy, and apparently neither does Dick Latvala on a roll. I'm not sure how he got so far from the original thoughts he jotted down about Cornell in his notebook in 1977—"There are shows where they excel on some of the above tunes, but overall, I haven't heard a finer show"—to his Deadnet Central thoughts—"The shows on 5/15, 5/17, 5/18 and 5/21 are each deserving notation, and although they don't match up with 5/22, they are each more satisfying than 5/8." But somewhere along the bumpy, long, winding road toward an official release of the concert, Latvala changed his tune about Barton Hall. It is certainly Latvala's prerogative as a fanatic to change his opinion. It's also the prerogative of Poo Face, wtf, and The Truth to air their opinions online.

That's the beauty of the Internet. It's the place to let your voice join the chorus of experts, pranksters, fanatics, and trolls. C'mon let's jam together! Cornell '77 is the best show ever. Cornell '77 is totally overrated. Cornell '77 is transcendent. Cornell '77 is bunk. Cornell '77 is the epitome of Grateful Dead musicianship. Cornell '77 is a donut without the jelly. Cornell '77 is barely worth mentioning. Let's talk about Cornell '77 all night long. . . .

A Band Out of Time

There is a continuum that I feel when we're playing "Dark Star" that I've felt all along. There's a sort of deep, dark-planets-and-space feel to it that I've always felt about that song.   —Bob Weir

There is a place in the universe where "Dark Star" is always playing. I don't mean that in the sense that somewhere someone is undoubtedly listening to a recording of "Dark Star." There is truth in that as well. But what I really mean is that "Dark Star" is woven into the fabric of the universe, or, better imagined, there is a room that exists somewhere in the cosmos and you can access that room through a door, and once you open the door you realize that the room exists exclusively as a place for "Dark Star" to play for all eternity. Whatever bits and pieces of "Dark Star" you have heard are beautiful and ornate, yes, but only snippets of the larger truth, which is that "Dark Star" began with one single note that was waiting patiently to be sounded, and once it was, the entire song began unfolding with no need of players, or a stage, or instruments, or even ears to hear it. Truly, it is wondrous to hear "Dark Star." But we need "Dark Star" more than "Dark Star" needs us. It strikes the tuning fork of our existence rather than the other way around. Nobody plays or hears "Dark Star"; we simply bear witness to it.

The Grateful Dead's great gift was as gatekeepers to the door behind which "Dark Star" played. Only the Dead could open that door. Once they did, the band members joined us while we became absorbed in its power for as long as they could keep the door from closing. Then we would listen to recordings of the most recent visit to the room and wait patiently for the next trip. Sometimes that could take months. One time it took 1,535 days. No matter. "Dark Star" was always there, playing just outside of time.

Are the Dead outside of time too? After spending a year listening obsessively to Cornell '77, it occurs to me that, musically speaking, they just might be. I don't mean "out of step" with the times, which is a different and more pedestrian concern. The Dead were never out of fashion, because they were never in fashion. Or, as we may remember what Bob Weir said to Tom Snyder on *The Tomorrow Show*, "I don't think we've stayed current. I don't think we ever were current."

It's true that the band was more or less popular in terms of ticket and album sales in any given year. But those numbers existed apart from the music and were barely attached to the Grateful Dead as a creative entity. They were as much a mystery to the members of the band as they were to the musical critics who were forced to contend with a group they would much rather dismiss out of hand. As one critic put it: "The criticisms are obvious and plentiful. These guys were nothing but a bunch of dirty hippies. Their voices sucked. They played 40 minute songs based around an average (at best) guitarist improvising over a basic scale. They went like 30 years between hit songs, if you can even call them hits. Yet they've been a fixture of popular music since the mid-1960s and had a dedicated fandom of hundreds of thousands for the whole time."

Jerry "Average (at best)" Garcia looked at it this way: "We always were anachronistic. We have always been out of time."

Love them or hate them, the Dead just don't go away. They won't go away. How can a band that exists out of time ever go away? In 2015, twenty years after Jerry Garcia died and the group disbanded, the remaining members—the "core four," if you will—took the official Grateful Dead name out of mothballs and immediately sold out two nights at Levi's Stadium in Santa Clara and three nights at Soldier Field in Chicago. The combined attendance number for the five concerts was 361,933, and the pay per view live streams of the shows set the record for the biggest PPV musical event in history, with more than 400,000 streams being broadcasted across all formats. All said and done, the shows turned a profit of $52.2 million.

But here's the thing: none of that matters. If we are truly and deeply talking about Grateful Dead music, none of that matters at all. In fact, I will go so far as to say there is no such thing as a show played at Cornell on May 8, 1977, either. Not because it was a hoax perpetrated by the U.S. government for the sake of mind-control testing or some such nonsense. No, this involves a different hoax entirely. My hoax theory is based on the belief that every time the musicians constituting the Grateful Dead played, they were simply acting as gatekeepers to the door behind which every note of Grateful Dead music exists and continues for all eternity. Cornell '77 doesn't exist, because there are no individual shows at all. There is simply one never-ending show called Grateful Dead music. It exists beyond time and has no location. It started with the first note played and will continue through all eternity. In my theory, becoming attached to any one specific show, or even the band members themselves, is nothing but folly. That sort of attachment is the true hoax. Listen to what Jerry is telling you. "We have always been out of time."

That is one way to look at Cornell '77. However, it is not the only way. The other way involves contemplating the event as a concert that was played by a band called the Grateful Dead in Barton Hall at Cornell University in 1977. Hoax or not, the latter is the view I've wrangled with in this book. That is the lens through which the interviews were conducted. That is how I will stumble forward to my final conclusion, which is this: *Cornell '77 is a damn fine Grateful Dead show.*

Is it the best one the band ever played? Absolutely, without a doubt, that is impossible to say. There were bum notes, blown transitions, and shaky vocals here and there. It *was* a Grateful Dead show, after all. Squeaky-clean polished performances were for Lawrence Welk or Donny Osmond. However, if you love Grateful Dead music, warts and all, it is impossible not to appreciate Cornell '77. It is an exceptional Dead show. Even if you hate the late 1970s version of "Dancin' in the Streets" and feel that the "Mama Tried" is undistinguished kitsch and—just for the hell of it—strip out every other song they played that night and evaluate it based solely on the "Scarlet" > "Fire," Cornell '77 would still be a must-hear sequence of GD music. Throw in the "Morning Dew" and you've hit epic levels of Grateful Dead excellence. In many ways, Cornell '77 earns its bones as one of the all-time great Dead shows based on those songs alone. To refine it further, the emotive power of "Morning Dew" and the dynamic and fluid transition between "Scarlet Begonias" and "Fire on the Mountain" are some of the best examples of what made the Grateful Dead special that you will find captured on tape. You can argue against that if you want. But you'll be wrong.

But by all means, let's argue. That's half the fun of being fanatical about anything—sports, films, the stock market, mathematical theorems, and, yes, your favorite band. Whatever ranking you may or may not give Cornell '77 (including following the anti-ranking wisdom of David Gans: "I'm not a big believer in top tens and ranking shit. It just bores the hell out of me"), the beauty of the show is that it was played at all. Whatever it may or may not be, it is singular Grateful Dead music: a moment of fully realized creativity that can neither be created nor destroyed, but only converted into different forms of energy. I've known mopey Deadheads who could take a perfectly fine Dead show and convert it into enough negative energy to paint a rainbow black. I've known starry-eyed Deadheads who could elevate the most standard run-through of "El Paso" into enough positive energy to light up every window between Rochester, New York, and Rosa's cantina (where Felina would whirl). As the old saying goes, "There's no accounting for taste." Or, as the new saying goes, "Haters gonna hate."

The day after the Barton Hall show, the *Ithaca Times* said of the concert, "The Dead kept to their solidly patterned style with the ever prominent guitar of Jerry Garcia carrying songs on for 20 minutes. Garcia's mastery of the guitar, while amazing, approached monotony by the latter half of the concert." Damn that boringly extended "Morning Dew" crescendo. There's just no accounting for taste, huh?

One of the things I love most about the Grateful Dead is that there is a show, a song, an era, a transition between songs, or even a particular sequence of notes, for every mood. Sometimes I feel almost guilty about how much Grateful Dead music I listen to. Almost. When it comes right down to it, though, I listen to the Grateful Dead every day because there is Grateful Dead music that fits every place—physical, psychological, spiritual—that I find myself in. To put it plainly, there is never a wrong time for me to listen to the Grateful Dead. I listen to lots of other music, too, and on any given week will dip my toe into every genre, subgenre, and sub-subgenre of music that's available. But chances are, for anywhere from five minutes to five hours every day, there will be Grateful Dead music playing in my life.

That is another reason that 5/8/77 has continued to be revered and passed down by subsequent generations of Dead fans. The show contains a little something for everyone. Want a sweet love song? Try on this gorgeous "They Love Each Other." Feel like a good stomp around your yard? Here's a ripping "Brown Eyed Women." How about a little slinky jazz-fusion while you make it with a groovy chick on your shag carpet? This "Lazy Lightning" / "Supplication" will work just fine. Need a good cry? Look no further than this heart-wrenching "Morning Dew."

Whether you want to dance, cry, sigh, whoop it up, cool it down, or just strap in and ride the full roller-coaster of human emotion, Cornell '77 has it all. This is the show to give to someone who's never heard the Grateful Dead and wants to see what all the fuss is about. It's also the show for hard-core Deadheads who never get tired of hearing the band during a peak tour. You can play a tune from Cornell for your mother, your lover, your brother, your rabbi . . . butcher, baker, candlestick maker, and proudly say, "*This* is the Grateful Dead! *This* is what I've been talking about all these years!" Thanks to Betty Cantor-Jackson's gorgeous original recording and the long-awaited and stunningly crisp official Rhino release of the show, the majesty, mastery, magnificence, and myth of Cornell '77 is available with, as they say, the push of a button. No matter how you listen to it, once you dial in the music and turn it up loud, the conclusion is always the same: *5/8/77 is a damn fine Grateful Dead show.*

Long live Cornell '77.

Long live the Grateful Dead.

Listening and Reading

The "Listening and Reading" section provides information on research sources that were utilized in the writing of *Cornell '77*. In many cases, information on the history of the Grateful Dead was gleaned and confirmed by multiple sources in addition to interviews. In those cases, I have provided endnotes for the primary resource that I used, but I give thanks to the other resources that allowed for the information to be confirmed.

All quotes, information, and anecdotes about Cornell alumni, including members of the Cornell Concert Commission, attendees of the Cornell '77 show, and Heather Horsley, were taken from original interviews that I conducted in the course of writing this book. I can't thank those individuals enough for sharing their stories with me so that I could share them with you. In the course of writing *Cornell '77*, I also conducted dozens of informal, off-the-record interviews with Grateful Dead fans about the Cornell show and various facets of Deadhead culture. While those individuals are not quoted directly anywhere in this book, I wish to acknowledge them for contributing to its writing and thank them for sharing their passion for the Grateful Dead.

The factual information given in the "First Set" and "Second Set" chapters of this book relied heavily on a select number of trusted sources. In addition to naming those sources in this section, I wish to single them out for specific note. Those key sources are *Deadbase 50* by John W. Scott, Stu Nixon, and Michael Dolgushkin, David Dodd's "Greatest Stories Ever Told" section on Dead.net, and Dodd's book *The Complete Annotated Grateful Dead Lyrics*. It should also be noted that the track time references given in the "First Set" and "Second Set" chapters are approximations taken from various online postings of the show, which each vary slightly; they are intended to get readers within seconds of the referred to musical moments.

In the case of the legal arguments around the "Betty Board" recordings, some interviewees wished to remain anonymous owing to ongoing negotiations and legal situations that were unfolding, as may now be apparent, up to the time of publication. I have respected their wishes while also taking the precaution of confirming any statements around the ownership of the Betty Board recordings with multiple sources. The story of the auction and reclamation of certain Betty Board reels was gleaned from interviews with some principals, including Betty Cantor-Jackson, as well as from Rob Eaton's essay "Betty Board Story," in *Deadbase 50*; Nick Paumgarten's article "Deadhead: The Afterlife," from the *New Yorker*; and Dean Budnick's article "What's Become of the Bettys? The Fate of the Long Lost Soundboards," from *Relix* magazine. I want to especially thank Betty Cantor-Jackson for granting me a candid, in-depth interview, and for making some of the best live Grateful Dead recordings ever.

The anecdotes and quotes that make up the bulk of the chapter "The Show That Never Happened" are taken from new interviews conducted for this book with Mark Pinkus, David Lemieux, Nicholas Meriwether, Dennis McNally, and Steve Silberman. I deeply appreciate the time and insights that each one shared with me.

RECORDS AND DISCS

The first three studio albums in this section are most relevant to the Dead's sound at the time of Barton Hall show:

Blues for Allah (United Artists, released September 1, 1975; 44 minutes, 13 seconds recorded time). The record rose as high as number 12 on the *Billboard* chart of pop albums in 1975.

Side One
1. "Help on the Way" (Jerry Garcia and Robert Hunter)— 3:15 (lead singer: Jerry Garcia)
   "Slipknot!" (instrumental) (Jerry Garcia, Keith Godchaux, Bill Kreutzmann, Phil Lesh, and Bob Weir)—4:03
2. "Franklin's Tower" (Jerry Garcia, Robert Hunter, and Bill Kreutzmann)—4:37 (lead singer: Jerry Garcia)
3. "King Solomon's Marbles"
   "Part 1: Stronger Than Dirt" (instrumental) (Phil Lesh)—1:55

"Part 2: Milkin' the Turkey" (instrumental) (Mickey
Hart, Bill Kreutzmann, and Phil Lesh)—3:25

4. "The Music Never Stopped" (John Perry Barlow and
Bob Weir)—4:35 (lead singer: Bob Weir)

Side Two

5. "Crazy Fingers" (Jerry Garcia and Robert Hunter)—6:41
(lead singer: Jerry Garcia)

6. "Sage & Spirit" (instrumental) (Bob Weir)—3:07

7. "Blues for Allah" (Jerry Garcia and Robert Hunter)—3:21
(lead singers: the Grateful Dead)

"Sand Castles and Glass Camels" (Jerry Garcia,
Donna Godchaux, Keith Godchaux, Mickey Hart, Bill
Kreutzmann, Phil Lesh, and Bob Weir)—5:26

"Unusual Occurrences in the Desert" (Jerry Garcia and
Robert Hunter)—3:48

Initial CD release was in 1995, by Arista Records. A remastered
and expanded version was released as part of *Beyond Description
(1973–1989)*, a twelve-CD box set issued in 2004 by Rhino
Records as a compilation of all the Dead's albums released during
those years by Grateful Dead Records and Arista Records.

Terrapin Station (Arista Records, released July 27, 1977; 35 minutes, 38 seconds recorded time). The record rose as high as number
28 on the *Billboard* chart of pop albums in 1977 and went gold, according to the Recording Industry Association of America.

Side One

1. "Estimated Prophet" (John Perry Barlow and Bob
Weir)—5:37 (lead singer: Bob Weir)

2. "Dancin' in the Streets" (Marvin Gaye, Ivy Jo Hunter, and William "Mickey" Stevenson)—3:16 (lead singers: the Grateful Dead)

3. "Passenger" (Phil Lesh and Peter Monk)— 2:48 (lead singers: Bob Weir, Donna Godchaux)

4. "Samson and Delilah" (traditional)—3:29 (lead singer: Bob Weir)

5. "Sunrise" (Donna Godchaux)—4:03 (lead singer: Donna Godchaux)

Side Two

6. "Terrapin Station Part 1"—16:17 (lead singer: Jerry Garcia)
   - "Lady with a Fan" (Jerry Garcia and Robert Hunter)
   - "Terrapin Station" (Jerry Garcia and Robert Hunter)
   - "Terrapin" (Jerry Garcia and Robert Hunter)
   - "Terrapin Transit" (Mickey Hart and Bill Kreutzmann)
   - "At a Siding" (Mickey Hart and Robert Hunter)
   - "Terrapin Flyer" (Mickey Hart and Bill Kreutzmann)
   - "Refrain" (Jerry Garcia and Robert Hunter)

The album was released for the first time on CD in 1987 and was reissued by BMG International, also on CD, in 2000. A remastered and expanded version was released as part of *Beyond Description (1973–1989)*, a twelve-CD box set issued in 2004, by Rhino Records, as a compilation of all the Dead's albums released during those years by Grateful Dead Records and Arista Records.

Shakedown Street (Arista Records, released November 15, 1978; 39 minutes, 4 seconds recorded time). The record rose as high as number 41 on the *Billboard* chart of pop albums in 1979 and went gold, according to the Recording Industry Association of America.

Side One

1. "Good Lovin'" (Rudy Clark and Arthur Resnick)—
   4:51 (lead singer: Bob Weir)
2. "France" (Mickey Hart, Robert Hunter, and Bob Weir)—
   4:03 (lead singers: Bob Weir, Donna Godchaux)
3. "Shakedown Street" (Jerry Garcia and Robert
   Hunter)—4:59 (lead singer: Jerry Garcia)
4. "Serengetti" (instrumental) (Mickey Hart and Bill
   Kreutzmann)—1:59
5. "Fire on the Mountain" (Mickey Hart and Robert
   Hunter)—3:46 (lead singer: Jerry Garcia)

Side Two

6. "I Need a Miracle" (John Perry Barlow and Bob
   Weir)—3:36 (lead singer: Bob Weir)
7. "From the Heart of Me" (Donna Jean Godchaux)—
   3:23 (lead singer: Donna Godchaux)
8. "Stagger Lee" (Jerry Garcia and Robert Hunter)—
   3:25 (lead singer: Jerry Garcia)
9. "All New Minglewood Blues" (Noah Lewis)—
   4:12 (lead singer: Bob Weir)
10. "If I Had the World to Give" (Jerry Garcia and Robert
    Hunter)—4:50 (lead singer: Jerry Garcia)

Arista Records released the album on CD in 1987, and it was later issued, also on CD, by BMG International in 2000. A remastered and expanded version was released as part of *Beyond Description (1973–1989)*, a twelve-CD box set issued in 2004 by Rhino Records as a compilation of all the Dead's albums released during those years by Grateful Dead Records and Arista Records.

So Many Roads (1965–1995) (Arista Records, released November 7, 1999; 386 minutes and 22 seconds recorded time). This is a five-disc box set by the Grateful Dead. Primarily consisting of concert recordings from different periods of the band's history, it also contains several songs recorded in the studio. All but one of the tracks were previously unreleased. The album was certified a gold record by the Recording Industry Association of America in 2000 and went to the position of 170 on the *Billboard* pop album chart that same year. Rhino rereleased this set of recordings in 2004.

Disc One
1. "Can't Come Down" (Grateful Dead)
2. "Caution" (Grateful Dead)
3. "You Don't Have to Ask" (Grateful Dead)
4. "On the Road Again" (traditional)
5. "Cream Puff War" (Jerry Garcia)
6. "I Know You Rider" (traditional)
7. "The Same Thing" (Willie Dixon)
8. "Dark Star" > "China Cat Sunflower" > "The Eleven" (Grateful Dead / Robert Hunter)
9. "Clementine" (Phil Lesh / Robert Hunter)
10. "Mason's Children" (Jerry Garcia / Phil Lesh / Bob Weir / Robert Hunter)
11. "To Lay Me Down" (Jerry Garcia / Robert Hunter)

Disc Two
1. "That's It for the Other One" (Grateful Dead)
2. "Beautiful Jam" (Grateful Dead)
3. "Chinatown Shuffle" (Ron McKernan)
4. "Sing Me Back Home" (Merle Haggard)

5. Watkins Glen Soundcheck Jam (mentioned on pp. 159–60)
6. "Dark Star Jam" > "Spanish Jam" > "U.S. Blues" (Jerry Garcia / Robert Hunter)

Disc Three
1. "Eyes of the World" (Jerry Garcia / Robert Hunter)
2. "The Wheel" (Jerry Garcia / Robert Hunter)
3. "Stella Blue" (Jerry Garcia / Robert Hunter)
4. "Estimated Prophet" (John Barlow / Bob Weir)
5. "The Music Never Stopped" (John Barlow / Bob Weir)
6. "Shakedown Street" (Jerry Garcia / Robert Hunter)

Disc Four
1. "Cassidy" (Bob Weir / John Barlow)
2. "Hey Pocky Way" (Zigaboo Modeliste / Art Neville / Leo Nocentelli / George Porter Jr.)
3. "Believe It or Not" (Jerry Garcia / Robert Hunter)
4. "Playing in the Band" (Mickey Hart / Robert Hunter / Bob Weir)
5. "Gentlemen, Start Your Engines" (John Barlow / Brent Mydland)
6. "Death Don't Have No Mercy" (Gary Davis)
7. "Scarlet Begonias" (Jerry Garcia / Robert Hunter)
8. "Bird Song" (Jerry Garcia / Robert Hunter)
9. "Jam Out of Terrapin" (Grateful Dead)

Disc Five
1. "Terrapin Station" (Jerry Garcia / Robert Hunter)
2. "Jam out of Foolish Heart" (Grateful Dead)
3. "Way to Go Home" (Bob Bralove / Robert Hunter / Vince Welnick)

4. "Liberty" (Jerry Garcia / Robert Hunter)
5. "Lazy River Road" (Jerry Garcia / Robert Hunter)
6. "Eternity" (Willie Dixon / Rob Wasserman / Bob Weir)
7. "Jam into Days Between" (Grateful Dead)
8. "Days Between" (Jerry Garcia / Robert Hunter)
9. "Whiskey in the Jar" (traditional)
10. "So Many Roads" (Jerry Garcia / Robert Hunter)

MP3S AND STREAMS

Three of the key shows to listen to while reading this book, in addition to the Barton Hall concert, are now available as part of the Rhino box set, *May 1977: Get Shown the Light*. Those shows are New Haven Veterans Memorial Coliseum 5/5/77, Boston Garden 5/7/77, and Buffalo Memorial Auditorium 5/9/77. Here is a list of other relevant shows and URLs to access digital streams:

The Spectrum, Philadelphia, 4/22/77

https://archive.org/details/gd77-04-22.sbd.miller.27747.sbeok.flacf
This show kicked off the Dead's East Coast tour that spring.

Hartford (CT) Civic Center, 5/28/77

https://archive.org/details/gd77-05-28.sbd.sacks.4983.sbefail.shnf
This show was the last of the spring's East Coast tour. In June the Dead would be back on the West Coast, and their tour would kick off on June 4 at the Fabulous Forum in Inglewood, California.

Cow Palace, Daly City, CA, 3/23/74

https://archive.org/details/gd1974-03-23.sbd.clugston-orf.1995.sbeok.shnf
Young Deadhead David Gans went to see this show, and a week later his buddy "Feldstein" had a reel of it. From *Cornell '77*,

p. 46: "There was this moment in 'China Cat Sunflower' when they get to the bridge, that E chord in the bridge, and Phil hit this note that rattled the whole building. And when we listened to it on the tape it distorted the tape too! It was like, 'Oh my god, that's so cool!'"

Nassau Coliseum, Uniondale, NY, 5/6/81

https://archive.org/details/gd81-05-06.glassberg.vernon.17697.sbeok.shnf
The "Bobby Sands show" attended by Dead publicist Dennis McNally. From *Cornell '77*, pp. 49–50: Weir dedicated "He's Gone" to Sands, and then, after the "He's Gone," McNally remembers, the band "went into this ten-minute blur of a jam that was just brilliant."

Grand Prix Raceway, Watkins Glen, NY, 7/27/73

https://archive.org/details/gd73-07-28.sbd.weiner.14196.sbeok.shnf
Steve Silberman at the age of sixteen made the trek to western New York with six hundred thousand other music fans. He would travel by ferry, Greyhound bus, and by catching rides with strangers. It was Silberman's initiation into the Grateful Dead, and, in many ways, adulthood. Or, as Silberman puts it, "Going to Watkins Glen was quite an ordeal for a little nerd from New York."

Kingswood Music Theatre, Maple, Ontario, 6/30/87

https://archive.org/details/gd87-06-30.matrix.hinko.13442.sbeok.shnf
First Dead show I attended.

Rich Stadium, Buffalo, NY, 6/13/93

https://archive.org/details/gd93-06-13.schoeps.ladner.8584.sbeok.shnf
Last Dead show I attended.

CONVERSATIONS

Angwin, Peter. By phone on December 24, 2015.

Burke, Stephen. By phone on February 3, 2016.

Cantor-Jackson, Betty. By phone on May 5, 2016.

Eaton, Rob. In person on January 18, 2012.

Ellenberg, Todd. Interview by Peter Conners on the radio show *Tales from the Golden Road*, hosted by David Gans and Gary Lambert, Sirius / XM Grateful Dead radio channel, December 27, 2015 (hereafter "On *Tales from the Golden Road*").

Gans, David. In person on November 9, 2010.

Gans, David. On *Tales from the Golden Road*.

Gilles, Lisa. By phone on December 30, 2015.

Gross, Louis J. By e-mail on April 7, 2016.

Horowitz, Richard. By phone on March 3, 2016.

Horsley, Heather. By e-mail on February 20, 2016.

Kesey, Sunshine. By e-mail on December 1, 2015.

Koh, Rick. On *Tales from the Golden Road*.

Krakow, Brad. By forwarded e-mail on January 22, 2010.

Lambert, Gary. On *Tales from the Golden Road*.

Lemieux, David. By phone on January 28, 2016.

Mattson, Jeff. In person on January 18, 2012.

Mattson, Mark. By e-mail on August 23, 2016.

McEvoy, Mike. On *Tales from the Golden Road*.

McNally, Dennis. By phone on June 13, 2016.

Meriwether, Nicholas. By phone on May 1, 2016, and August 19, 2016.

Moore, Jerry. Interview by David Gans for the radio show *Tales from the Golden Road*, hosted by David Gans and Gary Lambert, Sirius / XM Grateful Dead radio channel, January 2008. Thank you to David for sharing that interview with me for use in *Cornell '77*.

Narad, JoAnne. On *Tales from the Golden Road*.

Pinkus, Mark. By phone on March 10, 2016.

Prouty, Eve. By phone on March 12, 2016.

Richardson, Peter. By e-mail on June 7, 2016.

Robinson, Stephen. By phone on May 20, 2016

Ruderman, Dan. On *Tales from the Golden Road*.

Silberman, Steve. By phone on June 9, 2016.

Wagman, Bruce. By phone on January 1, 2016.

Wagner, Robert. By phone on December 22, 2015.

"Wasson, Bill" (pseudonym used at interviewee's request). By phone on January 31, 2016.

Zimmerman, Stu. By phone on August 26, 2016.

BOOKS AND ARTICLES

Allgier, Dick. "Revisiting a Dream ESP Experiment with 'the Grateful Dead.'" Mind-energy.net, September 8, 2007. http://www.mind-energy.net/archives/235-Revisiting-a-Dream-ESP-Experiment-with-The-Grateful-Dead.html.

Aloi, Daniel. "Grateful Dead Live on in Alumni Memories of Barton Hall '77." *Cornell Chronicle*, February 2010.

Brandelius, Jerilyn Lee. *Grateful Dead Family Album*. New York: Warner Books, 1989.

Brown, Toni. *Relix: The Book*. New York: Backbeat Books, 2009.

Browne, David. *So Many Roads: The Life and Times of the Grateful Dead*. New York: Da Capo, 2015.

Budnick, Dean. "What's Become of the Bettys? The Fate of the Long-Lost Grateful Dead Soundboards." *Relix*, March 11, 2014. http://www.relix.com/articles/detail/whats_become_of_the_bettys.

Burke, Stephen. "Ithaca Notes: The Perfect Blend." *Ithaca Times*, May 6, 2015.

Christensen, Mark. *Acid Christ: Ken Kesey, LSD, and the Politics of Ecstacy*. Tucson, AZ: Schaffner, 2009.

Conners, Peter. *Growing Up Dead: The Hallucinated Confessions of a Teenage Deadhead*. New York: Da Capo, 2009.

——. *JAMerica: The History of the Jam Band Festival Scene*. New York: Da Capo, 2013.

Constanten, Tom. *Between Rock and Hard Places: A Musical Auto-biodyssey*. Eugene, OR: Hulogosi, 1992.

Daley, Jim. *Grateful Memories: Ten Years on the Road Taping the Dead*. Self-published, 2015.

Dalton, David, and Rock Scully. *Living with the Dead: Twenty Years on the Bus with Garcia and the Grateful Dead*. New York: Little, Brown, 1996.

Dodd, David. *The Complete Annotated Grateful Dead Lyrics*. New York: Free Press, 2005.

Fenchel, Luke Z. "Revisiting the Grateful Dead's 1977 Barton Hall Show." *Ithaca Times*, February 10, 2010.

Gans, David. *Conversations with the Dead*. New York: Da Capo, 2002.

Gans, David, and Blair Jackson. *This Is All A Dream We Dreamed: An Oral History of the Grateful Dead*. New York: Flatiron Books, 2015.

Gimble, Steven, ed. *The Grateful Dead and Philosophy: Getting High Minded about Love and Haight*. Chicago: Open Court, 2007.

Goodman, Fred. "On a Roll." *Rolling Stone* 566, November 30, 1989. Reprinted in *Rolling Stone*, "Jerry Garcia Special Collectors Edition," October 2014.

Greenfield, Robert. "Owsley Stanley: The King of LSD." *Rolling Stone*, May 14, 2011.

Jarnow, Jesse. *Heads: A Biography of Psychedelic America*. New York: Da Capo, 2016.

Lee, Martin A., and Bruce Shlain. *Acid Dreams: The Complete Social History of LSD: The CIA, the Sixties, and Beyond*. New York: Grove, 1992.

Lesh, Phil. *Searching for the Sound: My Life with the Grateful Dead*. New York: Little, Brown, 2005.

Lytle, Mark Hamilton. *America's Uncivil Wars: The Sixties Era from Elvis to the Fall of Richard Nixon*. Oxford: Oxford University Press, 2006.

Marcus, Greil. *Lipstick Traces: A Secret History of the Twentieth Century*. Cambridge, MA: Harvard University Press, 1989.

Mattera, Adam. "How Disco Changed Music Forever." *Guardian*, February 25, 2012.

McNally, Dennis. *Jerry on Jerry: The Unpublished Jerry Garcia Interviews*. New York: Black Dog & Leventhal, 2015.

———. *A Long Strange Trip: The Inside History of the Grateful Dead*. New York: Broadway Books, 2003.

Meriwether, Nicholas G. "Revisiting Cornell '77." Rock and Roll Hall of Fame "Stories of Rock," June 2016. rockhall.com/stories.

Moody, Rick. "Swinging Modern Sounds #54: Jam Band Apotheosis." *Rumpus*, May 27, 2014.

Parish, Steve. *Home before Daylight: My Life on the Road with the Grateful Dead*. New York: St. Martin's, 2003.

Paumgarten, Nick. "Deadhead: The Afterlife." *New Yorker*, November 26, 2012.

Perry, Paul. *On the Bus: The Complete Guide to the Legendary Trip of Ken Kesey and the Merry Pranksters and the Birth of the Counterculture*. New York: Thunder's Mouth, 1996.

Richardson, Peter. *No Simple Highway: A Cultural History of the Grateful Dead*. New York: St. Martin's, 2014.

Scott, John W., Stu Nixon, and Mike Dolgushkin. *DeadBase 50: Celebrating 50 Years of the Grateful Dead*. San Francisco: Watermark Press, 2015.

Shenk, David, and Steve Silberman. *Skeleton Key: A Dictionary for Deadheads*. New York: Doubleday, 1994.

Silberman, Steve. "There's a Dragon with Matches Loose on the Town." Liner notes to *May 1977* box set. Rhino, 2013.

Stanley, Rhoney Gissen. *Owsley and Me: My LSD Family*. Rhinebeck, NY: Monkfish, 2012.

Torgoff, Martin. *Can't Find My Way Home: America in the Great Stoned Age, 1945–2000*. New York: Simon & Schuster Paperbacks, 2004.

Trager, Oliver. *The American Book of the Dead: The Definitive Grateful Dead Encyclopedia*. New York: Fireside, 1997.

Weiner, Howard F. *Grateful Dead 1977: The Rise of Terrapin Nation*. New York: Pencil Hill, 2015.

Wenner, Jann, and Charles Reich. *Garcia: A Signpost to New Space*. San Francisco: Straight Arrow Books, 1972.

WEBSITES AND BLOGS

archive.org/details/GratefulDead
owsleystanleyfoundation.org
www.talesfromthegoldenroad.com/
www.dead.net
www.dennismcnally.com
www.dicklatvala.com
www.gdao.org
www.gdhour.com
www.jerrygarcia.com
www.tristudios.com

2

Acknowledgments

For every book that is published, there is a huge cast of supporters, advocates, cheerleaders, family, and friends without whom the accomplishment wouldn't be possible. At the risk of missing some of the individuals who are among that number, I want to name the people who were instrumental in the writing of *Cornell '77*.

First and foremost, thank you to John Perry Barlow, Jerry Garcia, Donna Jean Godchaux, Keith Godchaux, Mickey Hart, Robert Hunter, Bill Kreutzmann, Phil Lesh, Ron "Pigpen" McKernan, Brent Mydland, and Bob Weir. Your music is the soundtrack to my life.

From the Cornell University faculty and staff, thank you to Daniel Aloi, Glenn Altschuler, Evan Fay Earle, Michael Engle, Marcie Suzanne Farwell, Connie Finnerty, Heather Furnas,

Lisa Gilles, Eileen Keating, Melanie Lefkowitz, Laura Linke, Liz Muller, Anna E. Pollock, and Theo Wolf.

For the the friends, allies, and interviewees who lent their support to *Cornell '77* in ways both large and small, thank you to Matt Adler, Pete Angwin, Neem Karoli Baba, Ken Babbs, BOA Editions, the BOTNET group, John Briggs, Stephen Burke, Bill Chaisson, Todd Ellenberg, Mark Frisk, David Gans, Mary Goodenough, Dean Heiser, Heather Horsley, Jason Johnson, Patrick Kavaney, Sunshine Kesey, Rick Koh, Brad Krakow, Gary Lambert, Carol Latvala, David Lemieux, Jordan Lowy, Jay Mabrey, Mark Mattson, Mike McEvoy, Nicholas Meriwether, JoAnne Narad, Mark Pinkus, Eve Prouty, Simon Radford, Ivette Ramos, Stephen Robinson, Dan Ruderman, Ira Rose and the Hanuman Chalisa Daily Chant Group, Cody Schneiders, John Schroeder, Steve Silberman, Robert Spivack, Three Heads Brewing, Tru Yoga, Doran Tyson, Bruce Wagman, Robert Wagner, Christopher Wallis, Todd Weiner, and Stu Zimmerman.

My deepest bow goes to publisher Dean John Smith and editor Michael McGandy from Cornell University Press. I am so grateful that they presented me with the idea of writing a book about Cornell '77 and thankful that they stuck with me through the occasionally harrowing process of getting it done on time. In addition to lending his editorial expertise, Michael helped make contacts with Cornell alumni and Cornell faculty and combed through the Cornell archives to find every piece of primary resource material available on campus that could be useful for this book. Publisher Dean Smith's great enthusiasm for this book (and for the Grateful Dead) often made my work a pleasure, and his careful reading and editorial notes were a blessing. Also, massive thanks to author and scholar Peter Richardson for recommending me to Michael and Dean as the "perfect person" to write this book. My involvement with this project started with Peter, and he continued to support my writing with information, feedback, and encouragement until its completion.

Photographer Jon Reis deserves special mention for his fantastic images of the May 8, 1977, show and for generously allowing his photographs to appear in this book. Those images fill in the story and give us a richer sense of the scene at Cornell and in Ithaca.

At this point, pretty much every author who writes about the history of the Grateful Dead owes a debt of gratitude to Nicholas Meriwether and the Grateful Dead archives at the University of California, Santa Cruz. I proudly count myself among that number. Nicholas is a tireless advocate for Grateful Dead scholarship and is always there with information, documents, contacts, and true Deadhead spirit. We are all lucky to have you, Nicholas.

I also want to give warm thanks to David Gans and Gary Lambert for dedicating an episode of their radio show, *Tales from the Golden Road*, on Sirius/XM's Grateful Dead channel, to the Cornell show, and for allowing me to conduct live on-air interviews during that episode. In addition to their generosity on *Tales from the Golden Road*, both Gary and David made themselves available for questions and provided key contacts throughout the writing of this book.

Thank you to my agent Linda Roghaar, who has been a wonderful ally and trusted advocate through every book that I have written.

Thanks and praises to all my families. Thank you to the Conners family for their ongoing support of my work. Thank you to the Senise family for warmly welcoming me into their fold during the writing of this book. Thank you to the children in my life who make every day an adventure: Whitman, Max, Kane, and Little

Max. Thank you to the family of Deadheads who are my fellow travelers down the golden road.

Finally, my most heartfelt thanks to Aimée, who became my wife and my life during the writing of this book. If, as Ram Dass says, "We are all just walking each other home," there is no one I'd rather walk beside than you.

Acknowledgments

Copyright information pertaining to lyrics quoted in this book.

Loser
Words by Robert Hunter
Music by Jerry Garcia
Copyright © 1972 ICE NINE PUBLISHING
    CO., INC.
Copyright Renewed
All Rights Administered by UNIVERSAL
    MUSIC CORP.
All Rights Reserved Used by Permission
Reprinted by Permission of Hal Leonard LLC

They Love Each Other
Words by Robert Hunter
Music by Jerry Garcia
Copyright © 1976 ICE NINE PUBLISHING
    CO., INC.
Copyright Renewed
All Rights Administered by UNIVERSAL
    MUSIC CORP.
All Rights Reserved Used by Permission
Reprinted by Permission of Hal Leonard LLC

Jack Straw
Words by Robert Hunter
Music by Bob Weir
Copyright © 1972 ICE NINE PUBLISHING
    CO., INC.
Copyright Renewed
All Rights Administered by UNIVERSAL
    MUSIC CORP.
All Rights Reserved Used by Permission
Reprinted by Permission of Hal Leonard LLC

Deal
Words and Music by Jerry Garcia and Robert
    Hunter
Copyright © 1972 ICE NINE PUBLISHING
    CO., INC.
Copyright Renewed
All Rights Administered by UNIVERSAL
    MUSIC CORP.
All Rights Reserved Used by Permission
Reprinted by Permission of Hal Leonard LLC

Lazy Lightnin'
Words by John Barlow
Music by Robert Weir
Copyright © 1976 ICE NINE PUBLISHING
    CO., INC.

Copyright Renewed
All Rights Administered by UNIVERSAL
    MUSIC CORP.
All Rights Reserved Used by Permission
Reprinted by Permission of Hal Leonard LLC 6

Supplication
Words and Music by John Barlow and Bob
    Weir
Copyright © 1976 ICE NINE PUBLISHING
    CO., INC.
Copyright Renewed
All Rights Administered by UNIVERSAL
    MUSIC CORP.
All Rights Reserved Used by Permission
Reprinted by Permission of Hal Leonard LLC

Brown-Eyed Women
Words by Robert Hunter
Music by Jerry Garcia
Copyright © 1972 ICE NINE PUBLISHING
    CO., INC.
Copyright Renewed
All Rights Administered by UNIVERSAL
    MUSIC CORP.
All Rights Reserved Used by Permission
Reprinted by Permission of Hal Leonard LLC

Row Jimmy
Words and Music by Jerry Garcia and Robert
    Hunter
Copyright © 1973 ICE NINE PUBLISHING
    CO., INC.
Copyright Renewed
All Rights Administered by UNIVERSAL
    MUSIC CORP.
All Rights Reserved Used by Permission
Reprinted by Permission of Hal Leonard LLC

Scarlet Begonias
Words by Robert Hunter
Music by Jerry Garcia
Copyright © 1974 ICE NINE PUBLISHING
    CO., INC.
Copyright Renewed
All Rights Administered by UNIVERSAL
    MUSIC CORP.
All Rights Reserved Used by Permission
Reprinted by Permission of Hal Leonard LLC

Acknowledgments

Fire On The Mountain
Words by Robert Hunter
Music by Mickey Hart
Copyright © 1978 ICE NINE PUBLISHING
    CO., INC.
All Rights Administered by UNIVERSAL
    MUSIC CORP.
All Rights Reserved Used by Permission
Reprinted by Permission of Hal Leonard LLC

Estimated Prophet
Words by John Barlow
Music by Bob Weir
Copyright © 1977 ICE NINE PUBLISHING
    CO., INC.
Copyright Renewed
All Rights Administered by UNIVERSAL
    MUSIC CORP.
All Rights Reserved Used by Permission
*Reprinted by Permission of Hal Leonard
    LLC*

St. Stephen
Words by Robert Hunter
Music by Jerry Garcia and Phil Lesh
Copyright © 1969 ICE NINE PUBLISHING
    CO., INC.
Copyright Renewed
All Rights Administered by UNIVERSAL
    MUSIC CORP.
All Rights Reserved Used by Permission
Reprinted by Permission of Hal Leonard LLC

One More Saturday Night
Words and Music by Bob Weir
Copyright © 1972 ICE NINE PUBLISHING
    CO., INC.
Copyright Renewed
All Rights Administered by UNIVERSAL
    MUSIC CORP.
All Rights Reserved Used by Permission
Reprinted by Permission of Hal Leonard LLC

The Other One
Words and Music by Bill Kreutzmann and
    Bob Weir
Copyright © 1968 ICE NINE PUBLISHING
    CO., INC.
Copyright Renewed
All Rights Administered by UNIVERSAL
    MUSIC CORP.
All Rights Reserved Used by Permission
Reprinted by Permission of Hal Leonard LLC

New Minglewood Blues
Words and Music by Jerry Garcia, Bill
    Kreutzmann, Phil Lesh, Michael Hart, Bob
    Weir and Brent Mydland
Copyright © 1967 ICE NINE PUBLISHING
    CO., INC.
Copyright Renewed
All Rights Administered by UNIVERSAL
    MUSIC CORP.
All Rights Reserved Used by Permission
Reprinted by Permission of Hal Leonard LLC

Notes

Prologue. Grown Up Dead

1   **The bus came by . . .** Quoted in Peter Conners, *Growing Up Dead: The Hallucinated Confessions of a Teenage Deadhead* (New York: Da Capo, 2009), 153.

1   **In a twist on . . .** Ram Dass, "Promises & Pitfalls: Spiritual Materialism" (Love Serve Remember Foundation, 2014), https://www. ramdass.org/?s=promises+and+pitfalls+of+spiritual+materialism.

3   **Years later, I would read . . .** Barry Silesky, *Ferlinghetti: The Artist in His Time* (Warner Books, 1991), 197.

5   **As Mark Pinkus . . .** Pinkus, phone interview with the author, March 10, 2016.

6   **Even the local reporter . . .** Mary Suma, "'Dead' Still Strong," *Ithaca Journal*, May 9, 1977, 4.

7   **Bestselling author . . .** Steve Silberman, phone interview with the author, June 9, 2016.

The Sex Pistols, Disco, and the Dead

11   **"I'm not that taken . . ."** Quoted in Peter Richardson, *No Simple Highway: A Cultural History of the Grateful Dead* (New York: St. Martin's, 2014), 222.

12 **Then Weir stared straight** ... Bob Weir and Jerry Garcia interview, *The Tomorrow Show*, May 7, 1981, https://www.youtube.com/watch?v=9zTrVY80kVo.

12 **In a twisted funhouse** ... Sex Pistols interview, *Today*, December 1, 1976, https://www.youtube.com/watch?v=0knFHyDD150.

13 **"That was how I felt when ..."** Marcus Greil, *Lipstick Traces: A Secret History of the 20th Century* (Cambridge, MA: Harvard University Press, 1990), 88.

14 **The statement was written** ... Peter Richardson, e-mail to the author, June 2016.

15 **"The real danger to society ..."** Here and below, Danny Rifkin, in KPIX Eyewitness News broadcast, October 5, 1967, https://www.youtube.com/watch?v=_0x6w5ikXKY.

16 **"When it comes to politics ..."** Richardson, e-mail.

16 **Garcia summed things up** ... Fred Goodman, "On a Roll," *Rolling Stone* 566, November 30, 1989. Reprinted in *Rolling Stone*, "Jerry Garcia Special Collectors Edition," October 2014, 57.

16 **In an open letter / free-verse poem** ... Ken Kesey, "Jerry Garcia: The False Notes He Never Played," *New York Times*, December 31, 1995, http://www.nytimes.com/1995/12/31/magazine/the-lives-they-lived-jerry-garcia-the-false-notes-he-never-played.html.

16 **"The last time hope ..."** Quoted in Adam Tanner, "Grateful Dead, Deadheads Unite for Obama," Reuters, February 5, 2008, http://www.reuters.com/article/us-usa-politics-gratefuldead-idUSN0462538720080205.

17 **"Elton John listens ..."** David Gans, *Conversations with the Dead: The Grateful Dead Interview Book* (Cambridge, MA: Da Capo, 2002), 13.

18 **"John Travolta flares ..."** Adam Mattera, "How Disco Changed Music Forever," *Guardian*, February 25, 2012, https://www.theguardian.com/music/2012/feb/26/disco-changed-world-for-ever.

19 **"Early clubs such as ..."** Mattera, "How Disco Changed Music Forever."

19 **"While the Dead played ..."** Jesse Jarnow, *Heads: A Biography of Psychedelic America* (New York: Da Capo, 2016), 54.

20 ***Rolling Stone*'s review** ... Gary Von Tersch, "The Grateful Dead: Shakedown Street," *Rolling Stone*, March 8, 1979, http://www.rollingstone.com/music/albumreviews/shakedown-street-19790308.

Cold Rain and Snow

23 **"I remember it being ..."** JoAnne Narad, radio interview with the author, December 27, 2015.

23 **Snow hadn't factored . . .** Robert Wagner, phone interview with the author, December 22, 2015.

26 **Between January 28 . . .** AP newspaper article, "Buffalo Remembers Infamous Blizzard of '77," *USA Today*, June 1, 2002, http://usatoday30. usatoday.com/weather/wbufbliz.htm.

26 **"My experience started . . ."** Narad interview.

28 **"And when we first . . ."** Phil Lesh, in *Anthem to Beauty*, VH1 documentary film, 1997.

28 **"That's why I started . . ."** Quoted in Jerilyn Brandelius, *Grateful Dead Family Album* (Warner Books, 1989), 193.

30 **In June 1973, Deep Purple . . .** All details pertaining to the June 12, 1973, Deep Purple show are drawn from Ithaca media accounts and press releases from Cornell's Office of Public Information. See Cornell Concert Commission Files, Rare and Manuscript Collections, Kroch Library, Cornell University, Ithaca, New York.

31 **"We thought it was going . . ."** Reported by Beth Saulnier, "Big Tents," *Cornell Alumni Magazine*, November / December 2012, http://cornell alumnimagazine.com/index.php?option=com_content&task=view& id=1491.

32 **The concert was performed . . .** Mike McEvoy, radio interview with the author, December 27, 2015.

33 **As much as Bill Graham . . .** Tris McCall, "John Scher: A Life in Rock Music, in New Jersey and Far Beyond," *Inside Jersey*, January 29, 2012, http://www.nj.com/entertainment/music/index.ssf/2012/01/john_ scher_four_decades_of_bri.html.

33 **"In working with John . . ."** McEvoy interview.

34 **"A portion of an anticipated . . ."** Susan Gilbert, "Dead Sell-Out Helps Commission Pay Debt," *Cornell Daily Sun*, May 1977.

34 **The Dead show of May 1977 . . .** Cornell Concert Commission, budget for Grateful Dead show, 1977. Cornell Concert Commission Files, Rare and Manuscript Collections, Kroch Library, Cornell University, Ithaca, New York.

Sonic Experiments

35 **"At one of the Acid Tests . . ."** Quoted in David Gans, ed., *Conversations with the Dead: The Grateful Dead Interview Book* (New York: Da Capo, 2002), 295.

35 **"I remember standing . . ."** Ken Kesey, *New York Times*, December 31, 1995, http://www.nytimes.com/1995/12/31/magazine/the-lives-they-lived-jerry-garcia-the-false-notes-he-never-played.html.

36   **Given his vocation . . .** Mark Hamilton Lytle, *America's Uncivil Wars: The Sixties Era from Elvis to the Fall of Richard Nixon* (New York: Oxford University Press, 2006), 194.

37   **Although it took the band . . .** Joshua Green, "Management Secrets of the Grateful Dead," *Atlantic*, March 2010, http://www.theatlantic.com/magazine/archive/2010/03/management-secrets-of-the-grateful-dead/307918/.

37   **Grateful Dead lyricist . . .** Dennis McNally, *A Long Strange Trip: The Inside History of the Grateful Dead* (New York: Da Capo, 2002), 386.

38   **The whole decision to allow . . .** Dennis McNally, phone interview with the author, June 13, 2016.

38   **The registry was created . . .** Mission statement on the Library of Congress website, https://loc.gov/programs/national-recording-preservation-board/about-this-program/.

38   **During the spring 1977 . . .** Paumgarten, "Deadhead: The Afterlife," *New Yorker*, November 26, 2012, http://www.newyorker.com/magazine/2012/11/26/deadhead.

39   **"I can always tell . . ."** Quoted in Paumgarten, "Deadhead."

39   **"In a poll of Deadheads . . ."** Howard Weiner, *Grateful Dead 1977: The Rise and Fall of Terrapin Nation* (New York: Pencil Hill, 2015), 56–57.

40   **"The thing from a non-taper's . . ."** Jeff Mattson, interview with the author, Rochester, New York, January 18, 2012.

40   **"Employer shall not . . ."** Cornell Concert Commission files, Cornell Rare and Manuscript Collections, Kroch Library, Cornell University, Ithaca, New York.

42   **"The real reason . . ."** McNally interview.

42   **"I said, 'Why don't we put . . .'"** David Shenk and Steve Silberman, *Skeleton Key: A Dictionary for Deadheads* (New York: Doubleday, 1994), 278.

42   **"I taped my first show . . ."** Here and continuing below, Rob Eaton, interview with the author, Rochester, New York, January 18, 2012.

44   **"I'm a native New Yorker . . ."** Jerry Moore, interview by David Gans, Siriuis/XM Grateful Dead Channel broadcast, 2008. Audio file provided by David Gans via e-mail. Subsequent material on Moore and taping is drawn from this interview.

46   **"When I was a young Deadhead . . ."** David Gans, interview with the author, Berkeley, California, November 9, 2010.

47   **"It was very important for us . . ."** Quoted in Shenk and Silberman, *Skeleton Key*, 277.

48   **"Several of the really senior . . ."** Steve Silberman, phone interview with the author, June 9, 2016.

49   **"The community of meeting . . ."** McNally interview.

50   **the band "went into . . ."** McNally interview.

50   **The name stuck . . .** From here on I will refer to Owsley as either "Bear"
      or "Owsley" with respect to that community. He would eventually
      legally drop the name "Augustus."

51   **"A few weeks later, dressed . . ."** Rhoney Gissen Stanley, *Owsley and
      Me: My LSD Family* (Rhinebeck, NY: Monkfish, 2013), 11.

51   **"Inside was a party . . ."** Stanley, *Owsley and Me*, 14.

52   **In fact, he was so prolific . . .** Martin Torgoff, *Can't Find My Way
      Home: America in the Great Stoned Age, 1945–2000* (New York: Simon &
      Schuster, 2004), 123.

53   **"I never set out . . ."** Robert Greenfield, "Owsley Stanley: The King of
      LSD," *Rolling Stone*, March 14, 2011, http://www.rollingstone.com/
      culture/news/owsley-stanley-the-king-of-lsd-20110314.

53   **"A few months before I met . . ."** Quoted in Gans, *Conversations with
      the Dead*, 293.

54   **"I knew we had to do something . . ."** Quoted in Gans, *Conversations
      with the Dead*, 316.

54   **With Owsley in the lead . . .** McNally, *Long Strange Trip*, 426. See pages
      300ff. of McNally's book for great accounts of the sound crews over the
      years from the late 1960 and well into the 1970s.

54   **As Nick Paumgarten noted . . .** Paumgarten, "Deadhead."

55   **That quest . . .** McNally, *Long Strange Trip*, 470–73.

55   **"The Grateful Dead's sound system . . ."** Quotations in this paragraph
      and the next from "1974: Wall of Sound Technical Specs," Grateful
      Dead Sources, December 23, 2012, http://deadsources.blogspot.
      com/2012/12/1974-wall-of-sound-technical-specs.html.

56   **"Owsley was a classic expression . . ."** Silberman interview.

57   **"Owsley was not an easy man . . ."** Ibid.

57   **"Bear was into creating . . ."** McNally interview.

58   **As Bear recounted . . .** Quoted in Gans, *Conversations with the Dead*, 335.

59   **Costs are estimated . . .** See the foundation website, http://www.
      owsleystanleyfoundation.org/page4/page4.html.

60   **More than a few . . .** See, for example, "Grateful Dead Haven't Stopped
      Growing Musically," *Baltimore Sun*, May 27, 1977, B5; "Dead Still
      Strong," *Ithaca Journal*, May 9, 1977, 4; "The Dead Return," *St. Paul
      Dispatch*, May 5, 1977; "Resurrecting the Dead," *Cornell Daily Sun*,
      May 6, 1977.

Just the Right Night

61   **"If you don't try . . ."** Peter Angwin, phone interview with the author,
      December 24, 2015.

63   **"I reckon we owe our musicians . . ."** Sandy Kohler List, "Grateful Dead: Musical Messiahs Come to Ithaca," *Good Times Gazette*, May 5–11, 1977, 18.

64   **The plan that Burke . . .** Stephen Burke, phone interview with the author, February 3, 2016.

64   **And then there was Louis . . .** Louis Gross, e-mail to the author, April 7, 2016.

65   **"Absolutely under no circumstances . . ."** Burke interview.

66   **"Hey, look at this! . . ."** Ibid.

66   **"They're really the seventh . . ."** Jerilyn Lee Brandelius, *Grateful Dead Family Album* (New York: Warner Books, 1989), 193.

66   **Social scientist Shaun . . .** Horace L. Fairlamb, "Community at the Edge of Chaos: The Dead's Cultural Revolution," in *The Grateful Dead and Philosophy,* ed. Steven Gimbel (Chicago, IL: Open Court, 2007), 24.

67   **"It could definitely be . . ."** Burke interview.

67   **Mark Mattson, who . . .** Mark Mattson, e-mail to the author, August 23, 2016.

68   **Perhaps, some venture, . . .** See the post from Mind Wondrin' and others at Archive.org, https://archive.org/details/gd77-05-07.sbd. eaton.wizard.26085.sbeok.shnf.

68   **Shows spoke to . . .** Nicholas Meriwether, e-mail to the author, August 19, 2016.

68   **So it is no surprise . . .** Burke interview.

68   **In Ithaca, unlike Boston, . . .** Rock Scully, with David Dalton, *Living with the Dead: Twenty Years on the Bus with Garcia and the Grateful Dead* (Boston: Little, Brown, 1996), 279–81.

69   **Burke remembers the band members . . .** Burke interview.

69   **They also played . . .** John W. Scott, Stu Nixon, and Mike Dolgushkin, *Deadbase 50: Celebrating 50 Years of the Grateful Dead* (San Francisco: Watermark, 2015), 38.

70   **Security staffing . . .** April 23, 1977, memo to Joe Patterson, superintendent of public safety at Cornell, from Doug Foulke, production manager for the Cornell Concert Commission, re security arrangement for Grateful Dead Show. Cornell Concert Commission files, Cornell Rare and Manuscript Collections, Kroch Library, Cornell University, Ithaca, New York.

70   **Their multipage contract . . .** Grateful Dead Productions, Contract Rider, 1977. Cornell Concert Commission files, Cornell Rare and Manuscript Collections, Kroch Library, Cornell University, Ithaca, New York.

71 **"Audiences were a little more fervent . . ."** Angwin interview. All subsequent quotes from Angwin are from this interview.

72 **"When weather permitted . . ."** Rosie McGee, *Dancing with the Dead—a Photographic Memoir: My Good Old Days with the Grateful Dead and the San Francisco Music Scene, 1964–1974* (Rohnert Park, CA: TIOLI Press & Bytes, 2012), 83.

72 **The Be-In was . . .** Peter Conners, *White Hand Society: The Psychedelic Partnership of Timothy Leary and Allen Ginsberg* (San Francisco: City Lights Books, 2010), 202–3.

74 **"There's a guy named Ron Rainey . . ."** Dennis McNally, phone interview with the author, June 13, 2016.

74 **Angwin was literally picked up . . .** Angwin interview.

75 **Quite a few tickets . . .** Dean Heiser, e-mail to the author, September 6, 2016.

75 **Stu Zimmerman, a student . . .** Stuart Zimmerman, phone interview with the author, **August 26,** 2016.

76 **Bill Wasson's entry . . .** Wasson, phone interview with the author, January 31, 2016. "Bill Wasson" is a pseudonym used to protect the identity of the interviewee at his request.

First Set

82 **Outside in the rain . . .** The coverage of the show in the *Ithaca Journal* of May 9, 1977, reported only rain before the show.

83 **It initiated a night of music . . .** While not academically vetted, Dead Base 50 is the most trustworthy clearinghouse of information about the Dead's set list and performance history and therefore is the publication I consulted most consistently while writing this book. While certainly esoteric—or maybe because they are esoteric—the set lists contained in Dead Base are among the chief points of discussion, debate, revelry, and celebration in Deadhead world. There is a reason Dead Base is called "the bible" by hard-core fans.

86 **In comparing the . . .** David Gans, interview with the author, Berkeley, California, September 9, 2012.

96 **"Early pot heads . . ."** Bill Kreutzmann, in e-mail sent to John Briggs on behalf of the author.

100 **"I like the setups in that . . ."** David Gans, *Conversations with the Dead* (New York: Da Capo, 2002), 29.

101 **"I didn't care . . ."** Peter Angwin, interview with the author, December 24, 2015.

101   **"I don't really think of that . . ."** Gans interview.

101   **"The rather fey treatment . . ."** Gary Lambert, interview with the author, December 27, 2015.

102   **Mary Suma . . .** *Ithaca Journal*, May 9, 1977, 4.

102   **Steve Silberman describes . . .** Silberman, "There's a Dragon with Matches Loose on the Town," liner notes to *May 1977* box set, limited edition, Rhino 2013.

102   **"I don't know whose idea . . ."** Blair Jackson and David Gans, *This Is All a Dream We Dreamed: An Oral History of the Grateful Dead* (New York: Flatiron Books, 2015), 250.

Second Set

105   **Between first and second sets . . .** Rick Koh, radio interview with the author, December 27, 2015; Stu Zimmerman, e-mail to the author, August 29, 2016.

106   **Mark Nathanson, a recent . . .** Quoted in Scott W. Allen, "Barton Hall Concert—The Grateful Dead (May 8, 1977)," Library of Congress National Recording Preservation Board, https://www.loc.gov/ programs/static/national-recording-preservation-board/documents/ GratefulDead.pdf.

108   **Jerry Garcia described . . .** McNally, *Jerry on Jerry: The Unpublished Jerry Garcia Interviews* (New York: Black Dog & Leventhal, 2015), 145.

111   **Hunter tells the apocryphal . . .** David Dodd, "Greatest Stories Ever Told: 'Fire on the Mountain,'" http://www.dead.net/features/ greatest-stories-ever-told/greatest-stories-ever-told-fire-mountain.

112   **"The basis of it is . . ."** Ibid.

113   **At only three dollars . . .** Wolfgang's Vault web store, handbill from the Grateful Dead show at the National Guard Armory St. Louis, St. Louis, Missouri, May 24, 1968, http://www.wolfgangsvault.com/grateful- dead/handbills/handbill/NGA680524_367.html.

114   **"I was very excited to hear 'St. Stephen' . . ."** Robert Wagner, phone interview with the author, December 22, 2015.

117   **"You look at Cornell . . ."** David Lemieux, phone interview with the author, January 28, 2016.

118   **"You may notice that . . ."** Brad Krakow, forwarded e-mail to the author, January 22, 2010.

120   **Canadian singer-songwriter . . .** David Dodd, *The Complete Annotated Grateful Dead Lyrics* (New York: Free Press, 2005), 32–33.

122   **"Gone were the half-hour . . ."** Steve Silberman, "There's a Dragon with Matches Loose on the Town," liner notes to *May 1977* box set, limited edition, Rhino 2013.

124 **The house lights blazed** ... Richard Ellenson, "The Grateful Dead: Living Up to a Legend," *Good Times Gazette* (Ithaca, New York), May 12–18, 1977.

124 **Worried about hypothermia** ... Letter from Alan B. Ley, MD, director of Cornell University Health Services, to Ronald B. Loomis, director of Cornell Student Unions, May 11, 1977. Cornell Concert Commission files, Rare and Manuscript Collections, Kroch Library, Cornell University, Ithaca, New York.

126 **The Catskill Mountain peaks** ... A summary of the storm's impact can be found at http://farmersalmanac.com/weather/2012/05/07/may-mayhem-a-freak-snowstorm-remembered/.

Betty Boards

130 **"Our teenage years were marked ..."** Heather Horsley, e-mail to the author, February 20, 2016.

131 **... a high school chemistry teacher** ... Nick Paumgarten, "Deadhead: The Afterlife," *New Yorker*, November 26, 2012, http://www.newyorker.com/magazine/2012/11/26/deadhead.

132 **"My late husband started ..."** Dean Budnick, "What's Become of the Bettys? The Fate of the Long Lost Soundboards," *Relix*, March 11, 2014, http://www.relix.com/articles/detail/whats_become_of_the_bettys.

132 **It was during the Dead's ...** Dennis McNally, *A Long Strange Trip: The Inside History of the Grateful Dead* (New York: Broadway Books, 2003), 494.

133 **"Brent was very insecure ..."** Betty Cantor-Jackson, phone interview with the author, May 5, 2016.

134 **"Brent wasn't treated badly ..."** Dennis McNally, phone interview with the author, June 13, 2016.

134 **"Brent and I split up ..."** Budnick, "What's Become of the Bettys?"

135 **"There was always a publicly stated rule ..."** Nicholas Meriwether, phone interview with the author, August 19, 2016.

135 **Roadies like Lawrence "Ram Rod"** ... Steve Parish, *Home before Daylight: My Life on the Road with the Grateful Dead* (New York: St. Martin's, 2004), 123.

135 **"They were the world's most macho ..."** Cantor-Jackson interview.

136 **Based on the fact that ...** Ibid.

137 **Given his knowledge of Dead bootleg ...** Rob Eaton, "Betty Tape Story," in John W. Scott, Stu Nixon, and Mike Dolgushkin, *Deadbase 50: Celebrating 50 Years of the Grateful Dead* (San Francisco: Watermark, 2015), 21–23. The material in the following paragraphs about Eaton's work on the tapes is from this same source.

140 **Grateful Dead archivist David Lemieux . . .** Lemieux, phone interview with the author, January 28, 2016.

141 **"I just dealt with the band . . ."** Cantor-Jackson interview. The rest of this section draws from this same interview.

143 **"There are two copyrights . . ."** Stephen Robinson, phone interview with the author, May 20, 2016.

144 **"We passed through a door . . ."** Paumgarten, "Deadhead."

144 **"We got ahold . . ."** Mark Pinkus, phone interview with the author, March 10, 2016.

145 **"I'm glad they got out there . . ."** Cantor-Jackson interview.

The Show That Never Happened

147 **"Yo this show is great but . . ."** Posted on http://www.setlists. net/?show_id=1009.

147 **When sixteen-year-old . . .** Here and below, Mark Pinkus, phone interview with the author, March 10, 2016.

151 **"It's having been able to hear . . ."** Here and below, David Lemieux, phone interview with the author, January 28, 2016.

152 **"I went to college . . ."** Here and below, Nicholas Meriwether, phone interviews with the author, May 1, 2016, and August 19, 2016.

157 **McNally would end up . . .** Dennis McNally, "Me and the Music Biz," essay, www.dennismcnally.com/music-biz/.

157 **He says of that year . . .** Here and below, McNally, phone interview with the author, June 13, 2016.

159 **"Because it was happening . . ."** Here and below, Steve Silberman, phone interview with the author, June 9, 2016.

163 **Forty years ago . . .** Richard Ellenson, "The Grateful Dead: Living Up to a Legend," *Good Times Gazette*, May 12–18, 1977.

163 **Discussion board comments . . .** All comments from the Setlist Program website, http://www.setlists.net/?show_id=1009.

164 **In a playful segment broadcast . . .** Bob Weir, "Weir Here: Tellin' Tales of Spring '77," June 24, 2013, https://www.youtube.com/ watch?v=ds_czmAJah4.

165 **Bob Weir built TRI . . .** Broadcast and facility description from tristudios.com.

166 **"A lot of folks think they were there . . ."** Weir, "Weir Here: Tellin' Tales."

167 **Track Listing Actual Source . . .** Posted anonymously at agitators.com. Although there is always track time variation on different recordings of the same show, these times match closely with all available versions of Cornell '77.

168 **After all, it is a well-documented . . .** Martin A. Lee and Bruce Shlain, *Acid Dreams* (New York: Grove Press, 1985), 32–33.

168 **During a run of shows at the Capitol . . .** Dick Allgire, "Revisiting a Dream ESP Experiment with 'The Grateful Dead,'" Mind-Energy, September 8, 2007, http://www.mind-energy.net/archives/235-Revisiting-a-Dream-ESP-Experiment-with-The-Grateful-Dead.html.

170 **Even the original Grateful Dead vault archivist . . .** Dick Latvala, http://agitators.com/gd/dick_1977.html.

171 **I'm not sure how he . . .** Ibid.

Epilogue. A Band Out of Time

173 **"There is a continuum . . ."** Quoted in Blair Jackson and David Gans, *This Is All a Dream we Dreamed: An Oral History of the Grateful Dead* (Flatiron Books, 2015), 367.

174 **"The criticisms are obvious . . ."** Jiminut, "10 Rock Bands You Either Hate or Love," Listverse.com, March 27, 2010, http://listverse.com/2010/03/27/10-rock-bands-you-either-hate-or-love/.

175 **"We always were anachronistic . . ."** Quoted in Fred Goodman, "On a Roll," *Rolling Stone* 566, November 30, 1989. Reprinted in *Rolling Stone*, "Jerry Garcia Special Collectors Edition," October 2014, 57.

175 **The combined attendance number . . .** Ray Waddell, "You'll Never Guess How Much the Grateful Dead Earned During Their Fare Thee Well Shows," *Billboard*, July 17, 1015, http://www.billboard.com/articles/news/grateful-dead/6634536/grateful-dead-fare-thee-well-earnings-concerts.

177 **Whatever ranking . . .** David Gans, radio interview with the author, December 27, 2015.

177 **"The Dead kept to their . . ."** Mary Suma, "Dead Still Strong," *Ithaca Times*, May 9, 1977.

Index

Academy of Music (New York City), 24, 63
Acid Tests, 28, 35–37, 51–52, 169
Adler, Matt, 64
Alpert, Richard (Ram Dass), 1, 51, 72
Alembic Sound Company, 55
Allman Brothers, 32–33
"Also sprach Zarathustra" (Strauss), 76
Altamont, California, 31
American Book of the Dead, The (Trager), 90
Anderson, Ian, 62
Anderson, Texas, 85
Angwin, Pete, 70–76
Avalon Ballroom (San Francisco), 132
Aykroyd, Dan, 14

Babbs, Ken, 35
Bakersfield sound, 88, 97–98, 126, 152;
    see also country and western music
Band, The, 98

Barlow, John Perry, 37
    lyrics, 95
Barton Hall
    acoustics, 6
    description of building, 5–6, 69
    use as ROTC drill hall, 107
Barton Hall, Grateful Dead Concert
    (5/8/77)
    attendance and tickets, 63–67, 74–75
    audience response, 81–127 passim
    conclusion and break–down, 124–125
    contract, 40–41, 70, 103
    Cornell Concert Commission and,
        29–34
    crowd and "Step Back," 105–107
    "Drums" > "Space," 117–118
    encore, 121–124
    first set, 81–104
    hoax, 167–170, 175–176
    media coverage, 6, 33, 63, 102, 163, 177
    Mother's Day, 25–26, 82, 99

Index

Barton Hall, Grateful Dead Concert
(5/8/77) (*continued*)
in National Recording Registry, 8, 38
part of May series, 39, 67–68, 126–127,
139
preparation at Cornell, 23–34
reputation, 4, 39–40, 73–75, 79, 83, 127,
147–171, 175–179
second set, 105–127
set–up and sound check, 67–70, 142
taping and, 38–39, 124, 127
weather, 23–34, 74, 81–82, 104, 124–125
Beach Boys, 73, 154
Beat Generation, 156
Berry, Chuck, 32, 55
Bessent, Malcolm, 168
Betty Boards, 7, 129–145, 151, 162
auction, 136
impact, 155–156
legal status, 143–145
possible official release, 144–145
restoration, 136–140
see also Cantor–Jackson, Betty; taping
Big Brother, 54, 72
Billboard, 18, 59, 88
Blue Cheer, 52
bootlegging. *See* taping
Brendan Byrne Arena (East Rutherford,
New Jersey), 153–154
Brightman, Candace, 10, 124
Brown, James, 159
Bruce Springsteen and the E Street Band,
33, 147
Buffalo, New York, 74
Buffalo Philharmonic Orchestra, 125

Candelario, Bill, 135
Cannon's Jug Stompers, 84
Cantor–Jackson, Betty, 39, 54, 125, 127,
144–145, 156, 179
career with Grateful Dead, 132–136
recording technique in 1977, 141–143
see also Betty Boards
Capitol Theater (Passaic, New Jersey), 1,
23, 32–33, 168
Carousel Ballroom (San Francisco), 54, 132

Carlyle, Arty, 47
Cash, Johnny, 99
Cassal, Neal, 165
Cayuga Lake, 25, 70
CBGBs (New York City), 2
Central Intelligence Agency, 167–168
Chimenti, Jeff, 165
Cincinnati, Ohio, 64
Clash, The, 147
Cole, Lamont, 65
Cole, Natalie, 73
Colgate University, 71, 73–75
Collins, Bootsy, 102
Concerts East, 30
Cooper, Alice, 32
Cornell Concert Commission (CCC),
29–34, 41, 70, 75, 118, 124
Burke, Stephen, 61–67, 69
Cornell Open Air Concert Series, 30–31
Horowitz, Robert, 61–62
McEvoy, Michael, 32–34, 61–62
planning for Barton Hall show, 61–67
Prouty, Eve, 62
Cornell Daily Sun, 33
Cornell students
Angwin, Peter, 61
Goldsmith, Nicholas, 31
Gross, Louis, 64–65
Koh, Harry, 105–106
Krakow, Brad, 118
Narad, Joann, 23, 26–27, 29
Wagner, Robert, 23–25, 29
Wasson Bill, 76–79
Zimmerman, Stu, 75, 105
see also Cornell Concert Commission
Cornell University
Bailey Hall, 31–33
Schoelkopf Field, 29–31
Statler Hotel, 70
see also Barton Hall; Cornell Concert
Commission
Constanten, Tom, 164
counterculture, 14–16
country and western music, 88–89, 98,
99, 152; *see also* Bakersfield sound;
cowboy songs

216

Index

cowboy songs, 83, 88–89, 98–99; *see also* country and western music
Creature from the Black Lagoon (1954), 26, 65
Curl, John, 55

Daily Mirror, 13
Dark Star Orchestra, 40, 42
Dass, Ram. *See* Alpert, Richard
Dave's Picks, 144–145, 164
Davis, Miles, 63
Day on the Green, 73
Deadbase (Nixon, Dolgushkin, Scott), 39, 109
Dead Relix. See *Relix*
Deep Purple, 29–31, 62, 124
Delhi, State University of New York, 74
Desolate Angel (McNally), 156
Dick's Picks, 144; *see also* Latvala, Dick
Didley, Bo, 116–117
disco, 9, 17–20, 101–103
Disco Biscuits, 48
Dobson, Bonnie, 120
Dr. John, 26
drugs, 77–79
    Garcia and, 134–135
    see also LSD

East Hill, Ithaca, 26
Eaton, Rob, 7, 42–44
    restoration of Betty Boards, 137–139
    see also Dark Star Orchestra
Ellenson, Richard, 163
Emerson, Lake, and Palmer, 77

fans, 27–29, 66–77, 94, 105–106, 178
    assessing Barton Hall show, 162–164
    fear of dangerous crowds, 31, 64, 74–75
    initiation rite, 161
Felt Forum (New York City), 63
Ferlinghetti, Lawrence, 3
Festivals East, 30
Fillmore East (New York City), 32, 59 76
Fillmore West (San Francisco), 1, 116

Frampton, Peter, 73
Frost Amphitheater (Stanford University), 73
Furman, Jim, 54

Gans, David, 17, 46, 53, 86, 101, 160, 177
Garcia, Jerry, 6, 7, 8, 10, 11, 69, 73, 75, 156–157, 158, 165
    assessing Grateful Dead, 11–12, 175
    Cantor–Jackson's departure, 133–135
    death, 2, 9, 35, 149
    Garcia (1972), 94
    Mu–Tron III effect, 102–103, 111–112
    performance at Barton Hall, 81–127 passim
    Reflections (1976), 90
    Rolling Stone interview, 16
    songwriting with Hunter, 90, 100
    Tomorrow Show interview, 11–12
    Travis Bean guitar, 95–96
    see also Jerry Garcia Band
Gaye, Marvin, 73
Ginsberg, Allen, 72, 108, 161
Glassberg, Barry, 43; see also *Relix*
Godchaux, Donna Jean, 10, 133, 165
    "Dancin' in the Streets," on, 102–103
    performance at Barton Hall, 81–127 passim
Godchaux, Keith, 10, 133
    performance at Barton Hall, 81–127 passim
Golden Gate Park, 71–72, 120
Goodtimes Gazette, 63, 163
Gordon, Mike, 165
Graham, Bill, 2, 14, 32–33, 54, 61, 73
    Bill Graham Productions, 136
Grateful Dead
    1970s, 11–21, 104
    1977, 4, 9, 133, 142, 155, 157, 164
    1980s, 2–3
    Bakersfield sound, 88, 97–98, 126, 152
    cowboy songs, 83, 88–89, 98–99;
        see also country and western music
    cultural currency, 11–12, 173–175
    disco and, 101–103

Index

Grateful Dead (*continued*)
  East and West coast shows compared,
    71–74, 115
  gambler themes in songs, 87, 88,
    93–94, 123
  jazz fusion sound, 94–95, 155, 178
  jester character, 78
  politics, 15–16
  road crew, 67–70, 135
  song writing, 85
  sound and Augustus Owsley Stanley's
    influence, 53–60
  spring tour 1977, 21, 23–24, 29, 60,
    67–68, 122, 124, 126, 139, 157
  storytelling, 83, 86, 87, 88, 91, 92,
    98
  subculture, 14–16
  "Touch of Grey" video, 129–131
  touring hiatus, 58–60, 156
Grateful Dead 1977 (Weiner), 39–40
Grateful Dead, concerts
  Avalon Ballroom (San Francisco,
    5/19/66), 85
  Berkeley Community Theater
    (10/27/84), 42
  Boston Garden (5/7/77), 25, 39, 67–68,
    82, 126, 139
  Boston Music Hall (6/9/76), 114
  Cameron Indoor Stadium (Duke
    University, 9/23/76), 24, 114
  Capitol Theater (Passaic, New Jersey,
    2/18/71), 87
  Carousel Ballroom (San Francisco,
    6/19/69), 116
  Cow Palace (Daly City, California,
    3/23/75), 55, 109
  Deercreek Music Center (Noblesville,
    Indiana, 7/2/95), 109
  Dillon Stadium (Hartford,
    Connecticut, 8/24/73), 24
  Festus National Guard Armory
    (Missouri, 5/24/68), 113
  Filmore East (New York City, 2/13/70),
    8, 59
  Filmore East (New York City, 2/14/70),
    59

Giza Sound and Light Theater (Egypt,
    9/14/78), 1
Greek Theater (U.C. Berkeley,
    7/13/84), 148
Hartford Civic Center (Connecticut,
    5/28/77), 67, 163
Memorial Auditorium (Buffalo, New
    York, 5/9/77), 8, 23, 39, 68, 125–127,
    139
Nassau Coliseum (East Garden City,
    New York, 5/6/81), 49–50
Olympia Theater (Paris, France,
    5/3/72), 91
Orpheum Theater (San Francisco,
    7/18/76), 75–76
Palace, The (Auburn Hills, Michigan,
    6/27/95), 84
Paramount Theater (Portland, Oregon,
    6/3/76), 60, 95
Portland Memorial Coliseum (Oregon,
    6/12/80), 111
Raceway Park (Englishtown, New
    Jersey, 9/3/77), 61
RFK Stadium (Washington, DC,
    6/25/95), 99
Rich Stadium (Orchard Park, New
    York, 6/13/93), 2, 7
Roosevelt Stadium (Jersey City, New
    Jersey, 8/6/74), 24
Roscoe Maples Pavilion (Stanford
    University, 2/9/73), 55, 89
Soldier Field (Chicago, 7/8/95), 91
Spectrum (Philadelphia, 3/22/77), 21, 60
Sportatorium (Pembroke Pines,
    Florida, 5/22/77), 69
Springfield Civic Center
    (Massachusetts, 10/2/72), 156
Springfield Civic Center
    (Massachusetts, 3/28/73), 24
Springfield Civic Center
    (Massachusetts, 4/23/77), 60
Thompson Arena (Dartmouth College,
    5/5/78), 43
Veterans Memorial Coliseum (New
    Haven, Connecticut, 5/5/77), 23,
    67–68, 139

Watkins Glen Raceway (New York, 7/28/73), 159–161
William and Mary Hall (College of William and Mary, 9/23/76), 114
Winterland Arena (San Francisco, 3/18/77), 20, 60, 102, 110
Winterland Arena (San Francisco, 3/19/77 and 3/20/77), 60
Winterland Arena (San Francisco, 6/7/77 and 6/9/77), 69
Winterland Arena (San Francisco, 12/31/78), 13–14
Grateful Dead, recordings
Anthem of the Sun (1968), 132
Aoxomoxoa (1969), 115
Blues for Allah (1975), 157
Europe '72 (1972), 146
Grateful Dead (1967), 85
Grateful Dead (1971), 155
History of the Grateful Dead, Volume One (Bear's Choice), 59
In the Dark (1987), 131
Live Dead (1969), 114, 115
Shakedown Street (1978), 20, 60, 85
Skeletons from the Closet (1974), 147–148
So Many Roads, 1965–1995 (1999), 159, 162
Steal Your Face (1976), 90
Terrapin Station (1977), 9, 60, 95, 101, 157
Grateful Dead, songs recorded and performed
"Alice D. Millionaire," 52
"Althea," 106
"Bertha," 67, 81, 87
"Brown–Eyed Women," 97–98, 150, 178
"Cassidy," 133
"Caution," 113
"China Doll," 89
"Cold Rain and Snow," 81
"Comes a Time," 126
"Cryptical Envelopment," 113
"Dancin' in the Streets," 101–103, 151, 176

"Dark Star," 77, 83, 113, 122, 125, 126, 148, 160, 173–174
"Deal," 93–94
"Eleven, The," 77, 113, 116
"El Paso," 88–89, 177
"Estimated Prophet," 39, 111–113, 115, 117
"Eyes of the World," 89, 117, 160
"Feedback," 113
"Fire on the Mountain," 20, 39, 60, 67, 102, 105, 110–111, 115, 126, 148, 150, 151, 152, 160, 175; *see also* "Scarlet Begonias"
"Franklin's Tower," 1, 7, 126
"Funiculi, Funicula," 69–70
"Good Lovin'," 67
"Greatest Story Ever Told," 87
"Help on the Way," 7, 126
"Here Comes Sunshine," 89
"He's Gone," 49–50, 166
"I Need a Miracle," 20
"Jack Straw," 39, 91–93
"Lazy Lightning," 39, 94–97, 178; *see also* "Supplication"
"Loose Lucy," 89
"Loser," 86–87, 93
"Mama Tried," 98–99, 176
"Me and My Uncle," 88, 99
"Mexicali Blues," 88, 99, 126
"Might as Well," 95
"Morning Dew," 39, 116, 119–121, 123, 150, 151, 152, 158, 175, 178
"Music Never Stopped, The," 67, 69, 126
"New Minglewood Blues," 39, 82–83, 84–86, 87–93
"Not Fade Away," 79, 113–114, 116–119, 126, 151, 152
"One More Saturday Night," 122–124
"Other One, The," 113, 126
"Playing in the Band," 87, 117, 122, 153
"Pretty Peggy–O," 67
"Promised Land," 55
"Row Jimmy," 89, 100–101
"Samson and Delilah," 95, 123

Grateful Dead, songs recorded and
performed (*continued*)
"Scarlet Begonias," 20, 39, 60, 67,
107–110, 115, 126, 148, 150, 151,
163, 175; *see also* "Fire on the
Mountain"
"Shakedown Street," 20
"Ship of Fools," 126
"Slipknot," 7, 126
"St. Stephen," 68, 77, 83, 113–116, 118,
119, 151
"Sugar Magnolia," 148, 149
"Sunrise," 133
"Supplication," 39, 94–97, 178; *see also*
"Lazy Lightning"
"Terrapin Station," 24, 60, 117, 126
"They Love Each Other," 90–91, 178
"Touch of Grey," 130–131, 148
"Turn on Your Lovelight," 77, 113, 125
"U.S. Blues," 55, 67, 81, 83, 90
"Victim or the Crime," 150
"Wave That Flag," 89
"We Bid You Good Night," 113
"Wharf Rat," 87, 153
"Wheel, The," 95
Grateful Dead Archives (U.C. Santa
Cruz), 135, 152, 154
Grateful Dead Properties, 144
Grateful Dead Scholars Caucus, 135, 152
Grateful Dead Songbook, The (1973), 78
Greek Theater (U.C. Berkeley), 73, 148
Gregory, Dick, 72
Grundy, Bill, 12–13
Gustin, Sam, 7

Haggard, Merle, 98–99
Hart, Mickey, 10, 16, 132, 149, 155, 157
Diga (1976), 110
"Fire on the Mountain," 110
performance at Barton Hall, 81–127
passim
Healy, Dan, 42, 43, 55
Heard, Clifford Dale, 135
Hendrix, Jimi, 52
hippie, 14–15
Holding Company, 54, 72

Holly, Buddy, 113
Horsley, Heather, 129–131
Hot Tuna, 77–78
Hornorton, Charles, 168
Hunter, Robert, lyrics, 3, 81, 87, 90, 93,
100, 105, 109, 111, 115

Ithaca, 28; *see also* Cornell; East Hill
Ithaca Journal, 6, 102
Ithaca Times, 177

Jackson, Blair, 160
Jackson, Rex, 132–133
JAMerica (Conners), 165
jam band, tradition, 36, 44, 48, 86, 165
Jarnow, Jesse, 19
Jefferson Airplane, 54, 72
Jefferson Starship, 32
Jerry Garcia Band, 32–33, 132
Jethro Tull, 62
John, Elton, 17
Judas Priest, 73

Kelley, Alton, 78
Kennedy, John F., 16
Kerouac, Jack, 156
Kesey, Ken, 14, 16, 35–37, 51–52
Keystone, The (Berkeley, California), 73
Kingfish, 73, 95
Kinks, 33
Kippel, Les, 47–48
Kleinhans Music Hall (Buffalo, New
York), 125
Kraus, J. R., 165
Kreutzmann, Bill, 10, 28–29, 66, 67, 71,
149, 165
performance at Barton Hall, 81–127
passim
Kreutzmann, Justin, 165
Kripper, Stanley, 168
KSAN (San Francisco), 76

Laguna Seca Raceway (Monterey, CA),
129–130
Lake Erie, 26
Lambert, Gary, 101

Index

Latvala, Dick, 49–50, 119, 135
  assessing Barton Hall show, 170–171
Law, Eileen, 78, 133
Leary, Timothy, 19, 51, 72
Led Zepplin, 73
Legion of Mary, 95
Lemieux, David, 117, 140–141, 145, 165
  assessing Barton Hall show, 151–152
Leonard, Dennis, 54
Lesh, Phil, 10, 16, 28–29, 35, 67, 149, 165
  performance at Barton Hall, 81–127
    passim
Lewis, Noah, 84–85
Library of Congress, 8, 38
Lipstick Traces (Marcus), 13
List, Sandy Kohler, 63
Long Island University, 32
Long Strange Trip, A (McNally), 8
LSD, 28, 51–60 passim, 72, 168; *see also*
  Acid Tests

Mainzer, Steve, 7
Mancuso, David, 19
Marcus, Greil, 13
Marcus, Steve, 42
Marshall Tucker Band, 62
Martha and the Vandellas, 103
Matrix (San Francisco), 1
Mattera, Adam, 18–19
Matthews, Bob, 54, 132
Mattson, Jeff, 40; *see also* Dark Star
  Orchestra
Mattson, Mark, 67–68
McGee, Rosie, 72
McKenzie, Scott, 13
McNally, Dennis, 8, 38, 42, 49–50, 57–58,
  74, 134, 156–158
  assessing Barton Hall show, 157–159
Meriwether, Nicholas, 68, 135, 152–156
  assessing Barton Hall show, 154–156
Merry Pranksters, 36, 51–52; *see also*
  Kesey, Ken
Messenger Service, 54
Miller, Denver, 165
moe., 48
Monarch Entertainment Bureau, 32

Moore, Jerry, 43, 44–46, 47, 48; see also
  Relix
More Than Human (Sturgeon), 28
Mouse, Stanley, 78
Move Me Brightly (2013), 165–166
MTV, 130–131
Mydland, Brent, 133–134

Nathanson, Mark, 106
National Recording Registry, 8
Neurotribes (Silberman), 48
New Riders of the Purple Sage, 62
Newsweek, 52
new wave, 2, 9
New York Daily News, 161
New Yorker, The, 54
No Simple Highway (Richardson), 16

Oakland Coliseum, 73
Obama, Barack, 16
Of Mice and Men (Steinbeck), 92
Oneonta, State University of New York, 74
Osbourne, Ozzy, 48
Owsley and Me (Stanley), 51

Parise, Felicia, 169
Parish, Steve, 135, 165
Parliament Funkadelic, 73
Patton, Charlie, 85
Paumgarten, Nick, 39, 54, 129, 144
Phish, 48, 165
Picasso, Pablo, 85
Pig Pen, 164
Pink Floyd, 77
Pinkus, Mark, 5, 144, 147–151
  assessing Barton Hall show, 150–151
  Rhino Entertainment, 149–150
Psychedelic Experience, The (Leary,
  Metzner, and Alpert), 51
punk rock, 9, 17–20

Quicksilver Messenger Service, 54

Radio City Music Hall (New York City),
  156
Raizene, Mark, 55

Index

Relix, 24, 43, 44, 48

Rhino Records. *See* Warner Music Group

Richardson, Peter, 16

Rifkin, Danny, 14–15

Robbins, Marty, 88

Robertson, Robbie, 98

Robinson, Stephen, 143

Rochester, New York, 74

Rodgers, Jimmie, 85

Rolling Stone, 16, 47, 48

Rolling Stones, 31, 147

Rosen, Charlie, 47

Rubin, Jerry, 72

Russo, Joe, 165

Sands, Bobby, 49

San Francisco Chronicle, 52

Saturday Night Fever (1977), 102–103

Saunders, Merl, 73, 95

Scher, John, 32–34, 61, 87

Scully, Rock, 68, 157

Scully, Tim, 59

Sex Pistols, 12–13, 17

Shearer, Harry, 14

Shurtliff, Lawrence, 135

Silberman, Steve, 7, 48–49, 56–57, 122, 159–162

    assessing Barton Hall show, 162

Silver Rarities, 7

Simpsons, The, 14

Snyder, Tom, 11–12

Stanley, Augustus Owsley, 35, 50–60, 72, 132

    Owsley Stanley Foundation, 59

Stanley, Rhoney Gissen, 51

Steinberg, Otto, 32

Sturgeon, Theodore, 28

subculture, 14–16

Suma, Mary, 102

Summer of Love, 72

Sutton, Shaun, 66–67

Syracuse, New York, 74

taping, 24–25, 76, 153

    Augustus Owsley Stanley's influence, 53–60

    Barton Hall show, 38–39, 124, 127

    circulation of Betty Boards, 139–140

    early concepts, 35–40

    fan culture and, 40–50

    first sanctioned, 42

    Free Underground Grateful Dead Tape Exchange, 47

    see also Betty Boards; Betty Cantor–Jackson

This is Spinal Tap (1984), 14

Time, 161

Tomorrow Show, The, 11–12

Turner, Rick, 55

Ullman, Montague, 168

Umphrey's McGee, 36

Vollman, William, 155

Wagner, Robert, 23–25, 114

Wall of Sound, 55–60, 89; *see also* Stanley, Augustus Owsley

Warfield Theater (San Francisco), 16

War Memorial Auditorium (Buffalo), 125–126

Warner Music Group (Rhino Entertainment), 7–8, 144, 149–150, 159

Watkins Glen, New York, 159–160

Weinberg, Marty, 47

Weiner, Howard, 39

Weir, Bob, 1, 5, 6, 10, 16–17, 48, 133, 149

    assessing Barton Hall show, 164–171 passim

    assessing Grateful Dead, 11–12, 173, 174

    cowboy songs and, 83, 88–89, 98–99

    performance at Barton Hall, 81–127 passim

Index

Kingfish and, 73, 95
Kingfish (1976), 95
"Take a Step Back" and, 106–107
Tomorrow Show interview, 11–12
TRI Studios, 164–169 passim
Weir Here, 166
Who, The, 64, 147
Wickersham, Ron, 55–58
Widespread Panic, 48

Winterland Arena (San Francisco), 13,
71–72, 98, 157
Wired, 161
Woodstock, 31

Yes, 32, 77

Zappa, Frank, 77
ZZ Top, 30